D0548525

Fixing and Avoiding
Woodworking
Mistakes

Fixing and Avoiding

Woodworking Mistakes

SANDOR NAGYSZALANCZY

The Taunton Press

Cover photo: Sandor Nagyszalanczy

for fellow enthusiasts

© 1995 by The Taunton Press, Inc.
All rights reserved.

First printing: 1995
Printed in the United States of America

A FINE WOODWORKING Book

FINE WOODWORKING® is a trademark of the Taunton Press, Inc.,
registered in the U.S. Patent and Tradmark Office.

The Taunton Press, 63 South Main Street, Box 5506, Newtown,
CT 06470-5506

Library of Congress Cataloging-in-Publication Data

Nagyszalanczy, Sandor.
    Fixing and avoiding woodworking mistakes / Sandor Nagyszalanczy.
    p.   cm.
    Includes index.
    ISBN 1-56158-097-X softcover
    ISBN 1-56158-115-1 hardcover
    1. Woodwork.   I. Title.
TT200.N24 1995
684'.08—dc20   95-19283
                                                CIP

About Your Safety

Working wood is inherently dangerous. Using hand or power tools improperly or
ignoring standard safety practices can lead to permanent injury or even death. Don't
try to perform operations you learn about here (or elsewhere) unless you're certain
they are safe for you. If something about an operation doesn't feel right, don't do it.
Look for another way. We want you to enjoy the craft, so please keep safety foremost
in your mind whenever you're in the shop.

To my darling Ann, who knows how to fix all the mistakes I make outside the woodshop with tolerance, patience and love.

ACKNOWLEDGMENTS

It's no mistake that sharing is the key to all wisdom. First, I'd like to thank the following people for their help with materials and supplies used in the research for this book: Jon Behrle at Woodcraft Supply; Kathleen Flores, sales manager at Colonial Saw (for help with the Lamello MiniSpot system); Chris Iero, sales representative at Mohawk Finishing Products; Tom Lie-Nielsen of Lie-Nielsen Tool; Steve Jackel and Sean Rovai at Jackel Enterprises (for supplying me with lots of good examples of bad lumber) and Carlo Venditto of CMT Tools.

For their technical information and assistance, I'd like to express my gratitude to professional wood finisher and instrument technician Michael Dresdner at Martin Guitar in Nazareth, Pennsylvania; Mark Hensley, woodworker and dovetail expert in Land O Lakes, Florida; Mark LaFond of Mark's Frame House, in Bemidji, Minnesota; and Griffin Okie, furniture designer/craftsman in San Raphael, California.

I'd like to say an extra-special thanks to Chris Minick, woodworker and professional finish chemist (and my finishing guru) in Stillwater, Minnesota. Through many fruitful conversations, I learned of new and exciting strategies for tackling many difficult finishing problems, methods that I hope all woodworkers can benefit from.

For their bravery (some would say foolhardiness), I must acknowledge my colleagues and cronies who shared the sometimes harrowing tales of their worst woodworking disasters, as well as the remedies they concocted in wisdom and desperation: Art Espenet Carpenter, Jim Casebolt, Mark Duginske, Tage Frid, Cliff Friedlander, Giles Gilson, Roger Heitzman, Jeff Hilber, Philip Hostetter, John Kriegshauser, John Lisher, Toshio Odate and Richard Wedler.

Finally, I'd like to make a most unusual acknowledgment: To withold thanks from Judge Michael Barton and the Santa Cruz Municipal Court system, whose denial of my request for jury-duty deferral forced me to write the lion's share of the last two chapters of this book in the back row of a cold and stuffy courtroom.

CONTENTS

INTRODUCTION

Most of the woodworkers I know are optimists. We commonly jump into the process of building things we've never built before, using methods that are untried or unpracticed, "boldly sawing where no one has sawn before." So why are we so surprised when we make mistakes? After all, stumbling into an occasional error is part and parcel of living in a less-than-perfect world.

Probably the worst thing about making a mistake is that it's painful twice: the first time when you discover you've made it, and again when you spend time correcting it. Mistakes must be paid for, sometimes in materials and money, always in time and trouble. Often they extract their greatest price in lost pride and self-confidence.

Mistakes have many causes: slips of the hand, errors in judgment, bad luck, poor materials, momentary distraction, cheap tools. Whatever the reason that caused a mistake to occur, one thing is for sure: You have to get past it before you can reclaim the pleasures of woodworking. But remedying even a small glitch can be surprisingly difficult. Part of what's so diabolical about woodworking mistakes is that they take so many forms and can strike at any time—a mismeasured face-frame member; a botched mortise and tenon joint; a ding in a freshly sanded tabletop; a cabinet door that wasn't glued up flat; a lacquer finish contaminated with sawdust. The fact is that while most woodworkers know all about how to set up a table saw, lay out a dovetail joint and sharpen a chisel, very little of that knowledge is helpful—or comforting—when trying to recover from a woodworking mistake.

This book offers you a comprehensive repertoire of repair strategies, methods and tricks for overcoming the boo-boos and blunders that occasionally darken every woodworker's shop door. The methods assembled in these 10 chapters come from my own 15 years of experience building custom furniture, along with the experience of dozens of my colleagues and other well-known woodworkers I first interviewed when I was Senior Editor of *Fine Woodworking* magazine, for an article on the subject of woodworking mistakes, which was published in issue #95, July/August 1992.

The first seven chapters of this book deal with repairing mistakes that may occur at any stage of a project, including parts that are cut too short, loose-fitting joinery, surface defects, warped parts, defective assemblies, and poor glue joints and finishes. The information is comprehensive, yet deals with specific problems encountered while building new furniture and cabinets. The text takes you through step-by-step repairs and offers alternative strategies wherever possible. I've generally eschewed techniques that require a lot of expertise to perfect, such as the professional finishers' method of shellac burn-in for the repair of dings and dents. Instead I've endeavored to present remedies that are easier to perform and yield undetectable results, so you can get back to building with that comfortable feeling that your project will look flawless when it's done. No one will ever have to know that you made the mistake in the first place (although many woodworkers are so proud of their mistake-mending prowess that they often introduce a new piece with the challenge: "I bet you can't find the spot where I dropped that C-clamp!").

The last three chapters present a collection of practices and strategies for avoiding woodshop mistakes. While following good woodworking practice is the best way to keep disasters from occurring in the first place, there are lots of little things one can easily do to prevent most common—and irritating—problems from cropping up: for example, calibrating all the tape measures in your shop so that they will yield the same measurements, and cutting longer frame members to length first, so that if you miscut one, you can use it for a shorter part. (Although the book doesn't discuss it explicitly, safe operation of all tools and machinery and the use of protective devices, such as push sticks and safety goggles, are the best way to avoid the worst woodworking mistakes, the ones that result in bodily injury.) Even if you don't follow my recommendations to the letter, studying them will help you to develop better "mistake radar," a sort of sixth sense of anticipating a problem and then finding a way around it. The book concludes with a comprehensive list of sources of supply that includes mail-order suppliers for most of the special tools and materials discussed in the text.

All the material in this book is aimed at making your woodworking pursuits more pleasurable and less costly (in terms of both time and money). And that is a desirable goal whether you're a veteran who's seen it all or a hobbyist just setting up your first shop. As my friend and traditional Japanese woodworker Toshio Odate told me: "You must learn to accept error, but also be prepared for it so that it doesn't inconvenience you."

PART 1
Fixing Woodworking Mistakes

I have often heard it said that the mark of good craftsmanship is how well you cover up your mistakes. For just as building flawless furniture or cabinetry is a matter of skill and experience, overcoming errors takes special knowledge and patient practice. What often separates seasoned woodworkers from novices is the size of their repertoire of mistake-mending tricks. Because there seems to be no end to the variety of goofs and gaffes that can beset you, devising and implementing a plan for getting out of a bad situation can call for as much inventiveness as it took to design and execute the work in the first place. The first part of this book presents mistake-mending methods that will help you in all aspects of woodworking, from selecting lumber to applying the finish. Chapter 1 tackles problems with parts that are cut too short or badly machined. Strategies for improving the fit of miscut joinery are presented in Chapter 2. Patching, puttying and covering up defects, such as dents, holes and gouges, are discussed in Chapters 3 and 4; Chapter 5 covers ways of overcoming natural defects in the lumber itself. Chapters 6 and 7 address the range of problems that can crop up during the assembly, glue-up and finishing of a project. While the material doesn't cover every possible contingency, there's a lot of good fodder here that will help improve the look of your finished projects (as well as enhance your enjoyment of woodworking) by quickly reducing the most maddening mistakes to mere passing memories.

CHAPTER 1
Dealing with Short and Miscut Parts

It's a painful realization when you try to assemble a door frame and discover that all the muntins have been cut too short, or that you've cut up all the rails for a cabinet face frame and forgotten to add extra length for the tenons. Sometimes the only thing to do is pull another board out of the lumber pile and start all over again, or clench your teeth and take another trip to the lumberyard. But what if there isn't another board left? Or the lumberyard isn't open or is 50 miles away? (Don't these things always seem to happen on a Sunday when the lumberyard is closed?) Then, it's time to strap on your thinking cap and try to weasel your way out of the dilemma.

You can recover from a surprising number of short-part blunders, usually in less time than it would take to make a new part from scratch (making parts over is usually preferable if wood is abundant and the operations and machine setups needed to remake the part are few). As if by some sort of arboreal magic, short, narrow or thin boards can be stretched to expand their dimensions. Molding, trim and decorative elements can be added either to extend a part's size or to cover the seam between undersized parts. And changes in joinery, the design of the subassembly or possibly the entire project can be effected to accommodate undersized parts.

Stretching a Board's Dimensions

What if the boards you've thoughtfully set aside for a pair of book-matched cabinet-door panels are just a little too short, narrow or thin? You can't just go out and buy a wider board because it won't match the color or grain of the lumber you've used for the rest of the project. You have to get out the "board stretcher," the name woodworkers have given to the ways of expanding one or more dimensions of a board to make it large enough for the desired part.

Diagonal scarfing to add width or length

If you cut a part too short, or can't find a board long enough to cut the part you need, you can employ a simple scarf joint to lengthen a frame member, molding or other part. One end of both the original part and the piece being added are mitered at complementary angles and then glued together. The miter angle of this kind of scarf joint should be shallow—25° or less—to provide as much long-grain to long-grain contact between parts, for better gluing and strength. You can make this steep-angle cut accurately with a portable circular saw (fitted with a sharp blade that's set square to the saw's baseplate) guided by a temporary fence clamped atop the workpiece—a metal carpenter's level

One way to extend the width or length of a board is to saw it apart diagonally, using a tapering jig, then slide the triangles together or apart along their hypotenuses until a board of the desired dimensions is achieved, and glue the pieces back together.

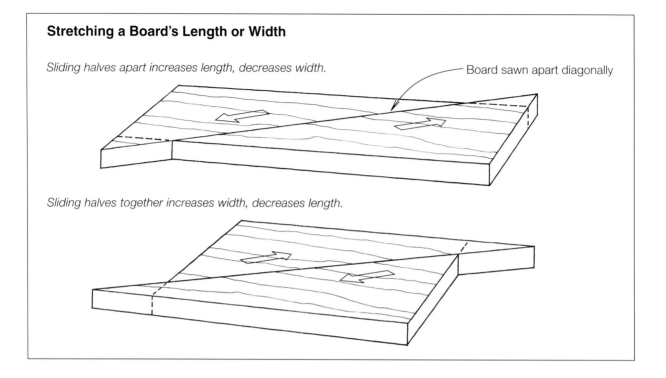

Stretching a Board's Length or Width

Sliding halves apart increases length, decreases width.

Board sawn apart diagonally

Sliding halves together increases width, decreases length.

or a straight board works just fine. Each cut end of the scarf joint can be trimmed straight and true using the clamped on fence to guide a flush-trim bit in a router.

You can also use the scarfing technique to increase the size of a "dimensionally challenged" part (that's the politically correct woodworking term). The part is first sawn in half diagonally, then the resulting wedge-shaped pieces are realigned to increase one dimension of the board. The wedges are then reglued into a solid part. In order for the method to work, you need to start with a board that is oversized in at least one dimension. You are in effect reducing the size of the board in one dimension in order to increase it in another. The technique works best on woods that have very bland grain or very straight grain.

The easiest (and most practical) way to employ the scarfing technique is for increasing the length or width of a part. The first step is to set up a tapering jig on the table saw to cut the board diagonally from corner to corner, as shown in the photo on p. 7. On your benchtop, reassemble the sawn wedges into the configuration of the original board and slide the wedges along their hypotenuse to change the size of the board. Sliding the halves apart increases the board's length; sliding them together increases its width, as shown in the drawing above.

When deciding upon the final position of the halves, watch for grain match across the hypotenuse. Subtle shifts in position can make all the difference between an obvious seam and one that's hard to detect.

If the diagonal cut is less than 30°, it's a good idea to add plate-joinery biscuits at even intervals along the hypotenuse. Besides strengthening the joint, the biscuits help to keep the pieces aligned when they are reglued. Before gluing, it's helpful to drive a couple of small brads into the edge of one hypotenuse, then clip them off very near the surface. They will prevent the pieces from sliding against one another—and out of position—when clamping pressure is applied. (For another way to keep parts from sliding, see p. 184.) To keep the pieces perfectly flat, I lay them on a sheet of waxed paper (to keep the glue from sticking), apply the bar clamps, then clamp the assembly flat on my benchtop, as shown in the photo below.

Once the glue has dried and the excess has been scraped from the joint line, it's time to trim the small triangles left at the corners of the revamped board. Depending upon whether you have extended the board in length or width, you will trim by ripping the scrap near the ends or by crosscutting the ends flush. Once the board is rectangular again, you can proceed to lay out the desired part and cut the board to final dimension.

When gluing up a "stretched" board, keep the halves from sliding along their diagonal edges by clamping them to the workbench. A sheet of waxed paper keeps the assembly from sticking to the bench.

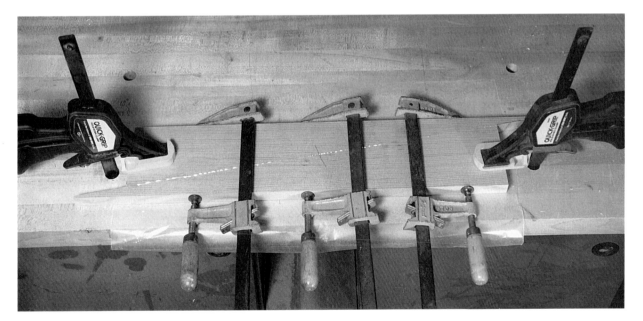

Veneering to add thickness

While the board-stretching method described above can be adapted to increase the thickness of a board (by resawing it across its thickness and sliding the resulting wedges together, you can make a board thicker while shortening its overall length), it is far more practical to thicken a part by adding a layer or two of veneer. On smaller parts and panels where only one side shows, you can add a thin layer of veneer to the back side, where it won't show. Thicker veneers (1/8 in. to 1/4 in. or more) can be resawn from stock, as described below. If you need to increase part thickness only slightly (3/32 in. or less) you can purchase and use regular sliced veneers. A layer of veneer can also be added to improve the mating of loose-fitting joints, as described on pp. 35-36.

Laminating veneer onto smaller parts is simply a matter of applying glue (yellow glue is just fine for most applications) and clamping the veneer flat to the part using a clamping block or caul to ensure flatness and full contact. Laminating larger panels is best done in a veneer press if you have access to one, or using the vacuum-bag method, as described in detail in *Fine Woodworking* #84 (pp. 68-70) and in #99 (pp. 72-75).

If the part or panel you wish to add thickness to is on the thin side to start with (1/2 in. or less), then adding veneer to only one side is likely to result in cupping. Conventional woodworking wisdom advises veneering both sides of a panel with veneers of the same thickness to equalize the forces created by seasonal moisture change that may distort the panel. If the panel is to be mounted or captured in a sturdy frame, you can often get away with veneering only the back side. If the thin panel must be flat and rigid on its own and you can resaw or find a veneer to match the face of the part, veneering both faces is best. If you can't find a matching face veneer and the edges of the panel won't show or can be banded, an alternative to veneering both faces is to resaw the panel and add the veneer layer to the center.

Here's one more handy trick you can perform by laminating a piece of thin stock to the face of a part. If you've been a little trigger happy with your router and rounded over the edges of parts that were meant to be joined flush, you'll end up with a quarter-round gap between parts when you assemble them. One way to cover this problem is to plane down the face of the rounded-over part, say a table leg or frame member, and glue on a new face of the same thickness (see the drawing on the facing page). An alternative strategy is to round over the end of the mating part as well, to create a reveal (see pp. 39-42), or to rabbet the edge and inlay a wood strip, as shown in the photo on the facing page. To prevent you from accidentally rounding over the wrong sections of a part again, try to do all your edge rounding *after* assembly whenever possible.

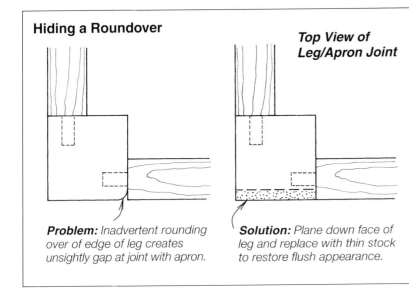

Hiding a Roundover

Top View of Leg/Apron Joint

Problem: *Inadvertent rounding over of edge of leg creates unsightly gap at joint with apron.*

Solution: *Plane down face of leg and replace with thin stock to restore flush appearance.*

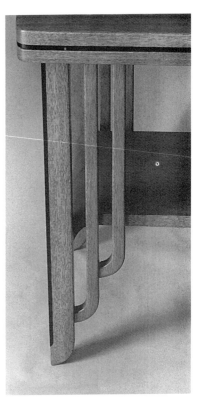

A dinged or improperly machined edge can be patched by rabbeting the edge and inlaying a strip of a contrasting wood. The edges of all four legs on the author's Honduras mahogany television table were inlaid with ebony strips to conceal a bad routing job.

Resawing stock to increase lumber coverage

Building a special blanket chest or display cabinet from a small flitch of highly figured boards you've stashed away for years is a pleasure. That pleasure is easily spoiled, however, if one of the parts gets miscut and you don't have enough wood in your stash to complete the project. Since the color and grain must match, you can't substitute different lumber. In this case, the best way to stretch the coverage of your lumber is to resaw some of the remaining stock into thick (about ⅛-in.) veneers and use them to face all the most prominent surfaces of your project—the top and front of the case, main door panels, and so on. The veneers can be laminated onto plain wood of the same species or, if the edges of the parts won't show or will be banded, a substrate such as plywood or medium-density fiberboard (MDF).

For resawing narrow boards into thin veneers, the bandsaw is the machine of choice. Most small bandsaws (14-in. or 15-in. wheels) can resaw stock that's at least 6 in. wide, and their thin blades consume a very small kerf in the bargain, so you get more veneer leaves from a given board. Fit the saw with a 3-TPI to 6-TPI (tooth-per-inch) skip-tooth blade that's ½ in. or ¾ in. wide (a wider, well-tracking blade has less of a tendency to drift). When cutting thin leaves, I prefer to surface both sides of the board and slice a leaf off of each face, then resurface and cut two more, repeating the process until the board is gone.

For ⅛-in. leaves of veneer, I resaw pieces ³⁄₁₆ in. thick, then thickness-plane them to ⅛ in. I use a marking gauge to scribe the lines of cut on the edge of the board. I clamp a shop-made resawing fence to the top

To make your own veneer, use a tall resawing fence on the bandsaw. The shop-made fence shown here has a dowel post that allows the angle of the stock to be varied for a straighter cut, yielding veneer sheets that are constant in thickness.

of the bandsaw table, as shown in the photo above. This resawing fence is described in detail on pp. 25-26 of my first book, *Woodshop Jigs & Fixtures* (The Taunton Press, 1994). The single-edge contact between the board and post allows the angle of the board to be adjusted as you follow the scribed line of cut to compensate for blade drift (the tendency of the blade to wander off the cutting line), which can easily ruin a thin veneer leaf.

After slicing enough leaves to cover your project's surfaces (and ideally a couple of extras), laminate them to your chosen substrate, either by clamping or with the vacuum-bag method. On wider panels, resawing allows consecutively cut leaves to be slipmatched or bookmatched, providing decorative options for showing off fancy grain to best advantage. Once again, conventional woodworking wisdom calls for veneering both sides of a substrate to keep the panel from warping. But if you live in a region of the country that has relatively stable annual atmospheric moisture, such as Arizona or Southern California, you can often get away with single-sided veneering of thick or frame-captured panels.

Adding Length by Adding Elements

Instead of using clever but time-consuming board-stretching techniques, you can often lengthen parts that are too short simply by adding other elements to the project. Depending upon the nature of the parts and the design of your project, there are several possible strategies. Connections between too-short carcase and cabinet parts can be hidden with moldings or decorative elements. Table or desk legs that aren't long enough can be extended with feet or separate bases. Narrow panels can be widened by cutting them apart and gluing in decorative strips of contrasting wood. Turnings can be lengthened by doweling on additional turned elements.

Moldings and trim

One of the easiest ways to fix the fit of parts that don't quite mate is to cover the gap with a simple molding or piece of trim. For example, if you've cut a divider for a display cabinet too short, you can scab on a strip of scrap wood to the end of the divider to make up the length, then cover the repair with lengths of molding (see the drawing below). Even if parts are cut to correct length, moldings can cover ragged edges, which are sometimes a problem with hardwood plywoods, which often have delicate face veneers that tear out badly when cut.

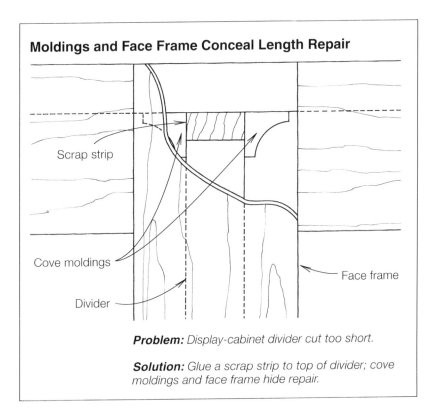

Moldings and Face Frame Conceal Length Repair

Scrap strip

Cove moldings

Divider

Face frame

Problem: *Display-cabinet divider cut too short.*

Solution: *Glue a scrap strip to top of divider; cove moldings and face frame hide repair.*

Adding a Molding to a Frame

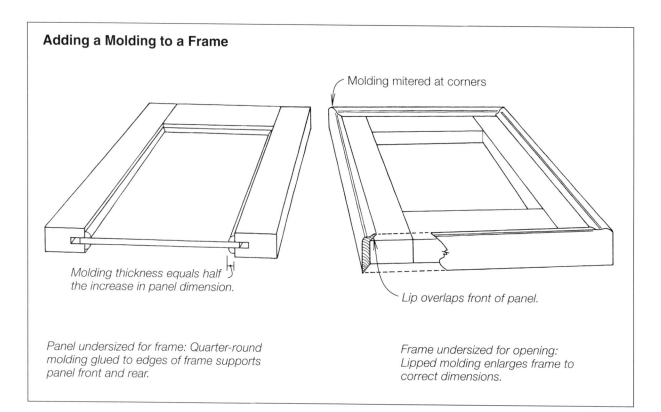

Molding mitered at corners

Molding thickness equals half the increase in panel dimension.

Lip overlaps front of panel.

Panel undersized for frame: Quarter-round molding glued to edges of frame supports panel front and rear.

Frame undersized for opening: Lipped molding enlarges frame to correct dimensions.

Creating a Reveal

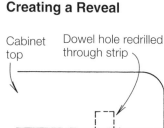

Cabinet top

Dowel hole redrilled through strip

Contrasting wood strip

Reveal

Side

Problem: *Display-cabinet side cut too short.*

Solution: *Glue a narrow scrap strip to top of side; decorative reveal at edge looks intentional.*

If adding a molding detracts from the clean look of the piece, you can make a virtue of necessity and turn the repair into a design detail. Just lengthen the carcase divider or side by adding a strip to its top edge (see the drawing above left). The strip, which can be made from the same wood or a contrasting wood, should be narrower than the thickness of the part. The difference in width creates a decorative space or "reveal" at the juncture of the side or divider and the top (for more on reveals, see pp 39-42).

Moldings can also be used to adapt a panel (mistakenly cut slightly undersized) to fit into its frame. For example, the inside edge of the simple frame shown in the drawing above is extended to accommodate a too-small panel by adding quarter-round molding frames (mitered at the corners) front and rear. If the frame has a shaped inside edge (such as a cope-and-stick frame), you can cut the frame members to suit the panel, recut the corner joints, and then add molding around the frame's outer perimeter to return it to original size. Similarly, moldings can be used to enlarge undersized doors or drawer fronts so that they will fit their jambs or carcase openings, as shown in the drawing.

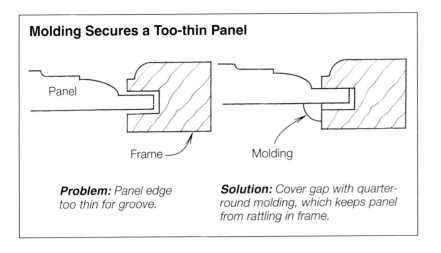

Molding Secures a Too-thin Panel

Panel

Frame

Molding

Problem: *Panel edge too thin for groove.*

Solution: *Cover gap with quarter-round molding, which keeps panel from rattling in frame.*

If things go awry while raising panel edges, you may be left with a panel that's too thin for the groove that captures it in the frame. For example, if the panel isn't fed smoothly or lifts during shaping, the raised-panel cutter (or blade in a table saw) can take a divot and leave a small dip in the shaped edge. The easiest fix is to take another pass and even up the shaped edge all the way around, but that leaves you with a panel edge that is thinner than desired. You can laminate veneer to the back of the panel, as described on p. 10, but another way (if the frame design allows it) is to add a small molding around the back of the frame, as shown in the drawing above. This technique will also work if you have accidentally dado-cut the grooves in the edges of the frame members too wide. Adding molding will also prevent panels cut from so-called ¼-in. imported plywood (which is typically ¹⁄₃₂ in. to ³⁄₆₄ in. undersized) from rattling in their frames if you've optimistically cut the frame grooves ¼ in. wide.

Another use for our versatile friends in the molding family is to cover gaps between a built-in cabinet and the space it is meant to fit into. If there isn't sufficient space around the cabinet's face frame to tack on a surface molding (full-overlay doors might need the clearance), adding a scribe strip to the edge of the cabinet's face frame will allow you to regain a tight, seamless-looking fit. This glued-on strip extends the edge beyond the surface of the cabinet side. The added strip is then scribed and trimmed as needed, so that the edge of the frame will conform to the irregularities of the wall the cabinet butts up against (all cabinets designed to fit against walls or into previously constructed spaces should already have scribes as part of their face frames, as discussed on pp. 151-153.

After discovering that he had accidentally cut the panels for the main doors of a stereo cabinet too narrow, Oregon woodworker Jeff Hilber cut each panel into three sections. He then reglued them, adding two strips of purpleheart wood to make each one the proper width. Photo: Jeff Hilber.

Another way to save the day with add-on trim is when adjustable shelves for a bookcase or storage unit have all been cut too short to rest on standard shelf pins set into holes drilled in the case sides. A wide, flat trim strip, planed as thick or thin as necessary to make up for shelf length, is glued over each row of previously drilled holes, as described on pp. 80-81.

Using decorative elements to stretch parts

One way to make a repair that lengthens a part inconspicuously is not to hide the error at all, but rather to add length with a design element. For example, if you cut the mitered casement around a door frame too short, you can square the ends off and fit plinth blocks (square blocks of wood with a turned design in the center, commonly seen in Victorian homes) at the top corners.

Similarly, a panel that is too narrow can be widened by cutting it apart and then gluing it back together with one or more decorative, contrasting wood strips laminated between the cut segments. Depending upon how the panel is cut apart and the kind of strips used, the laminating effect can range from subtle to dramatic. The panel may be cut in half or into thirds or quarters, and the cuts may be straight or curved, with strips cut straight or curved to match. By cutting a raised panel apart where the raised part meets the field, you can glue in wood strips of the same species, and yet still make it look as if it had been done intentially, rather than as a remedy. Curved cuts taken with a bandsaw or saber saw allow a panel to be reglued with thin, bent strips. Using a

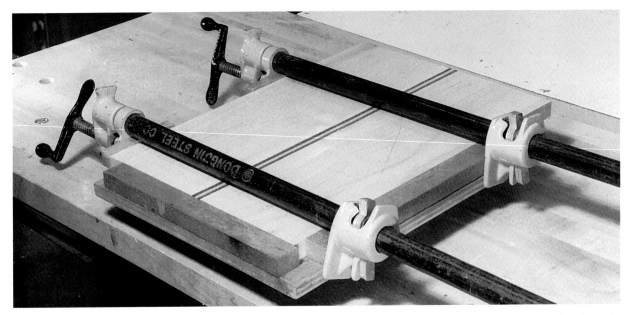

A cut-apart panel is glued back together on a base with lips on two adjacent sides that keep the parts aligned during clamping. One lip also acts as a clamp pad on one edge of the panel when pipe clamps are applied. A layer of waxed paper on the MDF base keeps the assembly from sticking.

contrasting-color wood for the strips can add panache and a strong visual element if done on a prominent door or carcase panel, as demonstrated in the doors of Jeff Hilber's stereo cabinet, shown in the photo on the facing page.

Regardless of whether you choose straight or curved cuts and strips, make them slightly thicker than the thickness of the panel so they can be planed or belt-sanded flush after the panel has been glued back together. When regluing the panel, it is very important to keep all parts properly aligned and flat. This is best done by laying the parts on a flat, square plywood or MDF base covered with a layer of waxed paper, which will keep the glued panel parts from adhering to the base. Strips of wood nailed to two adjacent edges of this base project above the surface to act as lips. Butting the panel parts against these lips during glue-up will help you keep them aligned, so the reglued panel will come out square as well as flat (see the photo above). After glue is applied and all parts of the panel are aligned, clamps can be fitted between one edge of the panel and the lip. The panel can also be clamped down on the base (if needed) to keep it flat as clamps are tightened.

Adding feet to lengthen legs

A simple but effective way to raise the height of a table, desk, chair or stool is to add feet to the ends of its legs. If the amount you need to raise the top or seat is small, you can fit a set of commercially made metal or plastic glides or casters. Most of these can be nailed or screwed to the bottom of any wooden leg; some adjustable metal feet

Feet Lengthen Legs

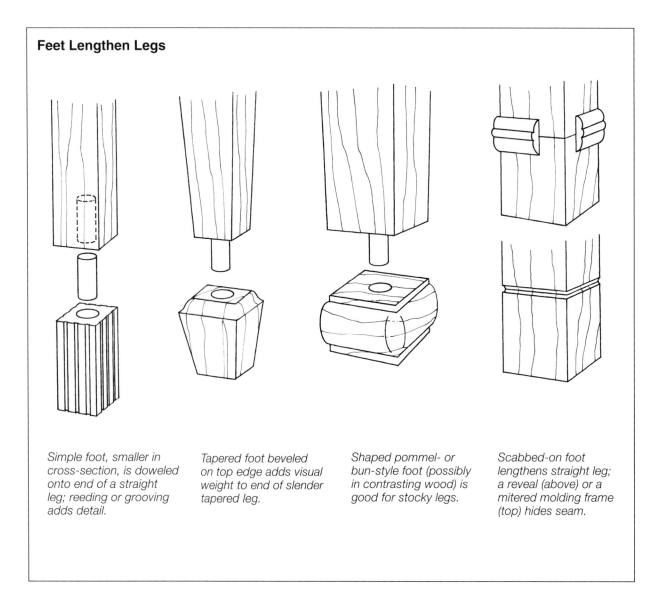

Simple foot, smaller in cross-section, is doweled onto end of a straight leg; reeding or grooving adds detail.

Tapered foot beveled on top edge adds visual weight to end of slender tapered leg.

Shaped pommel- or bun-style foot (possibly in contrasting wood) is good for stocky legs.

Scabbed-on foot lengthens straight leg; a reveal (above) or a mitered molding frame (top) hides seam.

have a screw thread that enables you to fine-tune height so the piece can be both raised and leveled on an uneven floor. If a greater height gain is required, say to raise a dining table because its apron is too low for adequate knee clearance, you can add separate wooden feet.

Feet can be fashioned to complement the style of the piece and the overall look you desire (for some examples of foot options, see the drawing above). If the piece is modern or contemporary in design, with straight or tapered legs, a simple way to extend each leg is with a short length of a contrasting wood. This creates a "visual" foot without changing the lines of the leg (see the photo at right). Feet may be larger or smaller in section than the leg itself. Indeed, you can even get away with adding a foot that's the same wood type and sectional size as the leg itself by hiding the juncture with a reveal or a strip of molding applied all the way around.

Height can also be added to the bottom of non-legged case pieces, such as dressers and stereo cabinets: On a traditional-style carcase piece, such as a highboy, you can gain altitude by adding a plinth-style base. If the piece already has a plinth base and is still too low, you may add a molding frame between the plinth and case bottom, or add bun or bracket-style feet to the bottom of the plinth.

Adding capitals, pommels or collars to turned parts

A spindle that's turned too short—or that has a section that's torn out or turned to the wrong profile—can be lengthened. Just trim it back lengthwise and dowel another turned section onto it (see the photo below). In fact, many longer turnings found on traditional furniture pieces, such as the corner posts on a pencil-post bed frame, were orig-

To add a little space under the apron for more comfortable seating, the legs of the author's bird's-eye maple table were extended with doweled-on ebony feet, tapered to match the clean, straight lines of the legs.

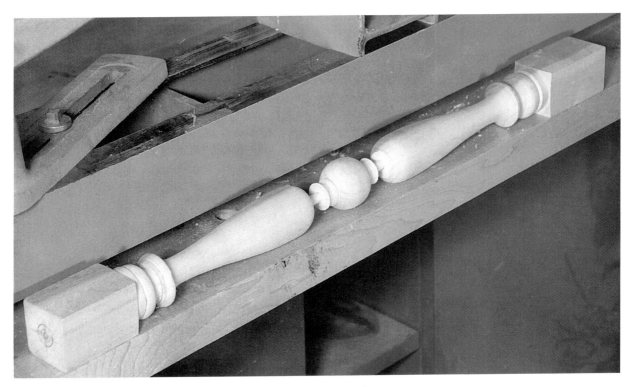

A part turned too short can be lengthened by splicing in a short turned element. As an example, here a pommel with coves on either side of it replaces a narrow bead that was cut out. The pommel is doweled to the ends of the sections on either side of it.

inally assembled from several segments turned separately and joined together with dowels or round tenons and mortises. This way, you can create turnings much longer than the maximum capacity of your lathe between centers.

Begin by trimming off the end of the too-short part. It can either be parted off on the lathe—cut through with a parting tool—or crosscut on a radial-arm saw, table saw or powered miter box. In order for the trimming to be undetectable, the cut should be made at a "transitional element" on the turning: the base of a bead, the corner of a cove, the edge of a ring. A dowel hole must then be made in the trimmed end. While this can be done with a jig on a drill press, to ensure concentricity, this job is most easily done on a lathe with a hollow tailstock. The extension turning can then be made, paying careful attention to the diameter and style of the end that will mate to the trimmed turning. The end element—bead, pommel, cove—should correspond to a natural sequence of turned elements along the length of the turning. The new, lengthened turning can be assembled by gluing in dowels, then clamping up. If you have a long enough lathe, you can clamp the assembly between centers by applying pressure with the tailstock. Thin spindles may need to be strapped to the tool rest to keep them from buckling when pressure is applied.

Adding Length by Changing Joinery

Even when parts are cut to the right length for the size of the frame, drawer or carcase, it's a common error to forget to add enough length for the joinery needed to connect the parts. Most traditional wood-to-wood joints require extra length in one or both mating parts. Mortise-and-tenon joints need extra length for tenoning on both ends of all rails; dovetails or box joints need ends to overlap by the thickness of the stock. The best way to compensate if stock length is inadequate for the intended joinery is to substitute another form of joinery, one that doesn't require as much length. Doweling, applying loose tenons or splines and plate-biscuit joinery all work by adding a third element—a dowel, tenon, spline or biscuit—to provide a strong connection between the parts being joined. Mating parts need only butt together and be machined to receive the connective joinery.

Dowels

Doweling is a traditional way to join most kinds of cabinet or furniture parts including face frames, door frames, aprons, tops and carcases. Dowels precut to length and grooved (for easier driving) are inexpensive to buy and simple to install in most edge-joined parts. If the edges of frame members don't show (or if you intend to plug the holes after-

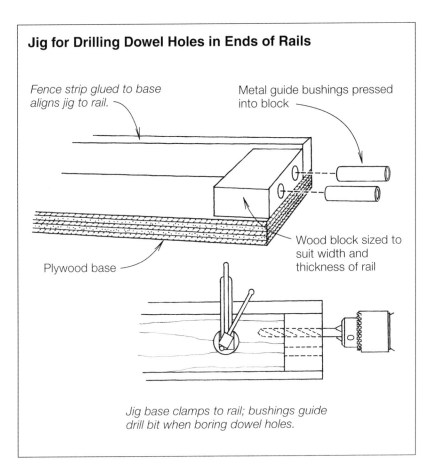

Jig for Drilling Dowel Holes in Ends of Rails

Fence strip glued to base aligns jig to rail.

Metal guide bushings pressed into block

Plywood base

Wood block sized to suit width and thickness of rail

Jig base clamps to rail; bushings guide drill bit when boring dowel holes.

wards), you can dowel together a frame by first butt-gluing the parts together (very weak by itself), then drilling holes and driving dowels through the stiles and into the rails while the frame is still in clamps. If blind doweling is desired, holes must be drilled in the mating surfaces of both parts with great accuracy so that the parts will align properly.

Locating the holes accurately is easy to do on carcase sides and wide frame members with a commercially made doweling jig, which has bushings to guide a bit in a portable drill. However, these guides don't work very well for doweling the ends of frame rails less than 3 in. wide; the jig won't clamp square and secure on such narrow parts. You can build a simple guide jig for drilling dowel holes in the ends of rails, such as the one shown in the drawing above. The jig has one or two steel or bronze bushing sleeves pressed into a solid wood block that is glued and screwed to a plywood base, which allows the jig to be clamped to the frame member. A fence strip screwed to the base ensures that holes will be drilled square to the end of the rail.

Loose tenons can compensate for stock cut too short for traditional tenons, and a box jig provides a convenient way to mortise the ends of rails. With the box clamped to the end of the rail, a top-piloted router bit in a plunge router follows the mortise template mounted to the top of the jig.

Loose tenons and splines

Loose tenoning is a technique that replaces the traditional tenon, cut on the end of one frame member, with a separate tenon long enough to seat into mortises chopped into the mating surfaces of both parts. Mortising of stiles can be done on a dedicated hollow-chisel mortising machine (such as the Delta 14-600), with a drill-press mortising setup, with a router-equipped joint-cutting machine (such as the JDS Multirouter) or by hand with a chisel and mallet. Most machine mortisers won't be able to handle end mortises in rails; these can be done by hand, but are easier with a router and box jig (as shown in the photo at left). Individual loose tenons are sliced from a "log" of tenon stock, cut to width and planed to thickness. If you choose to mortise with a router, the tenon stock must have rounded edges, which can be achieved on a router table by running all four edges of the stock over a roundover bit.

Just as loose tenons are best for joining frame members too short for standard mortises and tenons, loose splines are the components of choice for joining carcase parts that are too short for standard tongue-and-groove joinery. Like loose tenons, loose splines fit into slots routed in the mating edges of both parts. Loose splines yield strong joints in solid woods, plywood and composite materials such as MDF and particleboard. Slots for splines in the edges of narrow parts (about 12 in. or less) may be cut by running the part on edge over a dado blade in the table saw. Wider parts are best kept flat on the bench and edge-slotted using a slot-cutter bit in a router. The slot and spline can run the entire length of a joint or, on parts 12 in. and wider, short sections of spline can be fitted at regular intervals along the edge. The splines themselves can be cut from a good-quality plywood, such as ¼-in. Baltic birch, or from solid wood. If you choose the latter, cut the spline with the grain running the short way, for best strength across the joint line.

Plate-joinery biscuits

Another alternative for carcase panels and other wide parts that were originally meant to be connected with dovetails or tongue-and-groove joints is plate joinery. Using a dedicated machine (or a router fitted with a slot-cutter bit) you cut a series of crescent-shaped slots along the length of both parts; football-shaped biscuits glued into these slots create a strong joint in plywood, composite materials, or in the side grain or end grain of solid woods. An advantage of plate joinery over loose-spline joinery is that the portable plate-joinery machine can cut slots in the center of a surface after the cabinet or furniture piece has been assembled. Thus, you can cut slots and biscuit-join components that mate edge-to-face, such as cabinet dividers or shelves to bottoms or sides after the carcase has been assembled—a salvation if you forgot to cut the joinery for those parts before assembly.

Accommodating Miscut Parts

What's worse than making a mistake once? Making the same mistake a dozen times or more! One of the problems of generating parts from a cut list is that if your calculations are wrong (or if you've transcribed the figures on your list incorrectly), you might wind up cutting dozens of parts to the wrong length (to prevent measurement problems, see pp. 154-159). In such situations, it's usually not practical to replace or "lengthen" all miscut parts, especially if they have already proceeded through a series of subsequent machining operations. In lieu of performing a miracle or spending hours replacing bad parts, sometimes the best strategy it to figure out a way to make the best of the situation, using as many of the miscut parts that you have as you can, even if this calls for a change in the design of the project. It may sound drastic, but altering a few parts and ending up with face frame that has slightly different proportions or changing the entire design of the project to suit miscut parts is often much simpler and more expedient than starting over from scratch.

Wider Stile Compensates for Miscut Cabinet Rails

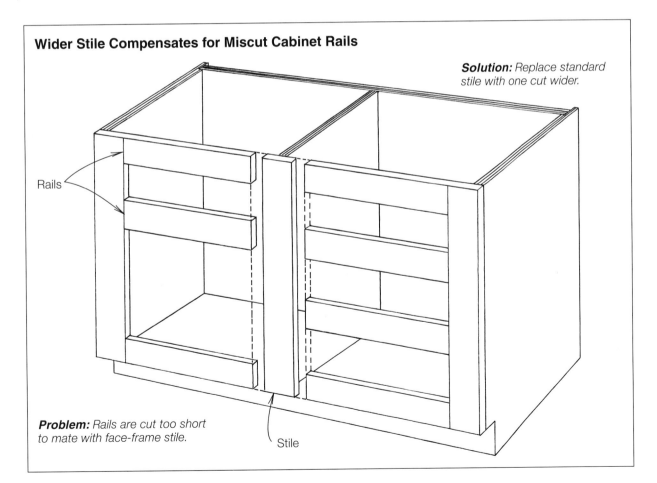

Solution: *Replace standard stile with one cut wider.*

Rails

Problem: *Rails are cut too short to mate with face-frame stile.*

Stile

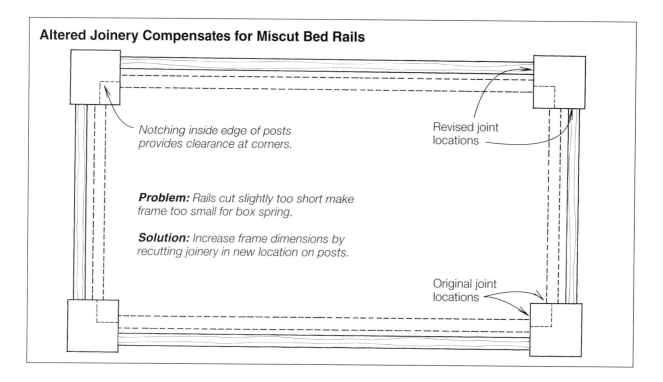

Altered Joinery Compensates for Miscut Bed Rails

Notching inside edge of posts
provides clearance at corners.

Revised joint
locations

Problem: *Rails cut slightly too short make
frame too small for box spring.*

Solution: *Increase frame dimensions by
recutting joinery in new location on posts.*

Original joint
locations

Making mating parts wider or thicker

In many situations, you can compensate for one set of miscut parts by changing the dimensions of a part (or parts) that mates with them. For example, if you've cut most or all of the rails for a cabinet face frame too short, cut the stiles wider to compensate. This way the outside dimensions of the frame remain the same, so the frame will still fit the carcase. If the stiles are already cut when you discover that the rails are too short, you might be able to recut and replace a single stile to compensate, as shown in the drawing on p. 23. Changing the dimensions of face-frame members can also be make up for an undersized door or drawer front, though you'll avoid this problem if you make these parts after the case is assembled (see pp. 170-171).

Sometimes just changing the location of the joinery can compensate for a sizing error, as in a bed frame whose rails are cut slightly too short for the box spring to fit. To compensate, change the location of the joint where the end of each rail attaches to the corner post (see the drawing above). With luck, this small change will increase the size of the frame enough so that it will accommodate the unalterable dimensions of the box spring. To add clearance at the corners, the inside edges of the corner posts can be chamfered or notched, as shown (you don't need to remove too much stock, since the corners of box springs are rounded). If the frame is joined with mortise and tenon, re-

After discovering that he'd accidentally made the laminated back slats for a set of walnut dining chairs too short, furniture maker Roger Heitzman decided to add a riser to the seats. The riser (above), shaped to look like an integral part of each carved seat, makes up for the ½-in. discrepancy and has mortises that accept the back slats. Heitzman was so happy with the look of this solution that he now includes risers on all similar dining chairs. Photo: Roger Heitzman.

locating the position of the rails on the corner posts will probably involve patching and recutting mortises (as described on pp. 73-74) or otherwise reworking the joints. Or you may have to compensate for the position change by altering the joinery, as described on pp. 20-22.

If you've erred and cut the slats or backsplat for the back of a rocking or dining chair too short, you have at least two ways of compensating: Make the chair's back top rail wider or make the seat thicker. Another solution that custom furniture builder Roger Heitzman came up with when he realized all the laminated slats he made for a set of dining chairs were too short was to add a riser at the back of the carved seats where the slats connected (see the photos above). The risers were laminated to the back edge of the seats and shaped to look like an integral part of each seat.

Nadim Hraibi and his corner table. Because the base assembly was laid out wrong, it had to be inverted to match the shape of the top, which had already been cut out. Photo: Richard Starr.

Changing the dimensions of a piece to suit the parts

If you've charged ahead and accidentally miscut many of the vital parts for a big project, say the sides and dust panels for a tall dresser, sometimes the best course of action is simply to resize the entire cabinet or piece of furniture to suit the existing parts. Unless the revised dimensions mean the piece won't fit the spot where it's meant to go, or if they make a piece of seating furniture uncomfortable, the change of an inch or two often makes very little difference in the look or function of a cabinet or furniture piece.

Richard Starr, Vermont woodworking teacher and author of *Woodworking with Your Kids* (The Taunton Press, 1990), comments, "Kids usually think a mistake is a fatality; it's usually not. If kids accidentally cut all the shelves for a bookcase too short, I usually try to talk them into making a narrower bookcase." When a major mistake upsets the entire project, Starr encourages his students to reset their sights. One of Starr's students was building a three-legged corner table with a triangular top (to fit an odd space in his mom's laundry room). However, the non-symmetrical shape of the top was not considered when the holes for the dowels that would join the stretchers and aprons to the legs were laid out, and consequently, the base assembly was built backwards. Instead of redoing everything, Starr realized that the base could simply be flipped over and the ends of the legs could be doweled into the top. The successfully finished piece and its proud maker are shown in the photo at left.

Changing dimensions of a piece after assembly

One of the most embarrassing situations that a professional woodworker can encounter is not to discover that the dimensions of a project are seriously off the mark—until the piece is delivered. It's a sickening, unforgettable feeling, standing there apologizing to a client, trying to act as if fixing the error is no big deal and hoping that the person won't lose all faith in you (or forget that you are still owed money for the job). There's little use in wishing that you had checked your measurements more carefully. But don't despair—there is often plenty of room for recovery.

The easiest-to-remedy situation is if you've built a cabinet too small. Unless the error is on a massive scale (there's a great scene in the rock 'n' roll parody movie "Spinal Tap" where the ersatz rock band designed a massive stage set based on Stonehenge that was somehow built exactly as drawn: 18 in. tall instead of 18 ft.!), you can usually fudge the difference between the size of the piece and the space it's meant to occupy with add-on components: a plinth-style base to raise a low counter or chest of drawers or a soffit to fill out the space above a built-in bookcase or an upper kitchen cabinet. To remedy smaller discrepancies, you can employ all manner of trim, scribe strips and more, as discussed more extensively on pp. 13-19.

But what if your project ends up too long, too tall or too deep? As luck would have it, most cabinets and furnishings based on rectangular carcases (dressers, bookcases, counters) can usually be cut down and trimmed out to appear that they were originally built that way. Most kitchen-cabinet counters have either a separate base that can be cut down or a kick space where they can be trimmed down to correct height. Similarly, bookcases can simply lose a shelf at the top, or a built-in dresser can have shallower drawers fitted top or bottom. Small carcases can be cut down on a table saw, but with large casework, you'll have to clamp on a fence and use a portable power saw. Electric panel-cutting saws are terrific for remedial work like this because of their small size and light weight, especially if you have to do the work on site.

Making hardware changes

Often, miscut parts don't announce themselves until you near the completion of a project, such as shelves cut too short or drawers made too wide (or narrow) or holes drilled for pulls spaced incorrectly. What's worse than making these mistakes in the first place is discovering them at such a late stage, when it's difficult or impossible to replace bad parts. Fortunately, you can often compensate for these problems by changing the hardware, and make do with the parts you've got.

Drawer glides and pulls Building drawers 1 in. narrower than the size of the opening is a common mistake (see p. 157). Such drawers can still be used if they are fitted with a pair of metal drawer glides. Most modern glides require ½-in. clearance on each side of the drawer, and some, such as Blum Epoxy, Amerock Frame-Tech, and Knape & Vogt 8400 series slides, come with a durable colored finish, making them suitable for the finest of woodworking projects. Conversely, if a drawer that was meant to be fitted with side-mounted metal drawer slides is built 1 in. too wide (leaving no room for side-mounted slides) switching to a single bottom-mounted slide, such Accuride's Series 1029 or Delta 100 series slides, can save the day.

If you've misdrilled holes for mounting drawer and door pulls and haven't missed the mark by much, you can avoid a difficult-to-hide patch job in several ways. You can change to a pull with the correct hole spacing. Some wire pulls are thick enough at the base to conceal holes drilled very slightly off the mark. Or you might fit two knob-style

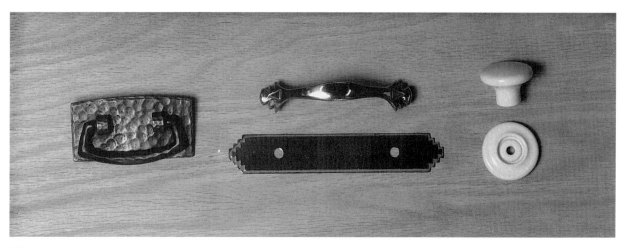

When holes are drilled a little off the mark, you can cover up the error by fitting a bail-type pull (left) or install a backing plate behind the pull (center) or knob (right).

pulls in place of one loop or bail-style pull, one in each hole. Round ball-type pulls are especially good for this. A third solution is fitting backing plates behind the existing pulls. Backing plates come in many styles and configurations (The Woodworker's Store stocks a good variety), some designed to work primarily with a specific pull, others made more generic to work with many different kinds of pulls (see the photo above). Some bail-style pulls have a built-in backing plate that will hide wayward holes. If you don't care to use a store-bought metal backing plate, you can make your own wood plates or use a pressed carving (there are several round patterns available). If the holes for the pulls are badly damaged or seriously off the mark, you can switch to a surface-mounted or recessed hardwood pull. These cover a large space in the area of the pull, and come in a variety of hardwoods to match (or contrast with) your drawers or doors (see the photo at left on the facing page).

Hinges Because hinges aren't often mounted until after the finish has been applied, mistakes with door sizes aren't caught until it's too late to alter wood parts. Here prevention is the best medicine: Make your doors after you've confirmed their correct size from the assembled carcase, as described on pp. 170-171. If you do end up with a door that doesn't fit, changing hardware can be a life-saver. For example, if a door designed for flush mounting on butt hinges turns out oversized, mounting the door with full-overlay hinges can make it functional. If you have mispositioned a mortise for a simple butt hinge (or cut the mortise to long or deep), you might be able to change to a larger-size

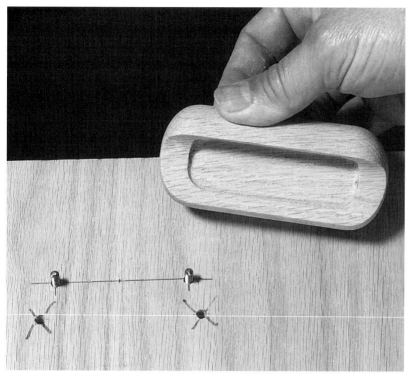

If holes for pulls are seriously off the mark, a surface-mounted hardwood pull can be substituted to cover up the misdrilled holes.

If you've trimmed an inset door too narrow and mortising for regular butt hinges would upset the narrow clearance around the door, you can install No-Mortise hinges.

hinge. If you've trimmed an inset door just a tad too narrow and mortising for regular butt hinges would upset the even amount of clearance around the door, you can switch to special No-Mortise hinges, as shown in the photo at right.

Adjustable-shelf holes Holes for adjustable shelves are easy enough to drill, but you can get into trouble if you're not careful while laying them out. A common error is to start a row of holes from the same location on both the sides and dividers of a case, without compensating for joinery. This may place the holes on one side $\frac{1}{2}$ in. or more out of level with the other—unacceptable for level shelves. One solution is to switch to surface-mounted adjustable shelf standards, mounting the metal rails over the rows of misdrilled holes. If you want to avoid metal hardware, you can glue on wood trim strips with newly drilled holes, as described on pp. 80-81.

CHAPTER 2
Improving a Poor Fit

Ideally, the parts of a properly marked and deftly cut joint fit together like a smooth hand sliding into a velvet glove. Dovetails and box joints interlock as if the halves grew together, and tenons slide into their mortises like pistons mating with their cylinders in a high-compression race-car engine. In the real world, however, joints are rarely perfect. Faulty layout—mispositioned pencil lines or scribe marks—or inaccurate sawing or machining can lead to a sloppy fit. If the joint is an essential structural connection, such as between legs and apron on a table or betwixt legs and stretchers on a chair, a loose fit seriously compromises strength and more than likely shortens the life expectancy of the piece. On exposed joints, such as dovetails that join carcase parts or a drawer front to its sides, poorly mating joints may not compromise much strength, but instead detract from the look of precision and quality that we all strive for.

If a tenon doesn't fit tightly in its mortise, try relieving its shoulder. Here a Dremel tool fitted with a spherical burr relieves the shoulder area of a large tenon, so that the shoulder will seat tightly against the mortised member.

Massaging Joint Fit

The easiest way to clean up the look of joints that aren't 100% perfect is to fine-tune their fit by "massaging" them in various ways. These techniques will help you tweak miter joints, dowel joints and other popular joints for a better fit and a clean final appearance.

Cutting a relief on poor-fitting joint surfaces

Often, joints won't close completely because of slight irregularities in their mating surfaces. Before recutting the end of a miter, butt or scarf joint, or the shoulders of a tenon that don't quite fit right, try relief cutting the surface of the joint just shy of the outer edges, as shown in the drawing on p. 32. You can remove a small amount of stock using a mallet and gouge, a riffler (a small rasp) or even a scraper. To save time, I often use a rotary burr in a portable electric die grinder or, for smaller joint surfaces, a Dremel tool fitted with a spherical burr, as shown in the photo above.

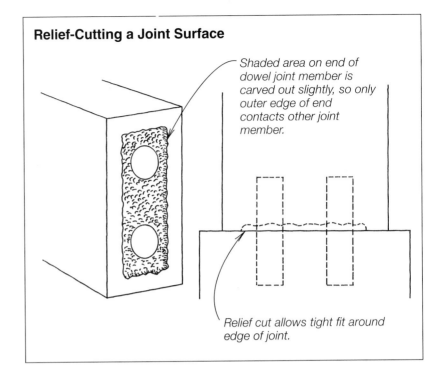

Relief-Cutting a Joint Surface

Shaded area on end of dowel joint member is carved out slightly, so only outer edge of end contacts other joint member.

Relief cut allows tight fit around edge of joint.

If the edges of your joint still don't meet properly after the joint surfaces have been relieved, trimming the joint to a proper fit is much easier than it would be with an unrelieved joint; you need only remove a small rim of material at the outer edge of the joint. The edges of a miter joint, for example, can quickly be trimmed to fit with a hand plane. Just be sure to take a fine cut; usually very little material needs to be removed to achieve a perfect fit.

Rubbing the tips of miters closed

The mitered corners of frames, moldings and other trim must be cut to very precise angles, lest they have unsightly gaps. That lack of fit shows up most prominently in joints where the members don't meet exactly at the tip, an indication that either the members have been cut at a more obtuse angle than called for or, in the case of molding or trim, that the edge they are attached to isn't square or true. An open miter that isn't too far off can be tweaked shut by carefully rubbing the miter tips, which bends the wood fibers to close the gap. The rubbing action is akin to burnishing the final edge on a sharp cabinet scraper. Rubbing should be done with a hard, smooth, rounded tool, such as a steel rod or the round shank of a screwdriver. I've used this technique successfully to close miter-tip gaps of up to $3/32$ in. With larger gaps, you'll want to relief-cut the joint surface before trimming (as described above) or glue in a shim.

Miter-tip burnishing works best on medium-density hardwoods, such as mahogany, walnut and oak, though it can also be done with dense species, such as maple and birch, as long as the gap is slight—$\frac{1}{32}$ in. or less. You can close larger gaps in these species by pounding the tips lightly with a smooth-faced hammer or mallet, but the procedure is not without risk: The short, brittle fibers of these dense woods tend to crush, resulting in a weak miter tip that also takes stains and finishes darker than the surrounding wood. Many softwood species, such as pine and cedar, are very pliable and can be burnished to close big gaps— $\frac{1}{16}$ in. or more. A little glue, spread into the miter gap with a fine pallet knife before burnishing, will help keep the tip closed.

Easing the fit of dowel joints

Because of inaccuracies in hole diameter or shrinkage or swelling of the dowels themselves, dowel joints are often too loose or too tight. A loose joint will do a poor job of aligning the parts it is joining and can easily exceed the gap-filling ability of the adhesive (most yellow aliphatic-resin glues are poor gap fillers). A tight dowel joint can be difficult or impossible to assemble, and trying to close up such a joint can damage or even break the joint members.

There are several convenient strategies for dealing with ill-fitting dowel joints. To remedy a loose joint, you can switch to a good gap-filling glue, as described on p. 34. Tight joints have a wider range of possible remedies. If the dowels you're using are significantly greater in diameter than their holes, you may do best to resize the dowels by driving them through a draw plate (see the photo at right). A draw plate is a metal plate with accurately sized holes that shave dowels to size and scratch in glue grooves as they are pounded through (see Sources of Supply on pp. 196-197). If dowels aren't too far from a good fit, you can try shrinking them in a regular household gas oven. Spread the dowels out on the rack and leave them in the oven overnight; the warmth of the pilot light should be enough. If you're in a hurry, you can try drying them for an hour or two in a 225°F oven.

Dowels too big for standard-size holes can have their diameters reduced by driving them through a draw plate, here held in a large machinist's vise.

A more direct approach to fixing too-tight dowel joints is to increase the diameter of the holes slightly. You can buy special oversized drill bits designed specifically for portly dowels (see Sources of Supply on pp. 196-197). A more flexible (albeit more expensive) solution is to purchase an indexed set of lettered drills. Designed for the machinist's trade, a typical jobber-length set of lettered drills ranges from size A (.234 in.) to size Z (.413 in.), with drill diameters increasing from one size to the next by between .004 and .010 in. A lettered drill set, which costs as little as $30 (see Sources of Supply on pp. 196-197) will allow you to drill both undersize or oversize holes for $\frac{1}{4}$-in., $\frac{5}{16}$-in. and $\frac{3}{8}$-in. dia. dowels.

Changing to a gap-filling glue

Glues differ in their ability to fill gaps, and one way to tighten loose joints is to change from hide glue, urea-formaldehyde or regular white or yellow PVA wood glue to an adhesive that has better gap-filling qualities. This way, you substitute glue for the air space that exists where there should be sound wood-to-wood contact inside the joint. The traditional approach is to make a stiff gap-filling paste from sawdust and hot hide glue (see pp. 57-58). Pack this mixture into a loose joint to tighten its fit and glue it at the same time.

Polyurethane adhesives, such as Gorilla Glue and Excel, have excellent strength and expand when they dry, qualities that would seem to make them excellent gap fillers. However, manufacturers caution that these glues don't provide structural bonding in gaps larger than 0.1mm. Further, polyurethane glues exude a foamy goo as they dry, making them very messy to work with. Hence, two-part epoxies (which can easily handle gaps of up to $1/16$ in.) are still the best choice for strengthening poor-fitting joints. Epoxy's lack of solvent means that it has extremely low shrinkage, an important characteristic if the joints are to remain sound. Avoid the five-minute-drying varieties though; these have a lower cured strength than standard epoxies (which typically set in one hour and cure overnight). Also, five-minute epoxies gel quickly, so it is more difficult to assemble and clamp your joints while the glue is still liquid. Once joints are assembled and clamped, don't wait for the glue to dry completely before removing the squeeze-out. This chore is best performed after an hour or so, when the excess is rubbery and beads or drips can be popped off with a sharp chisel or scraped off with the sharp edge of a scraper blade or a putty knife.

Incidentally, there's a product often found in hardware stores called Chair Loc that you might think would provide an ideal remedy for loose joints. This product is supposed to repair wobbly joints in old furniture by swelling them. While it is capable of expanding dry wood (only slightly, in my experience), Chair Loc isn't a glue—nor does woodworking glue bond readily to surfaces soaked with it, making it unsuitable for tightening loose-fitting joints in new constructions.

Shimming Joints

One of the most direct and effective ways to salvage a slack joint is to glue in a shim. The shim increases the dimension of the joint part where too much stock has been cut away, thereby restoring a snug fit between mating joint parts. Shims are easily made from veneer scraps or cut out of scrap stock and thicknessed as required.

Gluing shims to tenon cheeks

If you go to the trouble of cutting mortise-and-tenon joints for cabinet face frames or for other furniture members, you might as well go the extra mile to tweak their final fit so that the joints are snug and strong. But since joinery is essentially a subtractive process, joints can only get looser with subsequent machining. If a tenon is too loose in its mortise, it's easier to shim the tenon than to fool with the mortise. The shim fills the gap and restores the wood-to-wood contact in the joint. Thin veneers, typically sliced to between $\frac{1}{25}$ in. and $\frac{1}{32}$ in. thick, make a quick and handy shimming material. Shims can be added wherever they're needed. They can be glued to both sides of cheeks or edges of tenon, or on one side only to shift the position of the member relative to the mortise, if necessary (you might even trim a tenon, then shim it to shift the position of the member).

Veneer shims or thin shims cut from solid wood are great when the surfaces of tenons are flat and parallel. But if they have an unintended taper or angle slightly, you'll need a wedge-shaped shim (see p. 36). This will restore the tenons cheeks to parallel and help bring the shoulders of the tenon square to the surface of the mortised member.

Before gluing the shim on, you can easily check to make sure it's about the right thickness by slipping it into the mortise and dry assembling the joint. If the fit is good and you're ready to assemble the joint immediately, you can glue the shim to the tenon, then apply more glue and insert it into the mortise, using white or yellow PVA woodworking glue. If the shim fits well but the joint is still a little looser than you'd like, you can switch to a glue with better gap-filling properties, such as polyurethane adhesive or epoxy (see the discussion on the facing page). If you'd prefer gluing the shim to the tenon first and assembling the joint later, clamp or a give a tight wrap with tape to ensure that the shim will bond firmly to the tenon. Once the glue is dry, you can chisel off any excess and shave the shim or tenon as necessary for a final "piston" fit into the mortise.

Shimming dovetails and finger joints

The flaws that plague dovetail and finger joints usually are in the form of small gaps between the dovetail's pins and tails or between a box joint's fingers. If there are just a few gaps, the most cosmetically pleasing repair is to use what Tage Frid, professor emeritus of woodworking and furniture design, calls his "dovetail hammer." First, glue up the joint as usual. Then, with a thin-bladed saw, such as a dovetail saw or *dozuki,* cut down the ragged joint line to leave a clean kerf. The kerf should be slightly thinner than the shim, which is made from veneer of the same wood as the joint. Now, use your "dovetail hammer"—any hammer that's handy—to pound the shim and compress it slightly. Then apply white or yellow glue to the flattened shim (also work some glue into the kerf, using a thin knife) and insert it into the kerf, its grain oriented diagonally across the joint line. The shim is initially thinner than the kerf, so it is easy to insert, and the water-based glue quickly swells the shim back to its original thickness, leaving no gaps at the repair. After the glue dries, trim the shim and sand it flush.

If you've cut a joint that was laid out incorrectly—or if you set up your finger-joint jig with the wrong spacing to the index pin—the only reasonable solution is to remake one side of the joint, with the spacing set to match the incorrect spacing of the part already cut. If the joints between drawer sides and back have been miscut, you need only remake the back to match the spacing of the sides. If the joints between drawer sides and front have been miscut and you can't easily replace the front, you may have to recut the sides or shim each miscut joint.

Wedging Mortise-and-Tenon Joints

Wedging is a good way to tighten up the fit of a mortise and tenon joint. Wedges can be driven alongside a through tenon that's not wide enough for its mortise, Southwest style. Or they can be set into kerfs cut into tenons to expand them inside the mortise, a technique that can be applied to through tenons or hidden tenons.

You can make thin wedges in several ways. They can be split off an end-grain strip with a sharp chisel or sawn off with a handsaw. But I prefer to cut them on the bandsaw using the dual-fence cutoff jig shown in the photo on the facing page. The jig, which slides in the saw's miter slot, has two fences: one for square cuts, the other for cuts 5° off square. Start with a length of wedge stock, made from a side-grain strip of scrap wood as wide and thick as needed, and take cuts off the end with the scrap butted alternately against the leading edge of the 5° and square fences. Each cut will result in a wedge with 5° of taper. Most wedges for small tenons are about $\frac{1}{8}$ in. thick at the fat end.

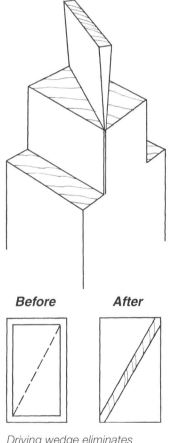

Wedges for tightening loose tenons are easy to cut on the bandsaw with a special two-fence crosscut guide made to slide in the saw's miter slot. Wedges are cut by alternately using the guide's square fence (rear) and 5° fence (front).

Tightening a Through Tenon with a Diagonal Wedge

Wedge driven into a diagonal kerf in end of through tenon drives halves apart.

Before   *After*

Driving wedge eliminates gaps between loose-fitting tenon and mortise.

Diagonal wedges

Through tenons are very easy to snug up with a narrow wedge running diagonally across the tenon (see the drawing at right). The wedge essentially drives the two halves of the tenon tighter into their corners of the mortise, snugging up the fit and leaving no gaps around the edge of the mortise. The method not only makes for a stronger joint, but also adds a nice decorative detail to the through tenon. For this reason many woodworkers like to wedge tenons, even if their joints are cut dead on.

To start, saw the tenon down its length using a dovetail saw, *dozuki* or another similarly thin-kerfed blade, with the cut running corner to corner. The direction of the diagonal cut doesn't really matter, except that you'll probably want all the cuts to run in the same direction if the joint has multiple tenons. Once the joints are glued and assembled, spread glue on the thin wedge (trimmed to be as wide as the length of the diagonal kerf) and drive it into the tenon, expanding it to fill the mortise. The wedge can be cut from a species of contrasting color or from the same wood as the joint, as long as it is a strong hardwood,

such as oak or birch. If the joint is cut in a softer species, such as mahogany, you should probably make the wedges of a harder wood, such
as maple, to ensure that they won't buckle when hammered in place.

Wedged tenons, Southwest style

Another way to fill out the space in a through mortise and tenon when
there's lengthwise play in the joint is to drive in wedges at either end.
This double-tenon look, commonly seen in through tenons used in
Southwestern-style furniture, is both easy to fit and distinctive in appearance (see the drawing below). Wedges are cut in much the same
fashion as for diagonal application, as described above, only they are
made as wide as the thickness of the tenon. Unlike diagonal tenoning,
you save time by not having to kerf-cut the tenons. Just assemble the
joint, glue and drive the wedges in, and trim them flush.

Foxtail wedges

A blind mortise-and-tenon joint can also be wedged, using a narrow tapered wedge called a foxtail wedge. This fits into a kerf cut into the
end of the tenon sawn down the middle parallel to its cheeks, as
shown in the drawing on the facing page. A foxtail wedge expands
the tenon when the joint is clamped up: The thick end of the wedge
hits the bottom of the mortise, which forces the wedge up into the
tenon, expanding it as the joint is driven home.

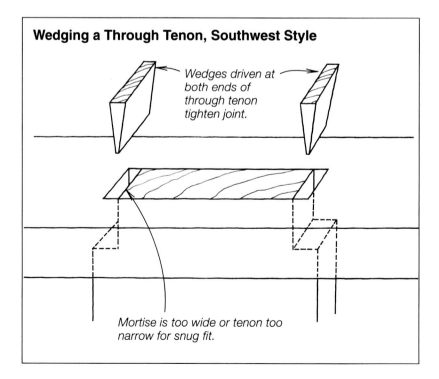

Wedging a Through Tenon, Southwest Style

Wedges driven at both ends of through tenon tighten joint.

Mortise is too wide or tenon too narrow for snug fit.

The trick to getting a good tight tenon-to-mortise fit with a foxtail wedge is in the sizing of the wedge, as well as the thickness of the kerf cut in the tenon. If the wedge doesn't produce enough expansion, the joint's fit will still be loose. If the wedge causes too much expansion, the joint won't fully seat or, worse, the mortised member will crack or split. What makes wedge and kerf sizing so difficult is that you can't make a dry run to try the fit (unless you mock up a test joint with the same degree of loose fit and clamp it up). Once the foxtail is fully inserted in its kerf, the parts being joined will be very hard to drive apart.

The best results I've had with foxtail wedges is to make them fairly stout, and make their corresponding kerfs in the tenon just thick enough to accommodate them. This is especially important if the tenons are long, as skinny wedges might misalign and foul as the joint is driven home. Keep the foxtail's degree of taper slight—only 3° to 5°—so that the wedge spreads the tenon only slightly when fully driven; most loose-fitting tenons require relatively little in the way of expansion for a snug joint.

Concealing Poor Fit

There are many parts of a cabinet or piece of furniture where a close fit is usually close enough. I know many woodworkers who cheerfully accept a less-than-perfect fit between kickplates around the bottom of lower kitchen cabinets, confident that no one on earth will ever get down on hands and knees just to inspect these joints. But there are also instances where nothing less than a perfect fit will do: the space around a recessed drawer front and its carcase frame, the seam between a showy veneered panel and its surrounding frame, the juncture of a subtly curved bedpost and the headboard it attaches to. If these parts don't meet in a flawless seam, the eye of the beholder is the first to know! Reveals and inlays are two devices for concealing poor fit that won't take a lot of work to implement and may even enhance the effect of your design.

Hiding problems with a reveal

Your ability to judge exactness of fit depends upon a clear view of the seam between two parts. If that juncture is meant to be a tight, even line where one part ends and the other begins, you'd be surprised at what a tiny variation the average viewer can detect. But if you obscure that boundary with a recessed seam that creates a little dark shadow (called a reveal by architects), you'll easily cheat the eye—the viewer won't be able to detect any misfit between the parts. A reveal is easily created by shaping the edge of one of the parts that connect. For

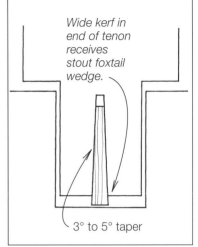

Wedging a Blind Tenon with a Foxtail Wedge

Pressing blind tenon home drives foxtail wedge up into kerf, expanding tenon and tightening loose fit.

Wide kerf in end of tenon receives stout foxtail wedge.

3° to 5° taper

The author's nightstand has legs that join to cutouts in the shelf that match the leg profile. The ragged edge left from the saber saw used to make the cutouts, as seen on the leg at right, is hidden when the cutout is chamfered, as shown on the leg at left.

example, look at the nightstand shown in the photo above. The irregular joint where the leg at right joins the divider is the result of a carelessly sawn notch. Chamfering the notch on the leg at left using a 45° router bit creates a reveal, giving the joint a clean, regular appearance. By this same method, you can improve the look of poorly cut cabinet sides, concealing tearout at the top edge of a carcase where the sides meets the underside of the top, as shown in the drawing on the facing page. If the carcase is already assembled, you might be able to cut this reveal using a scratch stock, a plow plane or (if the top doesn't overhang the sides too far) a slot-cutter bit in a router.

If you discover tearout along the edge of a plywood cabinet side after the face frame has been applied, you can trim the frame flush and create a reveal at the same time using a special router bit. The CMT flush and V-groove bit (#853-501) is like a regular ball-bearing-piloted flush-trim bit, with the addition of a V-shaped tooth that cuts a small groove directly over the seam between frame and cabinet side (see the top photo on the facing page). Similarly, you can clean up a ratty-looking joint between edge-glued parts by routing a shallow reveal with a regular V-groove bit, as shown in the bottom photo on the facing page.

To conceal a less-than-perfect connection between a cabinet's side and face frame, a joint can be routed with a flush and V-groove bit. Besides flush trimming the edge of the stile, the bit's small V-shaped tooth cuts a reveal that hides tearout along the glue line.

You can smooth out the look of a tawdry joint between edge-glued parts by routing a shallow reveal. Here, a V-groove bit in a router guided by a fence clamped to the panel has cleaned up a section of the seam.

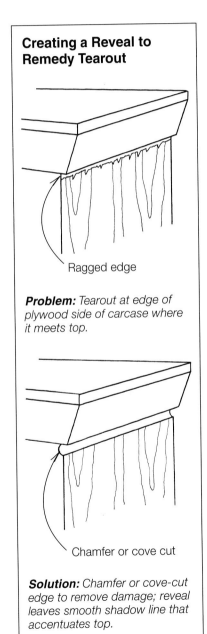

Creating a Reveal to Remedy Tearout

Ragged edge

Problem: *Tearout at edge of plywood side of carcase where it meets top.*

Chamfer or cove cut

Solution: *Chamfer or cove-cut edge to remove damage; reveal leaves smooth shadow line that accentuates top.*

If a poorly fitting recessed drawer front leaves an irregular line around its carcase housing, creating a reveal can be as easy as chamfering or rounding over the edge of the drawer front to varying degrees: more where the gap between drawer front and carcase seems too small, less where it appears to be nearly the right size. You can do chamfering with a small hand plane, rounding with a narrow strip of fine sandpaper used like a shoeshine cloth over the sharp edge of the drawer front. Reinforcing the back of the sandpaper with strapping tape makes the paper backing less liable to tear.

Installing an inlay over poor seams

Another way to disguise a poor fit is to rout a groove over the offending seam and insert a strip of decorative inlay. While this repair requires a lot more effort than simply routing a reveal, the technique can be a life-saver in situations where you must have a flat, continuous surface that appears seamless. For example, I once made a large round tabletop using a central panel of hardwood plywood surrounded by a segmented solid-wood frame. My miters on the frame were quite precise, but unfortunately I ended up with several shabby-looking gaps where the curved frame didn't butt up cleanly to the round plywood panel. Since this was a very even-grained walnut top, filling was out of the question; the repairs would have surely highlighted the irregular gaps. To save the top, I routed a ⅛-in. wide groove directly over the gap all the way around the top, using a pivoting circle jig to swing the router around at a constant radius (see the photo below). I then inlaid a thin strip of multicolored banding, a decorative inlay strip glued up

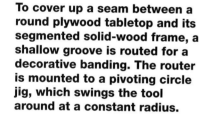

To cover up a seam between a round plywood tabletop and its segmented solid-wood frame, a shallow groove is routed for a decorative banding. The router is mounted to a pivoting circle jig, which swings the tool around at a constant radius.

from many different woods into a repeating pattern (these strips are available in a wide range of widths, patterns and color combinations; see Sources of Supply on pp. 196-197). The gentle curve of the groove allowed me to coax the straight inlay strip into place. After gluing down and sanding the strip flush and finishing the top, the irregular gap was completely hidden, and the inlay added a welcome bit of visual detail to the otherwise plain tabletop.

You can use inlaid banding or line inlays (narrow strips of veneer-thick wood) to conceal a poor fit between any panel and its frame, or between any adjacent parts glued together, say the seams between staves glued up into octagonal columns used for legs on a large desk or conference table. You can also use inlaid banding around the edge of a part, such as a drawer front, to conceal a dinged or badly damaged edge. Choose a banding pattern wide enough to conceal the defect and inlay it into a shallow rabbet routed around the part.

Replacing Bad Fasteners

The fit and strength of parts assembled into furniture or cabinetry often depend upon fasteners, such as screws or nails. Screws occasionally lose their grip in the wood or break from the force of being driven, and they can be a pain to remove and replace. Brads and small finish nails sometimes bend before they're hammered home. Here are some tips for refitting or extracting such troublesome fasteners without damaging the surrounding wood.

Extracting stripped screws

Modern screws have come a long way since the days when soft, zinc-plated steel and solid-brass screws were the only fasteners available to woodworkers. Today there are dozens of types of screws, many designed for specific functions: stainless-steel screws for attaching outdoor hardware, hardened-steel screws with fast-gripping threads and slender shanks for driving into hardwoods without pilot holes, special large-thread screws specifically designed to join MDF parts for European-style cabinets. But whatever the variety, when a screw strips out its threads, there's a problem to deal with.

The first step to fixing a stripped screw is to see how easily you can remove it. If the driver has damaged the slot or recess in the head of the screw to where the tip has little purchase left, try applying a drop or two of Screw Medic (see Sources of Supply on pp. 196-197). This special liquid increases the friction between the driver and the screw so you can apply more torque and stand a better chance of backing out the screw. Once the screw is removed, giving the threads more bite may be

To increase the bite of a stripped #12 screw, line the hole with small strips of "Mr. Grip" before the screws are replaced. The thin perforated metal can be cut with tin snips or a hefty scissors.

as easy as inserting a glue-covered toothpick into the hole. I find that square toothpicks (bought at the supermarket) work better for this than the round ones do. Break the toothpick off flush with the surface, wait for the glue to set (or use a thick cyanoacrylate adhesive, such as Satellite City's Special T, if you're in a hurry) and re-drive the screw.

If the screw spins in its hole but can't easily be removed, pull the screw out by temporarily gluing the tip of an old screwdriver into its slot with a fast-drying cyanoacrylate (or use one of the techniques for extracting broken screws described below). You can restore this more seriously stripped hole with "Mr. Grip," a product made up of thin strips of metal mesh (see Sources of Supply on pp. 196-197). These strips are cut to length with shears and pressed into the stripped screw hole before re-driving the screw (see the photo above). I haven't tried it, but the package says that Mr. Grip will also tighten loose rungs and round tenons in their mortises.

To repair a stripped screw hole, bore a tapered hole with a tapered reamer, then glue in a wooden cone and trim it flush with the surface. After a new pilot hole is drilled, a new screw can be driven.

If all else fails, you'll need to plug the hole and drill a new pilot hole before reinstalling the screw. One remedy is to fill the hole with a two-part epoxy putty, such as Quickwood (see p. 59), though you should wait until the epoxy cures (usually 24 hours) before drilling and re-placing the screw. A quicker solution is to glue in a tapered wood plug with cyanoacrylate. A special tapered reamer called a "wood screw hole restorer" (see Sources of Supply on pp. 196-197) makes a conical hole in the place of the stripped screw hole. The tapered wood cone is glued into the hole, then a new pilot hole may be drilled and a new screw driven (see the photo above). You can buy tapered wood plugs ready made (see Sources of Supply on pp. 196-197) or make your own by sharpening the end of a ¼-in. dia. or ⁵⁄₁₆-in. dia. dowel in a pencil sharpener, then cutting off the tapered end. In lieu of a special tool, you can also bore a plain ¼-in. or ⅜-in. dia. hole over the screw hole and glue in a cylindrical wooden plug, made with a standard plug cutter. For tighter-fitting plugs, I prefer to use Snug-Plug tapered plug cutters, available from Woodcraft; see Sources of Supply on pp. 196-197).

Once cones or plugs have been glued in place, make sure to drill a tapered pilot hole that matches the screw's root diameter (the size of the shank minus the threads) to prevent the screw from stripping out again. Tapered pilot bits for standard-size screws (#8, #10, etc.) are available from most woodworking-supply catalogs (see Sources of Supply on pp. 196-197). Before driving new screws, apply a little paraffin wax or Behlen's Slideez. Lubrication will make the screws less liable to strip out, and you'll also get more screws driven with one charge of a cordless drill/driver (I like Slideez because of its Crisco-like consistency that applies easily to screw threads; it also smells good). Never use soap to lubricate steel screws, as it can attract moisture that will rust them.

Screws are particularly apt to strip out when driven into the end grain of solid wood or the edge of MDF or particleboard panels. Boring a hole and inserting a plug made from the face grain or the side grain of a board will not only remedy the stripped hole, but will also give the screw more holding power than it would otherwise have had. An even better solution for these tough fastening situations is to drive a threaded insert into the workpiece that the screw must bite into and use a machine screw to join the wood parts. There are several different types of threaded inserts, including ones that are specifically designed to be driven into end grain or into composite materials, such as MDF (see Sources of Supply on pp. 196-197).

After an automatic center punch makes a dimple in the top of the screw and a small pilot hole is drilled, a #1 screw extractor driven with a tap wrench pulls the remains of a broken screw out of the stock.

Extracting broken screws

If a wood screw is discourteous enough to break off instead of strip, special measures—and special tools—are called for. The cleanest way I know to remove a screw that has some of its head showing requires a small-diameter drill bit and a spiral-flute screw extractor, available from a machinist's supply (see Sources of Supply on pp. 196-197). A #1 extractor is about right for #8 and #10 screws (as well as small finish nails); use a #2 extractor for #12 and #14 screws. The first step is to center-punch the stub end of the screw and drill a hole ($\frac{5}{64}$-in. dia. for the #1; $\frac{7}{64}$-in. dia. for the #2) , $\frac{1}{4}$ in. deep if possible. If the broken end of the screw is sharply pointed, making drilling a clean hole impossible, you're better off drilling a plug out around the screw, as described below. Carefully tap the end of the extractor into the hole and back the screw out, using a small socket wrench or tap wrench (see the photo at left). Take care to keep firm downward pressure on the extractor and to keep its shank perpendicular to the surface of the workpiece as you work, lest the hardened-steel shank of the thin tool suddenly snap.

A short length of copper electrical wire is inserted into a hole drilled into the shank of a broken screw and heated with a propane torch until the wood around the screw burns slightly. The remains of the screw can then be pulled out with needle-nosed pliers.

If the screw is especially tenacious and won't exit before the extractor strips out of its hole, more extreme measures must be applied. Insert a short length of solid copper wire into the hole drilled in the top of the screw head: 14-gauge copper wire fits snugly into a ⁵⁄₆₄-in. hole, and 12-gauge wire into a ⁷⁄₆₄- in. hole. Heat the end with a propane torch until the wood around the screw starts to smolder (see the photo above). The heat should liquefy resins in the wood and char the wood around the screw, making its removal easier. Quickly, while the screw is still hot, pull the screw out with needle-nosed pliers, or reinsert the end of the screw extractor and back the screw out.

If all other removal methods fail, you can drill a plug out around the screw, remove it, plug the resulting hole, then re-drill and fit a new screw. You can buy a special screw-removal tool (see Sources of Supply on pp. 196-197) that drills a cylindrical hole around the screw stub, as shown in the photo at right. Once the tubular drill gets below the end of the screw, the plug should break out, allowing easy removal. After gluing in a clean dowel or wood plug, drill a new pilot hole and drive the new screw. If you don't want to buy a special tool, you can use a regular ¼-in. plug cutter (which leaves a ½-in. dia. hole in the work). However, I'd suggest doing this only when extracting brass screws; if the plug cutter hits a steel screw it will be damaged.

A hollow-steel screw-removal tool bores a cylindrical hole around the shank of a screw that has broken off below the wood's surface. Once the screw is out, the hole can be plugged with a dowel and a new screw can be driven.

Pulling out a bent brad or finish nail is easy with a small cat's-paw style nail puller. A guard plate made from a scrap piece of plywood with a hole in the middle keeps the tool from gouging the wood.

Pulling bent brads and nails

Small finish nails and brads used to attach frames and moldings or mount trim can be tricky to remove if a glancing blow bends them over before they're driven home. Since these fasteners are often used for assembly of parts that have already been finished, the trick is to remove them without damaging the surrounding wood. If more than a nib of the nail's head is above the work's surface, the tool of choice is a pair of long-nosed locking pliers. These are capable of grasping very small brad heads with great authority, thereby increasing your chances of a clean extraction. Gently twist the brad from side to side as you pull up.

If the brad has been dealt a death blow and lies crumpled and embedded into the surface of the work, you'll need to perform a delicate operation. For such removal, I rely on a small Japanese nail puller called a Tiger Claw (available from The Japan Woodworker; see Sources of Supply on pp. 196-197). The 6-in. long Tiger Claw is a petite version of a nail puller commonly referred to as a cat's paw. It has two small claws with a sharply tapered slot between them that is used to snag the head of the brad. The trick is to lever the brad up and out without denting the surrounding wood. To protect the work surface, I set a guard plate over the nail, as shown in the photo above. The plate is made from a piece of 1/4-in. plywood with a 3/4-in. dia. hole bored through the middle.

A double-ended nail set used to countersink the heads of brads that attach molding and trim is easier to control when setting small brads, so the head doesn't slip off and accidentally make another hole that needs puttying.

If the head or shank of the brad is below the surface of the work, I carefully use one of the puller's points to lift it up, prying with the tool against the guard plate. Then, I hook the nail with the tool's tapered slot and, using a sideways rolling motion, pull it up and out. If the brad breaks off, I use a nail set to drive the nib below the surface of the wood. I prefer a double-ended nail set, as shown in the photo above, because it is easier to control than a regular long-shank nail set. This also prevents another problem: holes punched in moldings when the nail set slips off. Incidentally, another good way to drive and set small brads is to use a brad pusher, a tool with a hollow shank and plunger that uses hand pressure to drive brads.

If you've managed to pull a crumpled brad out, you should repair the area around the hole before driving a new brad. If you're working on a less visible area of the piece, this repair could just entail filling the dented area, as described on pp. 54-55. If the damage is in a more prominent area, filling will probably be a poor choice, since it won't hide the defect as well as the following repair will. The bent-over shank of a brad typically dents the fibers at the wood's surface. These fibers often can be steamed back out, as described on pp. 50-52. If the dent is on a convex unfinished surface, say on a length of bead trim or an ogee molding, and isn't too deep, you may be able to scrape or sand down below the surface of the dent.

If a bent nail has split the part it's driven through, glue the split back together, as described on p. 96, before driving a new nail. If splitting continues to be a problem, try blunting the tip of each nail before driving it; the nail will then crush fibers as it's driven instead of cleaving them apart. Another way to limit splitting is to drill a small pilot hole or use a nail spinner in an electric drill. This chuck-like device spins a nail so that it creates its own pilot hole as it is driven in.

CHAPTER 3

Raising Dents and Filling Gouges

They say the little things make a big difference. Well, when I'm building a new piece of furniture, I'm painfully aware of all those "little things." At times, they seem to multiply faster than I can keep them under control, and they often conspire to undermine my enjoyment of the entire project. The best relief is to keep after woodworking's little molehills—superficial dents, nicks and gouges—and fix them before they add up to a mountain of defects.

As is true throughout this book, the methods demonstrated in this chapter have been gleaned from my own experience and that of my learned colleagues in the fields of woodworking, wood finishing and furniture repair. And while professional furniture repairers have dozens of special materials and complicated techniques for tackling any problem, I've chosen to focus on two broad categories—steaming out dents and puttying gouges—techniques that I feel will be the easiest for the average woodworker to manage successfully. Hence, I've purposely chosen not to discuss several well-known repair methods in this chapter. For example, I have excluded shellac-stick burn-in,

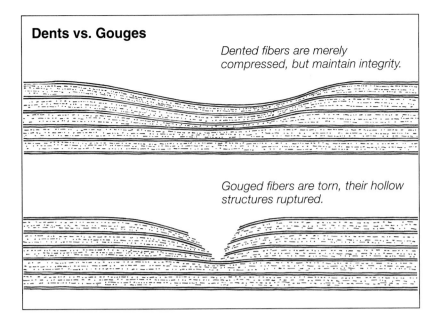

Dents vs. Gouges

Dented fibers are merely compressed, but maintain integrity.

Gouged fibers are torn, their hollow structures ruptured.

although it's a traditional way of repairing small dents and gouges. While the method can produce terrific results, burning in is difficult and risky, performed at or close to the last stage of the finishing process. A good burn-in requires a deft hand and the skill that comes only after years of experience. If you're set on using this technique, you'll find a thorough treatment of it in Michael Dresdner's excellent text: *The Woodfinishing Book* (The Taunton Press, 1992).

At the outset, it's important to distinguish dents from gouges (see the drawing above). A dent is a depression where the wood fibers near the surface have been crushed and compressed (imagine a handful of soda straws). In contrast, gouged wood has fibers that have been torn so that some or most of the fibers are actually broken. Expanding steam can reinflate compressed fibers (like blowing up a ribbed air mattress) to restore them to their former shape. But torn or severed fibers won't hold steam pressure and therefore don't expand as readily. Hence, for effective repairs, gouges need to be filled, as described on pp. 55-65, or patched, as described on pp. 67-74.

Raising Dents

Even when a clamp, dropped accidentally, appears to have left an otherwise perfect tabletop or cabinet door hopelessly scarred, do not despair: Most dents in wood can be miraculously raised, restoring the unblemished look of the surface. On unfinished wood dents may be raised with steam or with fumes from a drop of burning alcohol. Dents that are discovered after finish has been applied can be filled with additional drops of finish—a process called "doping in."

As you might suspect, softwoods and soft hardwoods like butternut and mahogany are more susceptible to denting than dense hardwoods like birch and maple, but the dents in soft woods are also usually easier to steam out. But regardless of species, steaming should be performed ahead of sanding, as coarse abrasive granules may sever grain fibers around the dent, making steaming less effective. To detect small dents on critical surfaces, like tabletops and wood counters, before sanding, you should raise the wood's grain with water (or, as R. Bruce Hoadley recommends, a damp cloth). Raising the grain not only reveals subtle dents you might not have noticed before, but also allows you to knock down the rough whiskers of the raised grain before applying stain or finish. After a dent is steamed, allow the wood to dry overnight before proceeding with final sanding and finishing.

One caveat before steaming: Whenever hollow wood fibers are crushed, the way they refract light changes. So even though you may have successfully raised a dent and restored the apparent flatness of a surface, you might still see a "dent" after finishing. Previously crushed fibers are also likely to take stain differently than the surrounding wood, so the restored area may stand out slightly.

Steaming out a dent

There are several effective methods for using steam to lift dents. The method you choose use will depend on the size of the dent and personal preference. Dents that are about the size of a bean can be raised with a regular electric soldering iron—mine is a pencil-style unit with a 25-watt element. Press the cleaned tip of the heated soldering iron into a clean, damp cloth directly over the dent for a few seconds, as shown in the photo at left. Keep the iron moving to avoid scorching the wood. Examine the dent after the area has dried; if it's not fully returned to level, repeat the process. In lieu of a soldering iron, you can use the tip of an old screwdriver or palette knife heated on a burner or with a propane torch.

The clean tip of a heated soldering iron is applied over a small wet cloth to steam out a small dent. The heat from the 25-watt iron takes only a few seconds to raise the dent.

Small dents in veneers can also be steamed out using this method (the substrate beneath the veneer is usually dented as well). But great care must be taken to keep heat and moisture to a minimum to avoid releasing the bond of water-based glues, such as hide glue, as well as thermoplastic glues, such as yellow and white PVA. In case the veneer does delaminate, glue it back down as described on pp. 115-116.

Dents the size of a penny and bigger usually respond better to the greater volume of heat produced by an ordinary household steam iron. Set the iron on the lowest steam setting (usually specified for wool fabrics) and iron the dent through a dampened cloth, as shown in the photo below. If your iron has a special steam-jet button, pressing it while the iron is over the dent will release a burst of steam that should help raise the dent more quickly.

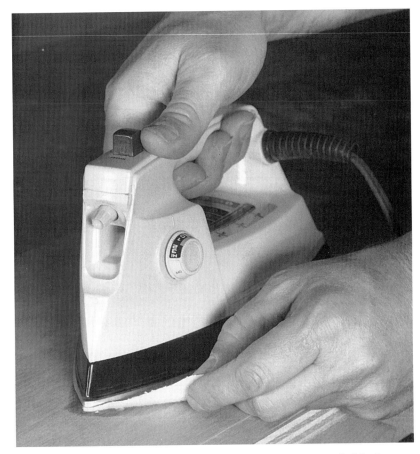

To raise a large dent in a lauan plywood panel, a household steam iron (set to a wool steam setting) is set over a damp cloth, which protects the wood from scorching.

A minuscule #80 drill chucked in a Dremel tool makes tiny holes in a dent. This technique can increase the effectiveness of iron-steaming dents in open-pore hardwoods, such as the red oak shown here.

To increase the effectiveness of ironing dents out of open-pore hardwoods, such as oak and walnut, drill or pierce small holes into the surface of the dent. These allow the steam to penetrate more readily and expand more fibers below the dent. If the holes are small enough (I use a large pin or a tiny #80 wire-gauge drill, as shown in the photo at left) and carefully confined to large open pores, the minute punctures will be virtually undetectable in the finished piece.

One other method remains for steaming out dents, and since it doesn't use water, it is ideal for repairs that need to be effected in great haste (you don't have to wait for moisture to evaporate from the area before applying the finish). I learned this method from finishing expert Michael Dresdner, who uses denatured alcohol as both the steaming agent and the source of heat. Begin by dispensing a single drop of alcohol into the dent, using an eyedropper and taking care not to get excess anywhere else—especially on your hands or clothing. Immediately set a match to the drop, which will burn briefly with a near-invisible blue flame (see the top photo on the facing page). Keep a wet rag handy, just in case things take a unexpectedly pyrotechnic turn. The gas emitted by the burning alcohol should swell out the dent in a few seconds. Repeat the process, if necessary, and commence sanding and finishing as soon as the dent is raised. I once read somewhere that this method will remove dents from finished surfaces, but I've ended up with scorched spots every time I've tried it.

Filling a dent by "doping in"

If you discover a small dent after the wood has been topcoated with a film-type clear finish, such as lacquer or varnish, you don't have to scrape or sand off the finish to steam the dent out. Instead, you can fill the dent with finish in a process called "doping in" to restore the look of a flat, blemish-free surface. You can also use the doping-in process to fix small chips that might occur in brittle finishes, such as lacquer.

Doping in entails applying a drop of the same finish used to topcoat the piece. (Mohawk's Transfil is a clear liquid filler specifically designed for doping in.) Apply the finish with a toothpick or a small brush (see the bottom photo on the facing page). After the drop dries and shrinks, you apply another drop and wait for it to dry, repeating the process once or twice more until the finish in the dent is built up to the same level as the surrounding finish. Doping in is most practical with a fast-drying lacquer or shellac finish, but you can use a slow-drying finish, such as varnish, by speeding up its drying time, as described on p. 189.

A drop of alcohol, applied with an eyedropper, burns nearly invisibly after it's touched off by a match. The brief burn can generate enough heat to raise small dents.

A brush is used to apply a single drop of lacquer to fill a small dent in a lacquered tabletop. After the drop dries, the process, called 'doping in,' is repeated until the finish in the dent is built back up to the level of the surface.

Once the doped-in spot is thoroughly dry, you can wet-sand the area flat with a piece of 400-grit sandpaper on a small felt-padded wood block before proceeding to topcoating. If at all possible, doping in should be done prior to the last application of top coat, which will help to conceal the repair. Final topcoating is essential with reactive finishes, such as varnish or polyurethane, to hide the faint lines (called "witness lines") that form around a repair where one coat has been sanded through to the other.

Puttying Gouges

For many woodworkers, putty is the "gatling gun" of the mistake-repairing arsenal—it can wipe out any defect. It's true that you can slap putty on all kinds of surface scars—dings, chips, screw holes, worm holes, cracks and gouges—as well as on gaffes such as misdrilled holes for mounting a door handle. But a hastily puttied patch is a real eyesore, and not much better than the flaw it clumsily covers. If you want the repair to look good, you will have to do a little planning and use a little restraint.

When faced with putty repairs, ask yourself these questions before slathering "miracle filler" all over your project. First of all, should you use putty or not? Try to save the putty for defects too small to be patched or dings that can't easily be repaired otherwise. If the defect is deeper than $3/16$ in. or bigger than a fingernail, you should probably correct it with a wood patch (see pp. 67-74). Second, choose the right kind of putty for the job and apply it at the right stage of construction or finishing, as described in the sections below. And finally, be prepared to follow up a puttying job in a prominent location with some artistic touching up, as described on pp. 126-129.

Filling raw wood with glue-and-sawdust putty

Most damage is inflicted during the cutting, machining and assembly stages of woodworking, and it makes sense to repair the damage as soon as it occurs. But even if you're lucky enough to find a can of putty that matches the color of the raw wood perfectly, it's unlikely that the puttied patch will match the surrounding wood after the project is stained and/or finished. Premixed putties in a can just don't take stain or finish the same way the raw wood does; they tend to become darker as they dry. That unfortunate fact leaves you with two alternatives: puttying after staining and sealing the wood, as described on pp. 62-64, or using a putty that absorbs finishes similarly to real wood.

As luck would have it, there is a putty you can mix up in your own shop that just happens to suit the second alternative. You probably already guessed that it's made from glue and sawdust, but wait—there's more to it. Putty made using ordinary white or yellow glue as a binder not only doesn't sand particularly well, but it also doesn't take stain or finish much better than many commercial putties. The not-so-secret secret is to mix the putty from sawdust and traditional hot hide glue. Hide glue works far better than synthetic glues because it is a protein, so its absorption characteristics are very similar to cellulose, the stuff wood fibers are made of. And the hide glue bonds with wood dust without changing its color, so getting a good color match is a breeze. (The putty does look slightly darker when wet, but dries to just the right tone.) Putty made from hide glue and sawdust is particularly great for patching a surface with lots of tearout due to poor planing on fussy, figured grain. You can fill all the defects at once, resand the surface and continue work, and not have to worry about having to do a meticulous job puttying up all those tearouts later on.

The sidebar on p. 58 tells you how to make a good hide-glue-based putty. You can use this mix fresh, or store it in your shop and just heat up a little whenever you need it. Apply this putty as described below, and fill holes and crevices proud of the surface to allow for shrinkage. Wait for repairs to dry at least a couple of hours before sanding. Incidentally, antique restorers often use a thickened putty made from hide glue and wood dust as artificial wood, to shape or cast "carvings" or small replacement parts. If you make a stiff mixture, you can use it to build up a broken edge or fill in missing parts of a carving.

Mixing your own putties for sealed wood

If you prefer to make your own putty for applying to a sealed wood surface that's to be clear coated (not stained), you can mix fine sawdust with regular shellac. Add just enough fresh shellac to turn the fine sawdust into a thick paste, and fill the defects as usual. The dried shellac putty dries quickly, and can be touch-sanded in less than one hour. Shellac, which is the "universal recipient" of the finishing world, is compatible with practically any top coat.

To fix checks and cracks on sealed wood in a hurry, make a mixture of fine sawdust and a drop or two of a thick cyanoacrylate adhesive, such as Satellite City's Special T. Cyanoacrylate is clear, bonds tenaciously, dries quickly, and dries hard enough to be sanded reasonably well in just minutes. (However, species that contain tannin, such as oak, can retard the drying of cyanoacrylates to the point where a putty mixed from these ingredients may not dry unless catalyzed by the addition of an accelerator; see Sources of Supply on pp. 196-197.) Finish chemist Chris Minick warns that mixing cyanoacrylates with exotic

Homemade Hide-Glue/Sawdust Putty

This recipe yields a small batch of putty (about 2 oz.), enough for dozens of small repairs. It can be stored for several months in a small jar or other airtight container.

1 oz. granulated hide glue (dry weight)
1½ oz. cool water (liquid measure)
2 to 3 drops iodine
1 oz. fine, clean wood dust

or

1-oz. package Knox gelatin
1 oz. cool water
2 to 3 drops iodine
1 oz. fine, clean wood dust

Start with powdered hide glue (see Sources of Supply on pp. 196-197) and mix 1 oz. glue granules with 1½ oz. cool water. If you don't have hide glue, you can substitute a 1-oz. package of Knox gelatin (which, believe it or not, is super-refined hide glue) and mix it with 1 oz. of water.

Whichever mix you use, let it set for a couple of hours, then heat it in a double boiler at about 140°F for about half an hour, checking the temperature with a candy thermometer (available at a housewares store). Let the mix cool, and add two or three drops of iodine (you can find it in the camping department of a sporting-goods store, as water-purification solution). The iodine prevents the perishable hide glue from going rancid, allowing you to keep it handy in the shop for some months. (Rancid glue stinks to high heaven.) Finally, reheat the mix and sprinkle in the sawdust, a little at a time and stirring constantly, until the mix has the consistency of creamy putty. Apply this putty warm, reheating it in a double boiler (or microwave oven) as needed.

While you can add any old sawdust to hot hide glue to make putty, it's best not to use sawdust created by sanding. Sawdust made during sanding is a combination of wood particles and the garnet, carborundum or aluminum-oxide grit that is shed from the paper; the little specks of grit reflect light, making a puttied patch glitter like a rhinestone cowboy. Instead, make up a batch of very fine wood dust by abrading a wood scrap that matches the area to be repaired with a fine file or riffler. Collect the wood dust on a clean sheet of paper, then strain it through a fine sieve before mixing it into the warm glue.

wood dusts can produce unexpected—and volatile—results, as the extractives in these woods can react with the adhesive and generate noxious fumes and heat. So when using cyanoacrylates, always work in a well-ventilated area and keep a bottle of solvent around, in case you glue your fingers together.

Using commercial putties

If you prefer to use a store-bought putty right out of the can, the best way to overcome color-matching problems is to fill defects after the wood has been stained and sealed. That way, you can select a standard putty color (or mix one, as described below) to match the surrounding finished wood and not have to worry about color disparity after finishing. The final coat of finish over the putty repair protects it and levels the surface.

In case you haven't looked in the finishing section of your local hardware store or woodworking supply catalog lately, there is a dazzling array of putties for woodworkers to choose from. These include powders that must be mixed with water, ready-mixed fillers that come in cans and tubs, two-part compounds that must be mixed or kneaded like clay before application, and wax-like filler sticks that can be rubbed into dings. Add shop-made concoctions to this list, and you can easily become what songwriter Joni Mitchell calls "the kind of crazy you get from too much choice." Let's explore each alternative carefully, so you start off with the right material for the job on hand.

Water-based and solvent-based putties Of all the various putty products, water-based and solvent-based putties are probably most handy to the woodworker. They come ready to use, are available in a wide variety of colors, sand well once dry, and can be mixed or tinted to match the color of your work (see p. 60). And, unlike older oil-based putty products, water- and solvent-based putties are compatible with virtually all finishes. Water-based acrylic latex putties, such as Amity Water-Based Wood Putty, Master Wood Filler, 3M Just-Like-Wood Putty and Wunderfil, can be thinned with and cleaned up with plain water. Solvent-based putties, such as Fil-O-Wood, Famowood and Wood-Tex Synthetic Wood, are thinned and cleaned up with acetone or lacquer thinner (some manufacturers also sell special thinning solvents). In general, water-based latex putties are easier to clean up after, more environmentally friendly and slower to set and cure than solvent-based putties. Solvent-based putties are water-resistant (some, such as Wood-Tex, claim to be waterproof) and tend to dry harder and with less shrinkage than their water-based cousins.

Epoxy putties Although they are not the most economical or speediest for typical filling jobs, two-part epoxy putties dry very hard and strong. They are totally waterproof, making them a good choice for outdoor applications. Products such as Araldite, Quickwood and Bond-Aide are two-part materials (a resin and a catalyst) that must be mixed together before application and harden in about 30 to 45 minutes. Quickwood and Bond-Aide are thick putties that come in sticks rather than cans. They are mixed by kneading the two parts, and then they can be molded to shape, like modeling clay. This plasticity makes them ideal for dings and gouges on the edges or corners of parts where the putty must stand up to physical abuse. Epoxy putties don't usually accept stain well—in fact, they don't take water-based stains at all. They can, however, be colored with universal tints and fresco pigments, though they don't accept deep colors as well as regular putties do.

Getting the right color

Most brands of putty come in a reasonable assortment of ready-mixed wood tones. When choosing putty color, make sure that its overall tone is slightly lighter than that of the wood (putties tend to dry lighter than their wet color). This will allow you to touch up the area and blend in the repair later (remember, touching up coats the repair area with transparent color, thus darkening the putty while blending in defects). And unless you brush opaque touch-up colors over them (which takes a real artist's eye and application technique), a dark spot isn't easy to lighten up.

Don't get distressed if you can't find a putty that matches the wood closely. You can mix like solvent-based or like water-based putties together, though I'd mix only the same brands together to avoid incompatibility problems. Further, all putties can be custom tinted with universal tints or fresco colors (see the section on color mixing on p. 126). Many woodworkers prefer to keep only one can of neutral or "natural" color putty, and tint it to make all their wood-toned putties. Universal tints come in small tubes you can buy at paint stores and home-supply centers; fresco powders are color pigments that come in small jars you can order from finishing and woodworking catalog suppliers; both are available in a wide range of standard colors as well as wood tones (see Sources of Supply on pp. 196-197).

To mix up a custom color, I first transfer a small amount of putty (enough for samples and to get the job done) to a plastic film canister, then add pigments to it until the color looks to be the right hue and about the same shade as my sealed finished sample—remember, most putties lighten up a little when they dry. If the wood is hard to match or the wood has areas of greatly different color, like zebrawood or rosewood, I mix several different-colored putties, each in a different film canister.

If you are repairing large or prominent dings, even the most carefully matched putty won't completely disappear (unless you're working with jet-black Gabon ebony). This is because most wood species contain many subtle hues; lowly putty has but a single color. Thus, aside from the tiniest pinholes, filled dings should be blended in with touch-up colors before final topcoating, as described on pp. 126-129.

Applying store-bought putty to sealed wood

Once you've chosen a putty, you're ready to apply it to fill the defect. Most paste putties can be applied right out of the can with a regular putty knife, but I prefer to use a putty knife I made by cutting off the blade on a regular palette knife (see the photo on the facing page). This smaller-bladed tool allows me to work more sensitively in the repair area without getting excess putty on adjacent wood surfaces, where it might fill the open pores of many species and show up later. For tiny nicks, I use a really narrow spatula (about $^3/_{16}$ in. wide), made by whittling down the end of a popsicle stick or a plastic kitchen pot scraper (these are sold in the housewares section of department stores).

You can fill deep scratches with putty to recover a level, smooth surface. But if the scratch is across the grain and has torn through fibers in the wood's surface, it will be very hard to hide. Unless you're prepared to do quite a bit of artistic touching up, it's usually best to sand or scrape below the scratch, back down to sound wood.

When filling small nicks, holes and gouges with a water- or solvent-based putty, I press the putty down firmly with the tool to pack the defect, leaving just a wee mound above the surface. After the putty starts to set (only a minute for solvent-based putty, a few minutes for water-based putty), I strike it flush with the sharp edge of my palette knife, as shown in the drawing below. After allowing the repair to dry an hour or more, I apply a second coat, leaving just enough putty proud of the surface so that once it shrinks a little, it will be very close to flush. The result is a tight patch that requires very little sanding.

A small putty knife, made by cutting down the blade of an artist's palette knife, does a neat job of filling holes and small defects. The narrow edge makes it easier to get the putty only where you want it.

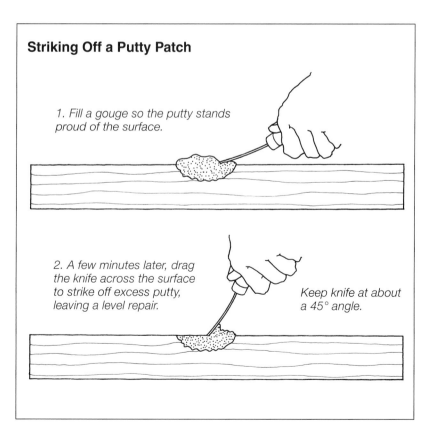

Striking Off a Putty Patch

1. Fill a gouge so the putty stands proud of the surface.

2. A few minutes later, drag the knife across the surface to strike off excess putty, leaving a level repair.

Keep knife at about a 45° angle.

Defects deeper than about $^3/_{32}$ in. must be filled in two or more applications, allowing the putty to dry for about one hour in between. You can make sure the putty is dry by touch sanding it; if forms powdery dust, it's dry, but if the paper clogs, it needs more time. To avoid ruining repairs on your work, putty a finish sample at the same time you putty the work and check the sample for dryness. Once the repair is dry, carefully sand with a fine-grit paper (180 to 320). Take care not to sand through the sealer coat and stain if one has been used. If you do, consult the discussion of toning repairs on pp. 123-125.

If you've puttied large patches on wood with big, prominent pores, such as ash, Roger Heitzman advises that you can avoid "shiny spots" on the final surface by etching in a few grain lines using the fine tip of an awl or the blade of a razor knife. You can then start touching up the repair, as described on p. 127, before applying the top coat, which seals the putty repair and protects it.

Okay, don't listen to your mother

If you insist on passing up good advice and decide to use a water- or solvent-based putty on raw, unstained wood, avoid heartache at finishing time by checking to see how good the final color match will be before you actually finish the piece. To do this, you'll need to fill a few holes on a scrap of new wood from your project. If you're repairing dings on a highly visible surface, make sure the sample has the same color and grain figure as the surface wood.

After the putty dries for about an hour, wipe the surface of the sample with mineral spirits, as shown in the photo on the facing page. Evaluate the color of the match under the same light source the piece will be seen in—direct or diffuse sunlight or incandescent, quartz or fluorescent lighting. This last step is necessary because, believe it or not, a puttied patch that seems a pretty good match in one kind of light may, in a different setting, stick out like a fluorescent-plaid shirt at a polo game. The unpredictable effects of metamerism come into play, as explained on pp. 192-193.

Using stick fillers after final finishing

Crayon-like stick fillers present an entirely different approach to filling defects. Products such as Touch Up Stik, J. E. Moser's Fill Stick, Retouch crayons and Patchal Pencils are made of a waxy, semi-hard putty that never hardens completely, and they are designed to be applied to defects after finishing (Michael Dresdner advises that regular kiddie crayons also work well). A similar product, Color Putty, is a semi-soft paste that comes in a jar; it can be used just prior to final topcoating.

Wiping down a puttied sample with mineral spirits is a good way to evaluate the color of a putty as it will look on the finished project. Here, a puttied crack (near the top of the sample) shows up darker than the surrounding wood.

Putty sticks are extremely handy for filling the holes left by nails or brads used to mount prefinished moldings and parts or install finished cabinets. They're also great for hiding little dings and scratches that can happen anytime after finishing. They come in an impressive assortment of colors (Mohawk's Patchal Pencils come in 50 different wood tones), and sticks can even be melted together to mix a custom color. I always carry an assortment in my travel toolbox, for on-site repairs after delivery of furniture pieces and installation of cabinets.

To fill a minor gouge in a finished surface, a small nail, held with locking pliers, is heated with a propane torch and set into the defect. A crayon-like fill stick is pressed against the hot nail, and the waxy filler flows down into the gouge.

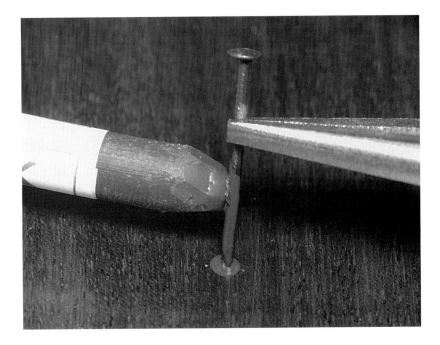

Repairs with putty sticks are made by rubbing the end of the stick over the repair area to deposit putty into the depression, then wiping the work surface with a cloth (dampened with mineral oil) to buff away the excess. A neat way to fill small nail holes and deep gouges is to melt the stick into the defect: Heat the end of a small nail or cheap scratch awl (heating ruins the metal's temper) over a stove burner or with a propane torch and set it into the hole. Now press the putty stick against the shank of the tool, allowing the molten putty to flow into the hole, as shown in the photo above. Scrape or buff off the excess, and you're done.

Filling voids with casting epoxies

In the mountains near my home, in Santa Cruz, California, redwood burl is an abundant and popular material for slab tables and countertops. And while it's gorgeous stuff, with lovely swirling grain figure, these burls are often fraught with cavernous voids, cracks and splits. Californian claro walnut slabs are also often loaded with these "features." While these are natural defects—no fault of the woodworker, who has merely cut into a slab and exposed them—they pose a problem in the functional sense. You know what I mean if you've ever set a drinking glass on a natural-slab tabletop, only to have your drink teeter on the edge of a gaping void and spill. Besides the fact that it would take an endless number of layers of store-bought filler to level these large natural voids, they just don't look good if you try to cover them up with a wood-toned putty.

Natural voids and fissures in large slabs of wood can be decoratively filled using black-colored epoxy, as shown here on the top of a California walnut dining table made by furniture maker Griffin Okie.

As they say in beauty school (which I'm glad to say I never attended), if you can't hide a defect, accentuate it. One effective way to deal with these big voids is to highlight them by filling the new wood with either a clear or colored casting epoxy. Just like the two-tube adhesive hardware-store epoxies, casting epoxy comes as a two-part mix, resin and catalyst. The material can be colored with universal tints or with fresco powders. San Rafael, California, woodworker Griffin Okie colors his void-filling repairs, like the one shown in the photo above, with lampblack. Okie uses a special resin mixture that's normally used for manufacturing prosthetic devices; this resin dries harder than regular epoxy, but is too toxic for non-professional use.

Before mixing your epoxy, make a careful examination of deep defects to be sure they don't have small fissures that go all the way through; you don't want your repair to wind up as a difficult-to-remove puddle on the floor! Check by placing a bright light above the defect, and tape up any areas on the underside of the surface that show any illumination. Now carefully measure the epoxy components as specified on the label and thoroughly mix them together. Pour the mixture directly into the defect and fill until it is just a tad proud of the surface (epoxy shrinks very little as it dries). If necessary, strike off the excess after the epoxy has set in an hour or so. Curing can take anywhere from overnight to several days, after which you can carefully wet-sand the epoxy using a fine-grit sandpaper and mineral oil to level and smooth the area.

CHAPTER 4
Patching or Concealing Defects

While little dents and gouges can be easily raised with steam or filled with putty, as discussed in Chapter 3, bigger problems don't go away so easily. Large defects that result from accidents, such as major gouges from misdirected hammer blows or blown-out grain and ragged holes due to careless or over-zealous machining, are hard to hide. Attempting to cover up such major wounds by troweling in gobs of putty is tantamount to conceding defeat. Unless you're remarkably talented with a touch-up brush, even the most casual observer will readily spot such poorly mended defects.

Achieving undetectable repairs on large defects usually means fighting fire with fire: What better material to replace bad wood than good wood? Patching a poorly routed slot or a misplaced hinge mortise takes more effort than just flipping open a can of filler, but the results are often remarkable. There are lots of remedies that can turn parts you might be ready to relegate to the firewood pile back into usable and seemingly unblemished components of your project.

A pattern for a dutchman patch is made by placing thin tracing paper over the diamond-shaped mortise that has been cut over the defect and rubbing with the flat of a soft-leaded pencil.

Surface Repair of Solid Wood

To patch any big problem area—large gouges, tearouts or misrouted sections—you have to select wood that matches the repair area as closely as possible. For this reason, I like to keep all the little scraps generated during a project until the piece is pretty well done (for some other good reasons to keep scraps, see p. 173). When selecting just the right scrap to cut a solid-wood or veneer patch from, it's important to consider not only how well the color and grain pattern of the patch fit the surrounding wood, but also grain direction. Light is reflected from wood fibers in different directions, often creating dancing patterns and figures. This phenomenon, called "chatoyance" (French for "to change luster like a cat's eye"), affects both the luster and the apparent color of the wood. A mismatch in the way a piece reflects light sometimes isn't caught until the finish goes on, because topcoating enhances the effects of light on the surface. Therefore, it's best to check the patch stock before beginning by wiping down both the workpiece and patch stock with mineral spirits (see p. 62). Then compare the match by laying the patch over the defect and examining it under sunlight or a strong lamp.

With any kind of patching job, make sure to seal the edges of the patch before inlaying it (shellac works well). This is especially important if you plan to stain the wood later. Otherwise, the open fibers of wood at the edge of the patch are likely to absorb more color than the surface grain and edge grain surrounding it, resulting in a dark line that follows the end grain.

Cutting in a "dutchman"

One traditional kind of patch for a deep or extensive defect on the surface or edge of the work is called a dutchman. Typically shaped like an elongated diamond, a dutchman is a fairly quick and simple to cut and works well on dark woods, where it's harder to detect. It's especially effective on gouges on the edge of the stock (see the photo below), where regular putty can offer only a weak repair.

To inlay a dutchman, start by chopping a shallow mortise ($\frac{1}{8}$ in. to $\frac{1}{4}$ in. deep) over the defective area. Next, lay a piece of thin paper over the mortise and shade the area around it with the flat part of a soft (#B) lead pencil (see the photo on p. 67). Now place this pattern over a piece of $\frac{3}{16}$-in. to $\frac{1}{4}$-in. stock, selected to match the repair area, as discussed above. Transfer the pattern using a sharp chisel or razor knife, then cut it out of the stock, trim and glue it in place, using any regular wood glue. If the repair is in the middle of a large panel, you can apply clamping pressure by weighting the patch or by using a go-bar, as shown in the photo on p. 116. The dutchman may be trimmed and sanded flush with the edge or surface after the glue is dry.

A dutchman is a good repair for gouges on the edge of the stock. It is a simple patch to cut and glue in place, and it works well on darker woods, such as this mahogany chair's apron, where it's hard to see.

Sawing and raising a tapered plug

On wood surfaces with particularly complex grain patterns, it's nearly impossible to make a patch match seamlessly with the surrounding wood. One possibility is to thickness-plane the part or panel thinner to bring the surface down below the defect. But there is a less drastic method for patching a uniquely grained wood surface without introducing a patch cut from another piece. This tricky repair requires cutting the wood around the defect into a tapered plug that's larger on the bottom than on the top. Once cut, the plug is raised (to make up for the kerf of the sawcut) and glued back in place (see the drawing below). The plug is then sanded or planed flush with the surface to remove the defect. (This leaves a hollow on the underside, which you hope won't show.) Since the surface of the leveled plug shows grain that's only slightly below the surface, it matches the surrounding grain almost perfectly.

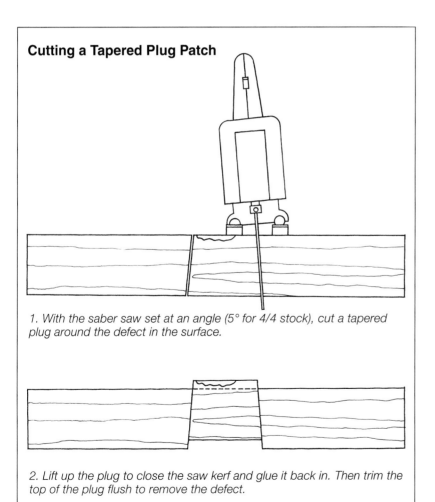

Cutting a Tapered Plug Patch

1. With the saber saw set at an angle (5° for 4/4 stock), cut a tapered plug around the defect in the surface.

2. Lift up the plug to close the saw kerf and glue it back in. Then trim the top of the plug flush to remove the defect.

To make a starting hole for sawing out a tapered patch, a ¹⁄₁₆-in. dia. bit is held at a 5° angle by a shop-made drill guide. The notch at the bottom of the guide lets you see the tip of the bit, so it can be placed accurately on the line that marks the patch.

In order to pull off this patching method, you have to make a clean, tapered cut to create a close-fitting plug. The big trick is starting the tapered cut to make the plug. The only practical way I know of to do this is to drill a series of closely spaced holes at the taper angle—5° off square is about right for most patches in 4/4 stock (use a correspondingly more acute angle if you're patching thinner stock; a lower angle, closer to square, on thicker stock). The holes creates a slot that a portable powered saber-saw blade can be inserted into. To guide the small (¹⁄₁₆-in. dia.) drill, I cut a guide block from dense maple with a hole drilled in it at the desired angle. A small notch at the bottom lets me see the tip of the drill, so I can place the holes accurately. The guide block is then clamped or held tightly on the work surface and moved over slightly after each hole is drilled (see the photo above). Four or five holes side by side make a slot big enough for a fine-toothed saber-saw blade with the saw's base tilted to match the angle of the holes. I cut the plug following an elliptical or oval line drawn around the defect. Then I proceed to raise the plug and glue it in place, belt-sanding the surface flush after the glue dries.

To repair a defect such as the pitch pocket at right in the photo, the Lamello MiniSpot (its base is seen at rear) is used to plunge-cut a hollow. Into this hollow is glued a wood patch shaped like a sailboat hull. After the patch is trimmed flush (at the arrow, left), it's difficult to detect.

The Lamello MiniSpot patch system

Buying a dedicated piece of equipment is a serious investment for any small shop. But if your specialty is working with pine, fir or any other wood that commonly requires patching due to resin galls, pitch pockets, pin knots or splits, there's no quicker solution than to use Lamello's MiniSpot system. This patching system uses a specialized portable machine that's very similar to a plate joiner to plunge-cut a slot shaped like a sleek sailboat hull into the wood over the defect (see the photo above). A wood plug of matching species and shape is then glued into the slot, and the surface is trimmed flush. Trimming can be done with a hand plane or belt sander, but the Lamello-Plano is a special flush-milling machine designed to clean up the patches lightning fast.

Wood patches are available in twelve commonly used species, including oak, walnut, mahogany, fir, pine and maple. (Lamello even makes a special machine that will make hull-shaped custom patches from your lumber.) For fixing long pitch pockets or splits, standard patches also come as long rods, or as double-width patches for covering knots or gouges. The MiniSpot machine is plunged and slid along a fence to cut a long groove for rod patches; double-width patches require two adjacent, parallel slots to be plunge-cut.

Bridging large gaps

Gaps that result from splits in the wood or joints that don't clamp up tight can be filled with putty, but a much cleaner remedy is to fill a gap with a thin wedge of matching wood. The wedge should be cut from a scrap that matches the color and grain direction of the workpiece.

If you're filling a gap between frame members that join at right angles, it makes for a cleaner repair to use a long-grain wedge; a short-grain wedge will absorb stain and finish more readily and become darker and more visible. If the gap is the result of cracking, or from a failed seam in an edge-glued panel, the gap isn't likely to run the full length of a surface. In that case, you'll need to feather out the ends of the wedge so that they match the tapering ends of the crevice (see the photo below). Before gluing, try the wedge in the gap to check the fit, taking care not to push the wedge too hard, lest it be difficult to remove without breaking.

For the cleanest repair, inject a conservative amount of glue into the crevice, just enough to bond both sides of the wedge without excess squeeze-out. You can use white or yellow glue, injected with a glue

Fissures, cracks or gaps due to poor fit at glue-up can be patched by gluing in a wedge. A belt sander is used to feather the edges and ends of the scrapwood wedge so they will fit the contour of the defect.

syringe, or you may prefer to use cyanoacrylate glue (which usually comes in a bottle with a spout thin enough to insert into narrow gaps) because it dries very quickly. Slip in the wedge and tap it down with just enough force to seat it—don't pound too hard or the wedge will buckle and break. Once the glue is dry, trim the protruding part of the wedge carefully, first by sawing it off close to the surface, then planing and/or sanding it flush. Resist the temptation to break off the protrusion, as this could tear the wedge below the surface of the workpiece.

Plugging miscut joints

If you've mismarked a joint and chopped a mortise or drilled a dowel hole in the wrong place, a wood patch can quickly put you back on track. The recut joint will be just as strong as if in unrepaired stock, and the patched area is likely to be mostly hidden by the joined members, so no one ever need know. Square-cornered mortises take a rectangular patch cut to match the mortise's length and width but a little higher than its depth to allow it to be trimmed flush (see the drawing below). If the patched area will be visible, make sure that the patch's grain runs in the same direction as the surrounding wood (i.e., if the mortise is on the edge of the stock, cut the patch edgewise as well, to make it blend in). To make a patch easier to insert, chamfer its leading

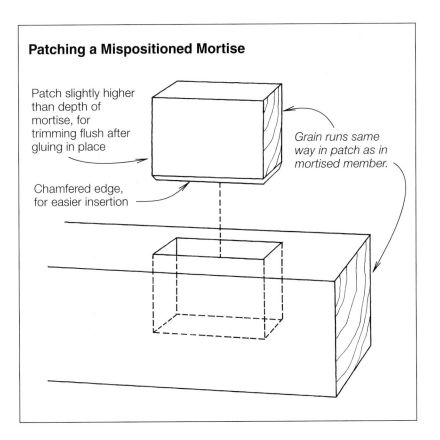

Patching a Mispositioned Mortise

Patch slightly higher than depth of mortise, for trimming flush after gluing in place

Grain runs same way in patch as in mortised member.

Chamfered edge, for easier insertion

edges so they won't hang up on the sides of the mortise. If the end of the patch will show after the new joint is cut and members joined, make sure to seal it, as described on p. 67. When trimming the patch after gluing it in, take care not to reduce or round over the mating joint surface, if the new joint will be recut in the same area.

Filling misdrilled dowel holes is child's play: Simply glue in a dowel cut about ³⁄₈ in. shorter than the depth of the hole, then top off the hole with a plug cut from the same wood as the workpiece. If the new dowel hole you'll be drilling will not intersect the old dowel hole, you can get away with just plugging the top of the hole. A tapered plug cutter, such as the Veritas "Plugger," produces a slightly conical plug that can be driven tightly in place without having to seat against the top of a dowel.

Patching Veneers

Defects such as fallen-out pin knots, insect holes, cracks and ingrown bark are common in many types of curly or burly veneers. Further, if you are thermo-bonding new veneer using a hot-melt adhesive sheet or a thermoplastic glue (such as hot hide glue or ironed-down aliphatic resin), splits and cracks can result from the heat of the iron used for application. Defects can also be caused by bonding the veneer to a substrate with a high moisture content. Even if the defect is discovered before veneer is laid, it's usually more practical to effect repairs after the veneer has been glued down.

Using a veneer punch

Small holes, checks and other defects in burl veneers are most easily repaired using a veneer punch. This special tool removes an irregular shape around a defect (see the photo at left), then cuts a matching patch from another piece of veneer to replace it. This method works best on burl and other heavily figured veneers where the busy grain pattern obscures the irregular contour of the patch. Before beginning, draw a straight line over the area of the defect, and then put a small pointed piece of tape on the punch to mark its orientation and align the point with the line. Now give the punch a sharp tap with a hammer, using enough force to pierce the veneer but not the crossbanding or substrate below. Carefully lift the patch out, working a thin palette knife or razor knife underneath to separate it from the crossbanding or substrate. If the glue bond is tenacious, you can usually loosen it by judiciously applying heat to the patch area; make a cardboard mask with a cutout matching the size and shape of the patch to protect the adjacent areas from the heat.

A veneer punch removes an irregular shape from a piece of scrap that is then used to patch a defect on a veneered surface. For a match that will make the patch hard to spot, the alignment of the punch to the grain of the veneer scrap is carefully determined and marked.

Because the cutter on the punch deforms the edge of the patch slightly, you'll get the cleanest results if you punch out the patch from the reverse side of the scrap (see the drawing below). Before cutting out the patch (if it's a critical repair, cut it from the same spot as the defect on another leaf of veneer from the same flitch), lay the leaf over the workpiece and mark its orientation relative to the line your drew earlier. Now lay the patching veneer on top of a very firm backing, such as a block of rock maple, and align the mark on the veneer punch before hammering out the patch. If you don't have an extra leaf of the veneer to spare for the patch, take great care in selecting a scrap and in aligning the tool, so that the grain will match the background. After cutting out the patch, wet it and the work with some mineral spirits to make sure the patch's grain reflects light the same as the work (see the discussion of chatoyance on p. 67). Glue the patch in place with the same adhesive and methods used to bond the rest of the veneer.

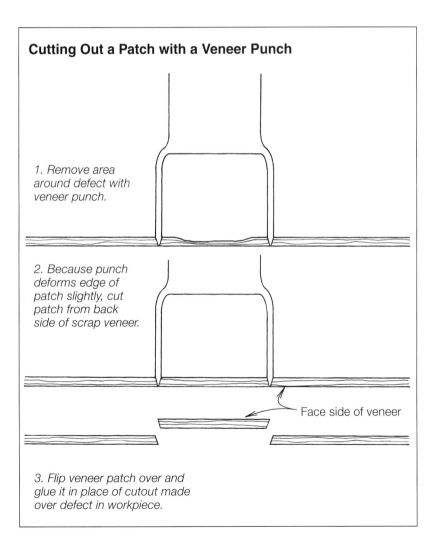

Cutting Out a Patch with a Veneer Punch

1. Remove area around defect with veneer punch.

2. Because punch deforms edge of patch slightly, cut patch from back side of scrap veneer.

Face side of veneer

3. Flip veneer patch over and glue it in place of cutout made over defect in workpiece.

To make a veneer patch less noticeable, cut out the offending area following the wood's grain lines. The cutout can then be used as a pattern for cutting a replacement patch from the same location of another leaf from the flitch.

Patching defects in non-burl veneers with straight or less busy grain patterns presents more of a challenge. Your best chance for a hard-to-detect repair is to cut out the veneer around the problem area following the natural grain lines, as shown in the photo above. On veneers with very distinct, straight grain lines, such as vertical-grain Douglas fir or other veneers that have been quartersawn, you may do best by removing an entire strip across a panel, from end to end, that includes the defect. On panel edges, it's best to replace the entire veneer edge band, rather than trying to patch a small part of it.

Repairing veneer sand-through

Another kind of veneering problem—sand-through—occurs all too commonly when the seam between a piece of solid wood and ply-wood, say between a cabinet side and a face frame, is power sanded. The face veneers on imported plywoods are so incredibly thin these days—some as little as $1/80$ in.!—that all it takes to sand through them is an abrasive thought (I call these "breath of hardwood" plywoods). They are certainly no match for a wood-hungry belt sander or random-orbit sander.

Despite asking all my learned colleagues (and saying my best prayers), I'm sad to say I've learned of no way to patch areas of veneer sand-through so that they are undetectable. I've tried gluing on veneer patches using all kinds of adhesives, but the edges of the patches always show after sanding them flat. If you have the problem, the only real opportunity for a remedy appears to be during the finishing process, when you can use a toning finish or touch-up colors and fake graining to hide sanded-through areas (see pp. 123-127).

Hardwood plywoods with thin face veneers can be protected during belt sanding by a thin sheet-metal mask. The metal is tacked to the underside of a stick, which is then clamped to the cabinet.

As with so many other errors, prevention is the best medicine (see chapters 8, 9 and 10). Try to sand seams between solid wood and veneer as little as possible. Instead, use a flush-trimmer bit in a router to pare a face frame or other member flush with a veneered surface. Then scrape and/or finish-sand with no coarser than 120-grit paper (preferably by hand with a sanding block or with an orbital sander). If you absolutely must belt-sand, use a belt no coarser than around 150 grit, and slow the belt speed down if the tool has variable speed. For added protection, shield the delicate veneer surface with a thin mask—I use a piece of .010-in. thick stainless steel I bought at a metal surplus yard, as shown in the photo above.

Cosmetic Cover-Ups

Sometimes you can run yourself into the ground trying to do an undetectable patch job, but some locations, such as the middle face of a top drawer, are so visible that virtually any patch that tries to match the surrounding wood will announce itself with tireless enthusiasm. If you are faced with such a glaring problem, rethink your strategy and figure out a way to cover up the flawed area, rather than trying to restore it to its unblemished former appearance.

Inlaying knots to cover blemishes

How we perceive the presence of a defect is highly subjective. Almost anyone would notice a hammer strike in the middle of a tabletop, since we expect the top to be flat and smooth. But if that same top had a knot in the middle, our eyes are likely to dismiss it, since we expect occasional natural defects in wood. You can put this perceptual phenomenon to work for you by cutting out and inlaying a knot over any prominent blemish, either natural or woodworker made.

First, find a good, tight knot in a scrap of the same wood you're working with, preferably with color and grain similar to the repair area. Resaw the scrap to a little more than 1/8 in. in thickness, then saw out the knot with a scrollsaw or bandsaw. Include a little point of grain at both ends of the knot (see the photo at left) to make the knot look more genuine in its new location. Set the knot over the defect, and carefully trace around it with a fine scribe or razor knife. Remove the bulk of the inlay area with a small straight bit (set to cut 1/8 in. deep) in a router or laminate trimmer. Complete the inlay by trimming to the scribe line with small chisels and carving gouges. Glue the knot in place, then belt-sand the surface flat. If you suspect the knot may contain resin that might later seep out, seal the knot with shellac before finishing.

Veneering over damaged surfaces

Filling, sanding or planing deeply torn grain or crater-like gouges in solid-wood surfaces can be more trouble than it's worth. If remaking the damaged part is too much work, a good alternative is to cover up the entire surface of the part with veneer. This solution is the most time-efficient if you happen to have a few leaves of veneer that match the wood of the part. If it's 1/32-in. thick veneer, you may not even have to pass the part through the planer to compensate for the slight additional thickness. If you don't have matching veneer and the surface must closely match adjacent parts, as on two bookmatched doors, here's another remedy: Thickness-plane (or sand) the part down to below the level of the defect, resaw it in half and add veneer at the center of the part to make up the thickness (see pp. 10-12).

Another effective type of veneering repair can be done to restore edges that have been incorrectly drilled or mortised for hardware. One common mistake is accidentally marking the mortises for simple butt hinges on the wrong edge of a door or face frame. This is easy to do, especially if you've got dozens to cut, say for an entire kitchen's worth of doors. While repairing an out-of-place mortise can be as simple as cutting and gluing in a thin, rectangular patch, this solution will almost always stick out like a hammer-struck thumb, especially if the repair is in plain view on an upper cabinet. A flaw covered up by veneering over the entire edge is much less detectable.

After selecting a knot in a scrap to inlay over a defect on your workpiece, resaw a slice about 1/8 in. thick. Then cut out the knot as shown. Including a little grain at both ends of the knot to make it look more natural when inlaid in its new location.

Start by gluing patches into both the bad mortise(s) and as any other properly cut mortises on the edge of the stile. If you have veneer on hand that matches the cabinet wood, you can then glue a strip of veneer over the patched edge. If not, take a $\frac{1}{16}$-in. to $\frac{1}{8}$-in. deep pass off that edge on the jointer and glue on a same-thickness veneer strip cut from the edge of a board similar in grain and color to the stile. Make the strip slightly wider and longer than the stile, so you can trim the overhang after gluing the strip on. Now recut the mortises correctly, touch-sanding the edges of the stile to make the veneer-strip patch virtually undetectable. Incidentally, this type of repair is also good if you blow out the edge of the stile while routing a wide mortise on a narrow stile; just joint the stile down slightly below mortise depth and glue on a strip of that thickness.

Ornamental carvings, moldings and inlays

Though somewhat limited in application, surface-mounted ornamental carvings, inlays and moldings can be used to cover up flaws, as well as to add visual detail to an otherwise plain piece of cabinetry or furniture. Readily available in dozens of shapes and patterns (see Sources of Supply on pp. 196-197), ornamental carvings are pressed (formed by a die rather than carved) from a blond hardwood plywood. They may be glued to the surface over the offending flaw. Of course, unless you're into asymmetry, the placement of these ornaments must be in keeping with the look of the piece. One very useful application is on drawer fronts and door frames to cover up misdrilled or badly torn-out holes for pulls. A round, oval, square or diamond-shaped carving will then function as a backplate for the pull. If one or more corners of a box or chest should become badly dinged, you can hide the damage by applying carvings in two or all four corners (see the photo at right).

Decorative moldings can be used to hide a wide range of faults, including unsightly edges that have been damaged or show poorly executed joinery, or to conceal screws used to join cabinets or mount them to walls. Like any moldings, these press-carved moldings are mounted with small brads or finish nails, although in some cases you can get away with attaching them with hot-melt glue. You can also dispense with driving and setting brads (and filling all those little holes) if you mount narrow moldings with pressure-sensitive 3M adhesive transfer tape. Professional picture framer Mark LaFond recommends using the super-sticky #969 adhesive transfer tape (often available at local frame shops), which comes in $\frac{1}{2}$-in. and $\frac{3}{4}$-in. widths. You can apply the tape either with a special applicator, shown in the photo on p. 80, or by rubbing the sticky side onto the molding, then peeling the backing off before pressing the molding firmly in place.

Surface applied pressed-wood carvings work to cover up dents and damage on the corner of the top of a basswood box. These ornamental carvings are inexpensive and come in a wide variety of sizes, shapes and styles.

To keep from splitting narrow, delicate moldings with brads, mount them with adhesive transfer tape instead. After rolling on a layer of highly tacky pressure-sensitive adhesive with the plastic applicator, press the molding firmly into place.

In similar fashion to the way moldings can be used to cover problem areas, thin wood strips can be used to correct problems with adjustable shelf pin holes. The strips are glued to bookcase or cabinet sides over previously drilled holes that have been spaced incorrectly, or shifted out of level from one row to another. The strips are drilled first, with holes in correct position. After the strips are glued on (see the top photo on the facing page), the holes can be made deeper if necessary to accommodate standard 3/8-in. long shanked shelf pins. The shelves themselves must be trimmed to account for the width of the strips, or you could notch them if you wish. If you've discovered a hole level problem before the casework has been assembled, you could run dadoes in the sides centered on the previously drilled holes and inlay redrilled strips flush, possibly making them from contrasting wood, for decoration.

For adding panache at the same time you're concealing a faux pas, ready-made decorative inlays are terrific. Often made from colorful woods in marquetry designs or mosaic patterns and available through woodworking supply catalogs in dozens of designs, these thin veneer inlays require only a shallow recess, between 1/32 in. and 1/16 in. deep. Recesses for round and rectangular inlays can be made accurately with a template and a bushing-guided router fitted with a straight bit. Templates for round inlays can be made from 1/4-in. thick Masonite, cut out with an adjustable circle cutter chucked in a drill press.

Grommets, escutcheons and metal corners

Another kind of patch job you can do to clean up the look of torn-out holes or poorly mortised recesses is to cover up their edges with grommets and escutcheons. For example, if the holes or routed slots you're machined in a stereo cabinet or computer desk for wiring come out ratty, there are many sizes and designs of cord grommets that could overlap and cover the edges of the hole or slot. Tearout is a common problem when drilling holes for adjustable shelves in imported hardwood plywood that has extremely thin face veneers. To clean up the look, resize the 1/4-in. holes with a 9/32-in. drill and install shelf pin sockets, as shown in the bottom photo on the facing page. Like tiny grommets, each socket has a small lip that will cover the edge of the hole around it. Further, they make the shelf support pins easier to insert and remove.

Escutcheons are small plates that surround locks and keyholes. If your keyhole mortise is ragged, simply fit an escutcheon plate to cover up the defect. Dinged or damaged corners of boxes and chests can be restored to a pleasing appearance by the addition of metal corners. Brass corners are inexpensive and are easily mounted with small brass brads, commonly called escutcheon pins.

If holes for adjustable shelves are off the mark, drill new, correctly spaced rows of holes on ¼-in. thick strips and glue them to the shelf sides over the misdrilled holes. After gluing, increase the depth of the new holes to allow them to accept the ⅜-in. long shanks of standard shelf pins.

Brass pin sockets cover up torn grain (likely to occur in plywoods with thin face veneers) around holes drilled for adjustable shelf pins. The sockets are driven into 9/32-in. dia. holes with a plastic mallet.

CHAPTER 5

Taming Wood's Tempestuous Nature

In contrast to the kinds of mistakes we woodworkers make ourselves—measuring parts incorrectly, cutting joints poorly, brushing on finish too thick—there are dozens of potential problems not of our own making, lurking in the lumber pile. Some, such as knots, reaction wood and fuzzy grain, are products of the way the tree grew. Others, such as unpredictable warpage and honeycombing in solid lumber or buckling in veneer, may result from the way the wood was dried and processed before it reached the lumber dealer. Regardless of whether the tree, the veneer mill or the dry-kiln operator is to blame, the woodworker who plucks the problem board from the pile is still the one who must deal with the wood's imperfections and correct them before they compromise the quality of the project.

Flattening Warped Parts

Many imperfections in wood, such as worm holes and small splits and checks, are best fixed with putty or a patch (as described in chapters 3 and 4). But twists, crooks, cups, bows and other deformations aren't as easy to tame. Changes in the temperature and the moisture content of the air act constantly upon wood's fibers, but they affect different parts of a board unevenly, depending upon the grain orientation. The resulting warpage can occur at any time, from when a plank is cut from the tree to when it's part of a finished cabinet or piece of furniture. Applying a coat of finish only slows the expansion and contraction that wood experiences; it never prevents it completely.

A lot of standard woodworking construction practices are meant to deal with solid wood's tendency to warp: Wide panels are held flat in frames; aprons keep tabletops in a level plane; dust panels keep the sides of a dresser true. The trick to all these constructions is to keep the wood parts flat without restricting their movement unduly (see pp. 183-184), as firmly joining wood crossgrain can result in some of the worst disasters, including gigantic splits, buckled panels and blown-apart joints.

Because the lion's share of wood movement typically takes place during drying, most warpage is removed when a board is machined into parts. Jointing can turn a bowed edge into a straight one; jointing and thickness planing can remove cup; and judicious planing can remove twist. Joinery is most accurate when it's laid out and cut when the stock is freshly dressed and edges are straight and true; machining warped parts often results in crooked joints that lead to twisted frames and carcases (see pp. 109-110). Despite our best efforts, machined stock often warps ahead of assembly and finishing, and we're left to try to coax it back to flatness.

Removing cup by humidifying or steaming

If you pull a cupped board from the lumber pile, it's clear that you have to plane the board on both sides until it is flat. However, a panel or tabletop that has cupped after its edges have been shaped and its surface has been sanded smooth calls for a different solution. A mild amount of cupping—say, ¼ in. in a panel 24 in. wide—shouldn't pose a problem with a panel that slides into a frame or is screwed down to an apron and is thereby flattened. Drawer sides and carcase parts are usually flattened when joined together at the corners. But greater degrees of cup (or a little cup in a panel that isn't flattened by the means of assembly) will need treatment to return it to flatness.

The oldest trick in the book for removing cup is to place the offending panel outside on a sunny day, cupped side down, on top of a lawn still damp with morning dew. The heat from the sun tends to shrink the wood fibers on the convex side of the panel, while the moisture from the grass expands the fibers on the concave side. On a cloudy day, you can substitute an infrared heat lamp for the sun and damp newspapers for the lawn, as shown in the photo at right. Either method can work wonders on mildly cupped panels and tops, even if they are made from dense hardwoods. The only caveat is that some of the cup is likely to

To remove cup from a panel on a dark or rainy day, place the panel atop some damp newspapers, cup side down. A heat lamp trained on the convex side of the panel provides the warmth that will hasten flattening.

To steam out a bad cup, a damp cloth is placed on the concave side and heat is applied with a steam iron, adjusted to a medium steam setting.

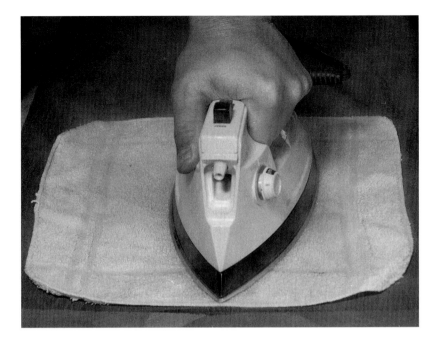

return after the panel cools and dries. I've had the best luck with this method when I've let the panel remain in the sun until it cupped slightly in the opposite direction. When the panel cools in my dry and shady shop, it springs back to flat, just as steamed wood bent to a tight radius relaxes to a slightly larger radius when it cools.

A more direct (and usually effective) means for removing cup from a panel relies on steam. The panel is placed on the benchtop, concave side up, with a damp cloth over it (see the photo above). It is then gone over with a household steam iron, set to a medium heat and steam setting. The idea is to keep the iron moving across the entire surface to heat and steam it as evenly as possible. Thin panels and parts can sometimes be flattened (or untwisted) by exposing the cupped side to the plume of steam expelled by a boiling kettle on a stovetop. Just wear gloves to protect your hands from the steam.

Once the cup in your panel has been reduced or eliminated, it's a good idea to get the panel sanded (or cut the joints on drawer and box sides) and finished on both sides as soon as the wood has dried. The finish will reduce the rate at which moisture is exchanged between the wood fibers and the air, thus reducing the tendency for the panel to cup again.

Removing cup by driving in splines

In cases of severe cup in a thick panel, flattening requires some major surgery. I once built a thick solid-cedar entrance door for a client's summer cabin. When gluing the door up from seven or eight separate boards, I debated which way to align the grain of adjacent boards. I chose to orient the "bark side" of each board toward the inside, reasoning that if the boards cupped, the entire door would cup in one direction. I could keep it flat with a pair of bolted-on braces. Well, the door cupped all right, but the force of the warpage was more than the braces could restrain. Try as I might, I couldn't flatten the door.

I decided that the only way to make the door usable was to saw a series of kerfs on the concave side of the door and glue a slightly oversized spline into each kerf. I made the kerfs with a narrow dado blade in my portable circular saw, running the cuts about halfway through the thickness of the door. To make the repair look like a decoration added on purpose, I spaced my cuts evenly and made the splines from wood of a contrasting color (walnut). I planed the spline stock about $1/32$ in. thicker than the kerf size and did a trial run without glue to make sure the splines would expand the cupped side of the door by the right amount. The only problem I had was getting a couple of the splines out after the dry run. I then applied the glue and drove the splines back in while carefully observing the door's cup. I stopped driving the splines home when the door was flat. I then planed and sanded the splines even with the surface of the door.

Flattening a wound top with a diagonal strap

Cup is simple to remedy compared to wind, which is the lengthwise twisting of a board or panel. While a badly twisted door frame or carcase will probably need to be rebuilt, there is at least one way I know of flattening a twisted solid-wood tabletop. I once labored patiently on the top for a small bird's-eye maple breakfast table (shown in the top photo on p. 19). I had spent hours hand-planing that top perfectly flat, trying to keep the squirrely grain from tearing out along the way. But, as luck would have it, the top developed a pronounced wind on the very day I was to deliver it to my client. The slender apron was too narrow to keep the top from twisting, and the poor table rocked badly because only two feet made steady contact with the floor.

In desperation, I racked my brain for a way to flatten the already lacquered tabletop. After discarding ideas for fitting support braces or adding weights to the underside of the top nearest the high corners, I came upon a solution: I fastened a $3/4$-in. by $3/8$-in. maple strip to the

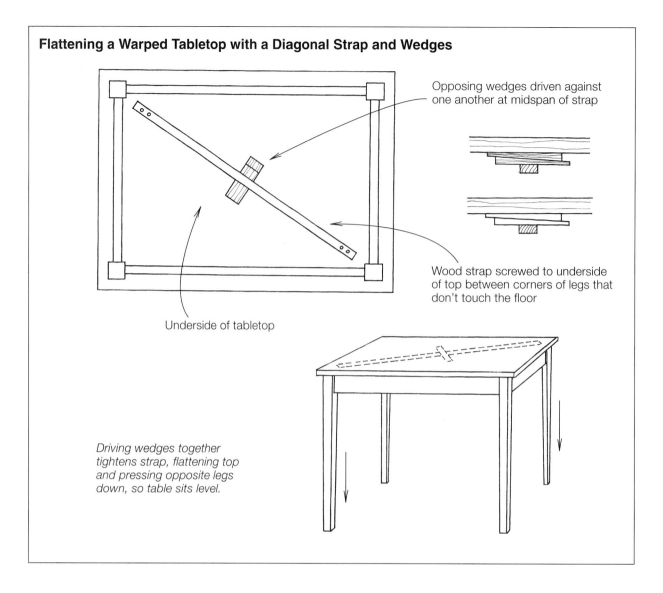

Flattening a Warped Tabletop with a Diagonal Strap and Wedges

Opposing wedges driven against one another at midspan of strap

Wood strap screwed to underside of top between corners of legs that don't touch the floor

Underside of tabletop

Driving wedges together tightens strap, flattening top and pressing opposite legs down, so table sits level.

underside of the top, running diagonally between the corners of the feet that didn't touch, driving two screws at each end. I then inserted a pair of dainty maple wedges at the center between the strip and top (see the drawing above). I then set the table on the flat surface of my saw table and drove the wedges in until all four feet rested solidly. Instead of trying to hide the tension strap from my client, I showed it to him right away, explaining that the wedges could be adjusted to make the table steady on his old uneven oak floor. He was delighted, although he didn't realize at the time that that strap was more of a repair than an innovation.

Flattening Burly or Curly Veneers

In the strict sense of conquering mistakes, flattening veneers with wild grain patterns before laying them is really a preventive measure. But as it is surely a sorry mistake to try to glue down stiff, bumpy and brittle leaves of veneer without overcoming their inflexible nature, we'll discuss how to flatten them here.

To tame unruly veneers, you have to treat the leaves with a mixture that rehydrates the cellulose in the wood, making the brittle fibers more pliable, then clamp them flat before gluing them down. The traditional formula for this preparation is a mixture of glue, alcohol, water, flour and glycerin. But as finish chemist Chris Minick points out, the glycerin in this mixture can cause more problems than it solves: Glycerin, the primary rehydrating agent, can take years to evaporate from the veneer. In the mean time, glycerin acts as a plasticizer for lacquer, inhibits the drying of water-based finishes and makes shellac finishes more susceptible to water spots and rings. Instead, Minick recommends a much better, simpler veneer-flattening concoction: propylene glycol. Though you can't easily buy this chemical in concentrated form, you can buy it already mixed to the proper 25% dilution for veneer treatment by purchasing a can of "recreational-vehicle water-tank antifreeze" from a recreational-vehicle dealer or supply house. This nontoxic antifreeze (not regular radiator antifreeze, which is toxic) costs only about $4 a gallon. It is dyed pink, but the color is very weak and doesn't seem to stain even blond veneers.

For veneer soaking, pour the antifreeze into a shallow tray. You can make one by fitting a sheet-polyethylene lining into the bottom of a long, shallow plywood box. Immerse the leaves into the mixture one by one, letting each one soak for about 10 minutes. Place each leaf on a couple of sheets of clean newsprint (not an actual newspaper, which can transfer ink to the veneer), sandwich the stack between two flat pieces of plywood and clamp or weight the assembly. Use moderate pressure (or weight) at first. If the veneers are severely buckled, don't try to flatten them in one application. Instead, repeat the process in 24 hours, this time applying more pressure until the veneers are flat.

Once the veneer leaves are reasonably flat and pliable, you should try to use them as soon as possible. If you must store them, keep them clamped between the plywood sheets, with clean, dry paper newspaper between the leaves. Glue the sheets down by whatever method you normally would use: hammer veneering, a veneer press, a vacuum bag, or ironing on with a thermosetting adhesive (a PVA glue).

Smoothing Fuzzy or Torn Grain

No matter how well I sharpen my plane blades and chisels, they occasionally let me down and I end up with an otherwise beautiful board with a surface that looks like I went over it with a meat-tenderizing hammer. But often, my tools and I deserve only part of the blame. The natural beauty of the wood itself often carries a price: Highly figured boards have complex grain that is often very difficult to surface without tearout. And stresses that develop as the tree grows can cause a poor bond between adjacent cells, resulting in wood that has fuzzy or woolly grain.

Firming up fuzzy grain

One of the most beautiful woods I've ever had the dubious pleasure of working with was western curly maple, a soft maple species with a remarkably swirly grain figure. Alas, despite its beauty, this wood resisted all attempts to smooth its surfaces—the grain seemed to tear and get fuzzy—even when it was orbital sanded with 180-grit paper! As was clearly the case with the soft maple, irregular growth in some trees results in tension wood that contains more cellulose than normal. The fiber structure of this wood doesn't sever cleanly, but instead leaves a woolly or fuzzy surface. Species such as pine, butternut, and mahogany (Honduras and lauan) often have areas of loose grain that become fuzzy when planed, scraped or even sanded. Staining such a surface (which may appear smooth unless examined with a hand lens) will result in a blotchy finish.

The most effective method I know for taming woolly wood grain is one I learned from Tage Frid. It requires coating the wood surface with a simple glue size prepared by mixing a diluted solution of hide glue and water. Start with dry hide glue, either granular or pearl hide glue (both are available from Woodworker's Supply) and mix about ½ cup of it with two cups of clear, cold water. Add the glue to the water, a little at a time, stirring all the while. Let the mixture stand for about 10 to 20 minutes, then brush a healthy coat of it on the fuzzy-grained wood surface that's been presanded to about 120 grit (see the photo on the facing page). Rub the size in with a damp cloth and let the surface dry overnight. The water in the mixture raises the fuzzy fibers, which the glue then hardens, so that subsequent sanding shears them off more cleanly. Any residual hide glue left in the wood after final sanding doesn't have a significant impact on clear finishes applied to the surface. If you plan to stain the wood, you should perform an experiment on a scrap to see how much the size (which acts somewhat like a sealer) retards the absorption of the stain, causing the wood to take color lighter.

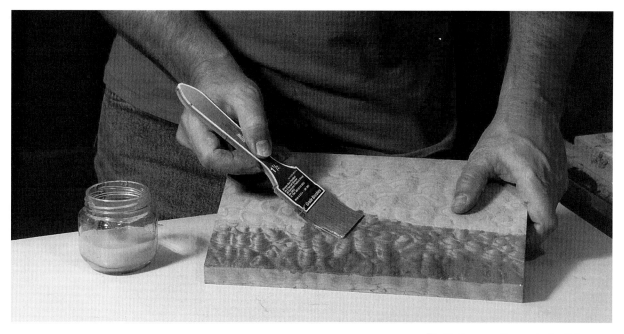

To tame woolly grain in this piece of western curly maple, a coat of glue size, made from diluted hide glue, is applied with a disposable brush. The protein-based glue firms up the soft fibers, making sanding easier, and takes stain and finish much like the wood itself.

Cleaning up torn grain on surfaces

Woods with fiddleback, curly, crotch and burl figure all have grain that changes direction, and thus are difficult to plane cleanly with a hand plane or with a standard thickness planer. Species with ribbon or stripe figure, such as bubinga, koa and lauan, are notoriously difficult to plane because of their interlocked grain configuration, with adjacent areas of grain run in opposite directions. There are several possibilities for cleaning up—or avoiding—torn grain in recalcitrant woods such as these. Methods including selective-direction hand and machine planing, scraping and abrasive thicknessing, all discussed in this section. If torn grain is too deep to clean up, you can use a layer of veneer to hide the damage, as described on pp. 78-79. Another remedy is to fill a torn-grain surface with hide-glue-and-sawdust putty, as described on pp. 54-56. You can also try filling areas of torn grain with sawdust and cyanoacrylate adhesive, as described on p. 95.

Abrasive thickness planers Stationary wide-belt thickness sanders and drum sanders are nothing short of miracle machines when it comes to cleaning up torn grain on fussy wood surfaces. And they are capable of thicknessing the wood evenly and to precise dimension. Even though these machines might be outside the budget (and space allowance) of a small shop, there's no reason not to avail yourself of the service that a wide-belt or drum sander can deliver. Such machines are a mainstay of most large cabinet shops, and the owners are often happy to rent you time on their machines to help defray costs. The belt

Planing from Two Directions

In many cases, the only way to clean up grain tears is to plane different areas of the surface in different directions. If the board has grain running in two clear directions, as occurs in a board that has been sawn from a curved portion of the tree, you can improve upon the surface by planing from one end of the board in one direction, then from the other end in the opposite direction (see the drawing below).

With a little care, you can also pull off this stunt with a stationary thickness planer. First, mark the grain direction on either end of the board, and also mark the area where the grain changes direction. Set the planer's depth and make a note of it for later. Now take a pass on one half of the board, running it in the appropriate direction for the grain on that half. Quickly raise the cutterhead when the grain-direction change mark reaches it. Then, reset the planer to the original cutting depth, reverse the board and take a pass on the unplaned section. This procedure will leave a slight irregular transition zone around the area of the mark, but it can usually be cleaned up quickly with a scraper, a hand plane or a belt sander.

Planing Changing Grain from Two Directions

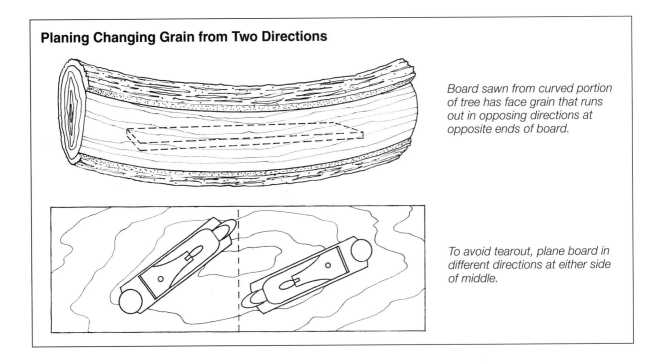

Board sawn from curved portion of tree has face grain that runs out in opposing directions at opposite ends of board.

To avoid tearout, plane board in different directions at either side of middle.

power feeds on these units can process a lot of stock in a short time; I've had an entire kitchen's worth of door panels sanded (at coarse and fine grits) in less than 20 minutes—at a cost of about $30. Since most large units will handle panels 48 in. to 60 in. wide, you can even run tabletops. Just be careful if you're sanding resinous woods down to a fine grit. There's one shop that will never let me back in, after I ruined one of their $100 belts thickness-sanding some rosewood shelves down to 180 grit!

If you need to dimension boards on a regular thickness planer before abrasive planing them, make sure the planer knives are sharp. Dull knives can easily cause tearouts on curly woods that go more than $\frac{1}{8}$ in. below the surface. While you can thickness-sand below these defects to eliminate them, it takes more time (and money, if you're renting time), and the thickness of the panel will be reduced significantly. With really touchy woods, it's best to plane surfaces within $\frac{1}{32}$ in. to $\frac{1}{16}$ in. (or more) of the desired thickness, then switch to abrasive methods and work down to final dimension.

Portable sanders If you don't have access to a stationary thickness sander, you can still do wonders with a good portable belt sander or random-orbit sander. A well-tuned belt sander with a clean, smooth-tracking belt can do a thoroughly acceptable job of cleaning up torn-grain surfaces. To help keep the unit flat when belt sanding large surfaces, such as an entire tabletop, fit the unit with a sanding frame, as shown in the photo below. Offered as options by some manufacturers, including Bosch and AEG, sanding frames keep the belt even with the work surface and prevent gouging. They also regulate the depth of cut to some degree. Random-orbit sanders, available in both electric

Large expanses of torn grain on a tabletop can be cleaned up with a belt sander. Fitting the unit with an optional sanding frame helps to keep the sander level and prevents gouges, so the top comes out smooth and flat.

and air-powered versions, are light in weight and can sand below torn grain quickly and cleanly. But while they remove stock as rapidly as disc sanders without leaving heavy scratches, random-orbit sanders are terrible at maintaining a flat surface on large panels.

Regardless of your choice of power-sanding tool, it's important to use a light touch and keep the unit moving across the entire work surface to keep sanding as even as possible. Work over the surface with a succession of grits, lest you end up with deep scratches, which can mar the finished look of a surface as much as the torn grain that the sanding was meant to remedy.

Hand planes and scrapers A well-tuned hand plane with a sharp blade can do a wonderful job of cleaning up a torn grain surface without leaving grit scratches, as abrasives do. The plane should have an exceptionally well-honed blade and a properly fitted chipbreaker set very close to the cutting edge (about 1/64 in.). Set the plane for a paper-thin cut and, if the plane has an adjustable throat, set it as small as possible (this keeps pressure on the chip just ahead of the blade, so it has less propensity for lifting and tearing out). I've had great results planing tricky grain using a low-angle block plane or a Lie Nielsen jack plane, which has its blade set at a low angle (available from Woodcraft). In areas of interlocked grain where planing only with the grain is impossible, work the plane across the surface at an angle to the predominant grain direction, keeping the plane blade at a skew to the direction of cut, as shown in the drawing below. You can also clean up a torn or blown-out edge by running it over the jointer with its fence set skewed relative to the cutterhead (if your fence can't be realigned, fasten a tapered-wedge auxiliary fence to its face).

Planing Interlocked Grain at an Angle

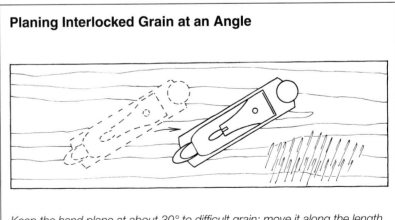

Keep the hand plane at about 30° to difficult grain; move it along the length of the board so that the blade slices the wood cleanly.

If areas of torn grain aren't too deep, you may prefer to use a hand-held cabinet scraper or a scraper plane instead of a hand plane. Scrapers can be used very sensitively to remove stock in the area of the fussy grain and feather the cut into adjacent areas, so that the area scraped clean doesn't appear too hollow. Further, a properly sharpened scraper can be used with the grain, against it or even across it without introducing scratches into the surface.

Cleaning up torn grain on shaped edges

Just as planing figured wood can result in pitted surfaces, routing and shaping can produce shaped edges with torn grain. Sanding takes care of the minute scars, and filling with hide-glue putty takes care of deeper tearing. But if the degree of tearing is too deep to sand away or conceal, you might do best to recut the shape, taking another light pass with a sharp cutter or bit. To lessen the likelihood of tearout, climb cut the edge at a very slow rate of feed.

Climb cutting—feeding with the bit engaging the stock in the same direction as the router is moving (see the drawing below)—encourages chips to break off ahead of the cut, rather than splintering the grain behind the cut. This is the same principle as hand planing with the grain, rather than against it. Climb cutting can make it more difficult to control the feed rate, since the spinning bit pulls the router forward. To discourage this tendency, take only shallow cuts when climb cutting. If you own a variable-speed router, you'll find it easier to take a climb-cut pass (and you will be less likely to burn the wood) if you rout with the speed reduced by 25% or even 50% (for larger-diameter bits). If reshaping reduces the width of a part excessively (as it might on the shaped front edge of an adjustable shelf), you can restore the part to its original width by adding a wood strip to the opposite (rear) edge, which is presumably straight, unshaped and less visible.

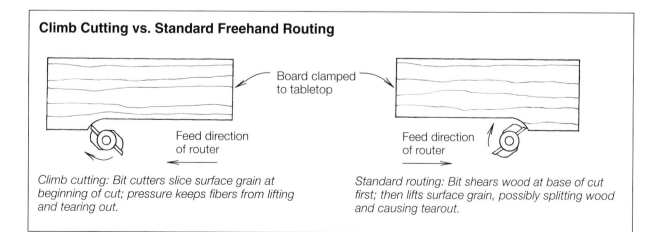

Climb Cutting vs. Standard Freehand Routing

Board clamped to tabletop

Feed direction of router

Feed direction of router

Climb cutting: Bit cutters slice surface grain at beginning of cut; pressure keeps fibers from lifting and tearing out.

Standard routing: Bit shears wood at base of cut first; then lifts surface grain, possibly splitting wood and causing tearout.

Dealing with Splinters

Some woods seem to develop splinters as readily as rose bushes put forth thorns. When a corner or edge suddenly snags and splinters, there's no sense in ignoring it and leaving it for a later repair. Puttied edges are difficult to hide and require more trouble in the long run than just fixing a splinter right away. This is easiest to do is when the splinter is only partially detached. Get a little glue under it, tape it down and sand it smooth later. A great way of gently working yellow or white glue up under a splinter, all the way up to where the detachment begins, is to put a little on a short length of unwaxed dental floss (see the photo below left). Carefully work the floss back and forth to get glue as far up into the split as possible. If the floss snags, just pull it straight out.

After gluing, put a small piece of tape over the repaired area to hold the splinter firmly in place. The tape prevents you from accidentally snagging the area before it can be sanded smooth. It will also remind you to check that area later, to confirm that the repair is sound and the area is clean of excess glue. While probably any tape will work, I prefer to use 3M's 2090 Scotch brand Long-Mask blue masking tape, because it leaves no residue that might interfere with staining or finishing later.

If the splinter has completely come off, make a quick search of the area to find it. Even if your shop isn't immaculately clean, you can usually find the splinter by rounding up a few likely suspects from the bench or floor and checking to see if they fit. Take care while replacing a splinter not to crush or break any of the fine fibers at its root (the fat end), as this will cause the area to absorb more stain or finish and bring attention to the repair site. If the edge of a part is so badly splintered that it cannot be repaired cleanly, you might consider rounding the edge over instead of trying to repair it. Use a regular hand plane, or a roundover bit or 45° chamfer bit chucked in a router.

Quick repairs with cyanoacrylate

Regular white and yellow woodworking glues do a fine job of bonding splinters, but take a while to set and can make a mess of the surrounding wood, if you're not careful. Consequently, many woodworkers prefer to use fast-setting cyanoacrylate adhesives (known as "super glues" or as "CA" by wood turners and modelmakers). Cyanoacrylates are quick and easy to apply, and most varieties dry extremely fast, so you can fix a splinter, reattach a split-off chip or repair a broken turned bowl and resume work immediately. To effect a repair, apply a drop of a thin cyanoacrylate adhesive (I use Satellite City's "Hot Stuff") and allow it to wick into the split by means of capillary action. Replace

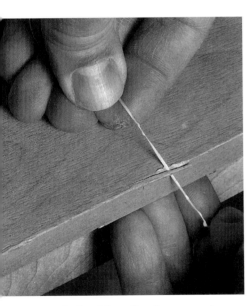

A short length of unwaxed dental floss is handy for applying glue beneath an attached splinter before it is taped back down. Pulling the floss gently back and forth works the glue all the way to the base of the splinter.

broken-off splinters before gluing; just take care to hold the splinter with tweezers or press it in place with the tip of a pin or small screwdriver. Don't use your fingers—you might become literally attached to your work. To keep excess glue that could repel stain or finish to a minimum, treat minute splinters by putting a tiny drop of glue on the point of a pin and apply to the split. You can also use a thin tube applicator tip, which is available with some brands of cyanoacrylates (see the photo below).

Even though thin cyanoacrylates cure quickly (in 10 to 30 seconds, depending on the humidity of the wood), you can speed repairs even more by spraying the area with a CA accelerator (such as Satellite City "Hot Shot"). It's also good to spray the repair area on woods that contain tannin, such as oak and walnut, to neutralize the surface (the tannic acid inhibits the glue's ability to dry). Alternatively, you can wipe the area with ethyl alcohol.

Because they dry so quickly, cyanoacrylates are terrific for repairing problems that crop up in the course of carving or lathe turning. Carvers can reglue chips that break off accidentally, and can refine or recarve the area minutes later. Turners can repair splinters, small splits and cracks quickly, with the spindle or vessel still on the lathe, and then resume turning. Professional turner Giles Gilson even uses cyanoacrylate to mend broken rims and parts of turnings by fitting parts back together and wicking the adhesive into the seams (see the photo below). He also uses more viscous cyanoacrylates (such as Satellite City's "Super T" or "Special T") to strengthen areas of soft or punky wood when he prepares damaged or spalted wood blanks for turning.

Giles Gilson uses cyanoacrylate to mend broken rims and parts of turnings by fitting parts back together and wicking the adhesive into the seams.

Correcting Other Lumber Defects

Defects in lumber such as splits, cracks, honeycombing and loose knots have a more subtle impact on a project than badly warped parts do. But they can conspire to ruin an otherwise well-built cabinet or piece or furniture just as surely as the worst warped tabletop or fuzzy-grained panel.

Gluing splits

The solid appearance of wood, while delightful to behold, doesn't reveal the material's true nature. Wood is made up of innumerable bundles of hollow fibers, like cellulose tubes bound together with lignin. Far from being an inert material, these tubes continue to exchange moisture with the air, expanding and contracting with the seasonal fluctuations in humidity. Since these movements are not equal across the different dimensions of a wooden plank or part, adjacent bundles of fibers often pull apart, resulting in separations as small as fine checks and minor splits or as large as obvious cracks that can run the full length of a board.

Splits that occur at the end of a part can often be closed up by applying glue and clamping them shut. This approach is preferable to filling them, in that closing them provides a cleaner repair than putty. Also, unless it is glued shut, a split due to uneven drying might increase in size later on, in which case the putty will probably fall out. You should always try clamping a split dry first—apply firm clamping pressure, but don't overdo it. If your clamps (and your forearms) are straining to apply enough pressure to close the split, it's likely that another split will open nearby, even if the glue keeps the repaired one closed. Patch the split instead, as described on pp. 72-73, or use a butterfly key, as discussed in the next section.

If a split clamps shut without brute force, work white or yellow glue or clear epoxy into the crack using a palette knife or a piece of stiff card stock cut from an old business card or playing card. For narrow splits that go through the part, try working the adhesive in with a length of unwaxed dental floss. Clamp and allow the glue to set. Unless a river of glue exudes from the repair, resist the temptation to wipe the excess away. It is much cleaner to scrape off stray drips after they have dried rubbery hard.

Mending cracks with butterflies

Large, prominent cracks, often present in heavy slabs and planks made into countertops and tabletops, can be successfully filled with epoxy, as described on pp. 64-65. An alternative way of treating such fissures (especially those that run out to the edge of the surface) and keeping them from enlarging due to the inevitable effects of seasonal humidity changes is to install a functional and decorative butterfly key. This small inlay, with two flared ends that look like two dovetails joined at the narrow ends, is inlaid across a crack (see the photo at right). The grain of the key runs at right angles to the crack, for strength.

You can mortise and inlay a butterfly key just as you would any other inlay. Make the butterfly first from stock that's between one-third and one-half the thickness of the cracked surface. For best fit, the sides of the butterfly should be tapered slightly inward. Transfer the key's outline to the workpiece with a sharp knife. After carefully chiseling around the outline, you can use a laminate trimmer or a small router fitted with a small-diameter straight bit to waste the majority of the mortise. Use the chisel again to refine the fit. After applying glue, drive the butterfly key home, leaving it a little proud of the surface. Plane the key flush after the glue dries. If the key is large (1 in. or more across), you can drive a screw into each wing from underneath to make sure it will stay put.

Strengthening honeycombed lumber

If a board dries too quickly, the stresses that develop in the wood may be great enough to cause internal separations of the fibers. The cracks and voids that develop are commonly called honeycombing, and are most commonly seen in 8/4 and thicker commercially dried hardwoods, such as red oak and ash. Although severe honeycombing can usually be spotted in the form of large cracks on the surfaces of the board and deep fissures on the ends, honeycombing can go unnoticed until parts are cut and ready to sand. At that point, you might find yourself trying to sand or plane a surface to get below a small crack. But instead, you find that the crack just keeps getting bigger as you reveal more of the fissure! And filling or patching a crack or two isn't your biggest problem: Honeycombing can seriously weaken a board. I once built a base for a music stand from red oak that literally fell apart after I left it overnight under a heat lamp to speed the curing of the finish.

Obviously, it's best to avoid honeycombed lumber altogether. If you find one honeycombed board in a stack at the lumber yard, be suspicious of other boards in that stack; if one board honeycombed from improper drying, it's likely that others did too. But if you've ended up with honeycombed parts and don't want to remake them completely from other stock, there are still some things you can do. First, test the suspected part by giving it a few sharp raps with a rubber, plastic or rawhide mallet. If honeycombing is extensive, you may hear a hollow

A butterfly key, inlaid across a large crack in the end of a heavy slab, keeps the crack from becoming larger over time. This rosewood key contrasts attractively with the board, which is walnut.

To discourage further splitting of deep surface cracks, inject visible fissures with epoxy, using a disposable syringe. Inject the glue until it protrudes slightly above the surface, then scrape flush after the epoxy has cured.

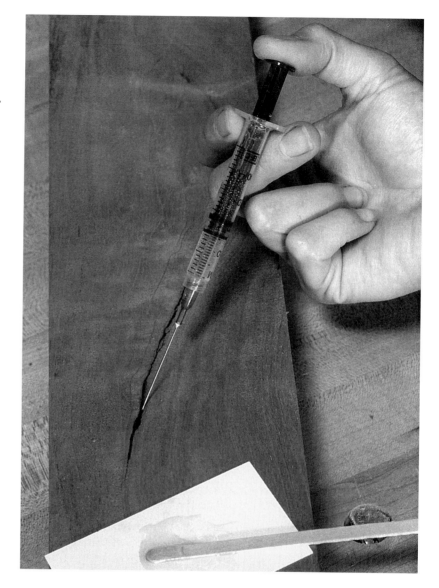

"thunk" or the part may split into pieces. If the wood falls apart cleanly, you can glue the pieces back together with a strong adhesive with good gap-filling properties, such as polyurethane glue or epoxy. If you hear a hollow thunk, but the part seems reasonably sound, you can discourage further cracking and splitting by injecting any visible cracks (the ones that get bigger when sanded) with epoxy. Use a fine-tipped, disposable syringe (see the photo above) loaded with regular two-part epoxy that has been thoroughly mixed—avoid five-minute epoxy, which is more viscous and harder to inject. You can use the epoxy clear, or color it to match the color of the wood as it will look when finished (see the discussion of coloring putty on p. 60).

A loose knot is glued back into its socket with epoxy, colored with fresco powders to resemble the color of the knot. The underside of the socket is covered with masking tape and epoxy is brushed on both knot and socket before the knot is driven in place.

Gluing loose knots in place

A knot in a pine plank may appear as tight as a pair of denim jeans after their first washing. But after a while, that same knot can become as loose as a pair of baggy swimtrunks. The time it takes to loosen can be as little as the few weeks it takes you to build a piece—if you're working with high-moisture-content lumber that's trying to reach equilibrium with your dry workshop.

Unless the expelled knot is mistaken for a chew treat by the shop dog, it (the knot) can usually be glued back in place without much ado. The act of shrinking usually leaves a gap between the knot and its socket in the wood, so you should use good old gap-filling epoxy to create a successful bond. After sealing the entire area on the underside of the knot site with masking tape, I lay the workpiece flat on the benchtop, coat the sides of the socket with epoxy and drive the knot in place (see the photo above). If any part of the gap around the knot remains unfilled, I pour in or inject a little more epoxy. If the gap is sizable, I may use universal tints or powdered pigments to color the epoxy to match the knot. When the glue has cured, I level the area, as described in the section on filling voids with epoxy on pp. 64-65.

CHAPTER 6
Assembly and Gluing Problems

Sometimes it feels like it's taking forever to cut out and machine all the parts for a big project. And then time speeds up: All of a sudden, components come together, sometimes in a single day, and assume the full likeness of a stereo cabinet, bathroom vanity or side chair. This is the moment of truth where you find out if the parts fit together correctly or not. It's time to stand back and admire your work, or to retreat to the drawing board.

Joints that won't go together or don't mate properly are problems that can arise for a number of reasons. They can be fixed before or after assembly, although getting a glued-up assembly apart can require quite a bit of finesse. The gluing process itself is fraught with pitfalls that can thwart you in the home stretch. Difficulties can arise from applying too little glue, or too much, from the way surfaces are machined, and even from the oily nature of the wood itself. Like all woodworking difficulties, mistakes made at assembly time are seldom fatal, but require resourceful repairs.

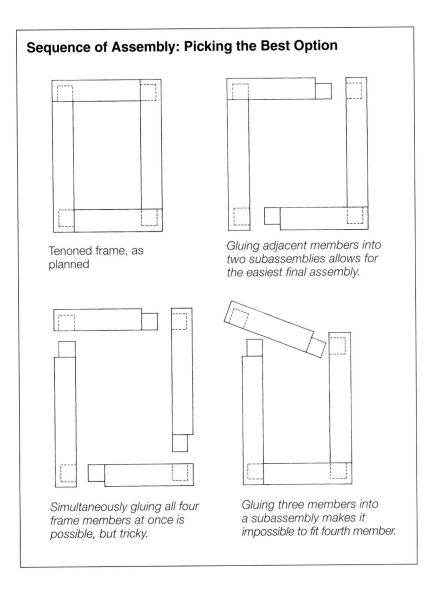

Sequence of Assembly: Picking the Best Option

Tenoned frame, as planned

Gluing adjacent members into two subassemblies allows for the easiest final assembly.

Simultaneously gluing all four frame members at once is possible, but tricky.

Gluing three members into a subassembly makes it impossible to fit fourth member.

Overcoming Adversity in Assembly

Discovering that parts don't go together correctly can happen at any of three stages: before the glue has been spread, during the glue-up or after the glue has dried. A dry run will uncover most assembly problems before the glue has started flowing (see pp. 179-180), when remedies are much easier to undertake: Ill-fitting parts can be altered or remade, and joints that don't mate can be recut. A dry run also reveals insidious problems, such as joints that appear to be straightforward on paper, but may be tricky (or impossible) to assemble in real life. For example, the tenoned frame shown in the drawing above is easy to assemble one way, harder in another and impossible in a third.

By discovering assembly difficulties early on, you can decide on the correct order that parts should be assembled, and decide on sub-assemblies that make the most sense.

An arduous assembly often can be made easier by altering joints slightly. For example, consider the crest rail of a chair back, shown in the drawing below. The rear legs have enough flexibility to be spread so that the stubby rail tenons can slip into their mortises. The problem is engaging all the back slats into their mortises on the underside of the rail at the same time. One solution lies in trimming the top of the rail's tenons to allow the rail to engage in a raised position, providing clearance for fitting the slats in place. Once the slats are engaged, the rail is lowered into final position, as shown in the drawing. Since the rail tenons have lots of glue area, the gap above them doesn't compromise the strength of the joints significantly.

Trimming a Tenon to Allow Assembly of a Chair Back

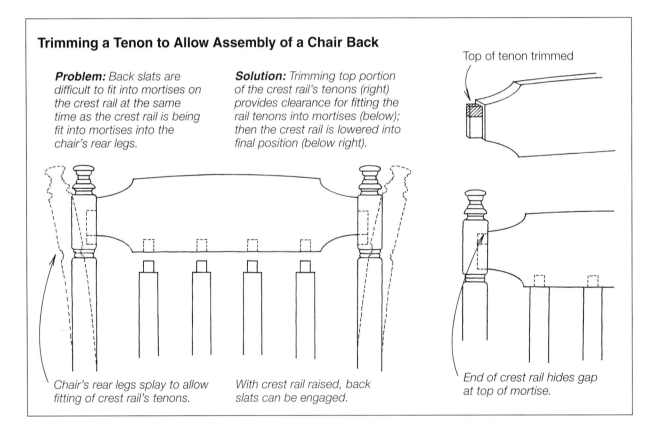

Problem: *Back slats are difficult to fit into mortises on the crest rail at the same time as the crest rail is being fit into mortises into the chair's rear legs.*

Solution: *Trimming top portion of the crest rail's tenons (right) provides clearance for fitting the rail tenons into mortises (below); then the crest rail is lowered into final position (below right).*

Top of tenon trimmed

Chair's rear legs splay to allow fitting of crest rail's tenons.

With crest rail raised, back slats can be engaged.

End of crest rail hides gap at top of mortise.

Melee in mid glue-up

It's every woodworker's nightmare to discover in the middle of a glue-up that things aren't going quite as expected: Joints won't drive home completely, parts don't fit, or the carcase won't square up. Then the adhesive sets, and your problem sits there on the bench with clamps askew and glue oozing from every joint. If the problem is localized, say one or two joints that won't close, it's probably best to leave things alone and mend the errant joint after the entire assembly dries, as described in the next few sections.

If the situation is more serious—for example, an entire carcase that won't go together—you must act quickly to avert disaster. Your best hope is to disassemble the entire piece so that you can recut joints or rework parts as necessary. Quickly, wriggle all the joints apart, using a soft-faced mallet or a spreader clamp if needed, as described on pp. 104-106. If you're fortunate enough to be using hide glue, just wipe any excess off the joint surfaces and let them dry; new glue will bond to them when you reassemble later.

If you're using a white or yellow PVA and plan to reglue the assembly within 24 hours, wipe the glue off of the joint surfaces with a damp sponge. When you're ready to reassemble, simply dampen the surfaces or edges with glue on them with a moist sponge, apply fresh adhesive and clamp the parts together. Intricate joints, such as dovetails or box joints, can be exposed to steam before regluing. If you will be unable to reglue PVA-coated parts within 24 hours, you must wash all the glue off before it has had a chance to set. Otherwise, you'll have to scrape dried glue off each joint later. This is because PVA adhesives, as well as plastic-resin (urea-formaldehyde) glues, don't bond well to themselves after they have cured—see pp. 112-113.

The most effective method I've found for washing off still-wet glue is to take the parts outside and blast them with a high-pressure nozzle on a garden hose. For better efficiency, connect the hose to the faucet on your water heater (set to between 130°F and 150°F). Wash the parts down completely to get all the glue off, scrubbing joints if necessary, then set them aside to dry. Remember that any glue that ends up on the surfaces of parts will show up as spots in the stain or finish, so make sure you do a thorough job.

Joints bonded with epoxy or resorcinol adhesives should be taken apart and left until the glue sets rubbery hard. Then the glue can be scraped off completely with a chisel or a scraper blade (these glues also won't redissolve).

Disassembly after glue-up

Some problems aren't discovered until after the glue has dried. These may include misaligned parts, unsquare frames or carcases, or parts assembled with the wrong end up or face out. Anything that can be assembled can be disassembled, but you don't want your project to end up looking like it was taken apart by a disgruntled gorilla with a 20-lb. sledgehammer. There are several ways to coax a glued-up joint apart and wind up with parts that can still be repaired and reassembled.

Joints bonded with hide glue are the easiest to deal with. Disassembling these is a cinch: Just inject denatured alcohol through a small hole drilled into each joint at an inconspicuous location. The alcohol softens the glue. Hide glue also softens readily when exposed to heat and moisture, and joints usually fall apart easily after steaming or after a few ladles full of hot water are poured over them.

Steam and heat Modern PVAs and polyurethane glues form bonds that are much stronger and more moisture resistant than "old-fashioned" hide glue. But they are also much harder to take apart once the glue has set. Because white or yellow PVA glues are thermoplastic, heat and moisture are your best tools to weaken their bonds and facilitate disassembly. Moisture is an effective medium for transferring heat, so an ordinary steam iron can introduce heated moisture into a joint through $\frac{1}{4}$ in. or even $\frac{1}{2}$ in. of solid wood. Set the iron to a steam setting and apply medium-high heat to a damp cloth placed over the joint area for a minute or two before attempting to wiggle, press or pound the joint apart, as described below. If the iron has a steam-jet setting that forces steam out of holes in the bottom of its sole, by all means apply a series of blasts to speed things along. Open-pore woods such as oak and walnut respond best to these treatments, as their pores allow the passage of moisture much more easily than denser species, such as maple and birch.

Forcing joints apart Even after the glue in the joints has been softened (as described above), separating a joined assembly can be difficult. Frames with tight-fitting joints can be hard to take apart even if they've just been clamped together in a trial dry run. To avoid damaging parts during disassembly, you need to apply a lot of force, but as gently as possible. One of the more controlled ways of separating misjoined parts is to reverse the action of a clamp and push the members apart. This method can be used only on an assembly with surfaces that provide purchase for clamp jaws to press against without damaging sharp corners or shaped edges; square frames and carcases are the best candidates. There are several commercially available clamps that can do a good job of providing the pressure needed to drive joints

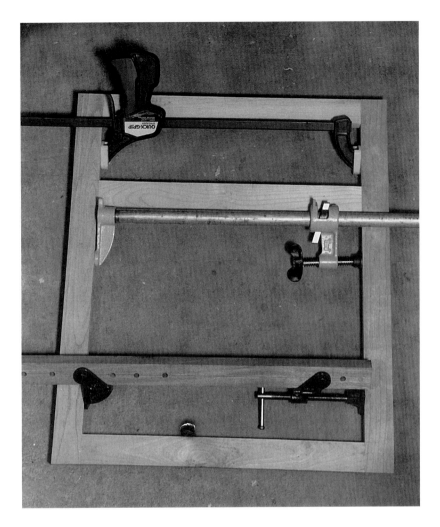

The members of an incorrectly made face frame can be separated without destroying them by applying force with spreader clamps. Shown here (bottom to top): a Record bar clamp, Jorgensen's #56 pipe clamp and Vise-Grip's Quick-Grip Spreader (the first two have their heads reversed for this job).

apart, including the Vise-Grip Quick-Grip Spreader (designed specifically for this duty), Record bar clamps and Jorgensen #56 pipe clamps, as shown in the photo above.

Before attempting to drive glued-up joints apart, apply steam heat, as described on p. 104, and twist the assembly or tap the joints with a mallet to try to break or loosen the glue bonds. It's a good idea to score the juncture between the parts before pressing joints apart. This prevents unsightly (and difficult-to-repair) grain tearouts from occurring on the mating surfaces around joints. Gradually apply force with the reversed clamps or spreader, and leave them in place if the parts don't come apart right away. Be sensitive about the amount of pressure you apply: There's no sense in destroying an assembly just to dismantle it.

Also, be mindful of the consequences if parts do separate all of a sudden. A heavy carcase with a lot of pressure forcing it apart may suddenly explode like a bomb. Parts thrown across the room can not only injure you, they also can get dinged up badly and be more work to fix than they're worth.

If you don't have a reversible clamp or spreader (or if you're just looking for a way to release anger), you can try pounding pieces apart with a heavy mallet or a small sledgehammer. For solid blows with protection against marring parts, I highly recommend Dead Blow mallets; these are made from cast high-impact plastic, and their heads contain lead shot suspended in oil, which virtually eliminates bounce after each strike. If you use a regular hammer or sledge, protect all striking surfaces by clamping scraps of wood to them. To avoid causing more damage than you already have, pound judiciously and, as with reverse clamping, anticipate where parts will go if they separate suddenly.

If an assembly just refuses to come apart no matter what you do, it will probably be most productive to cut it apart and redo the joinery, as described in the next section.

Repairing an Assembled Face Frame

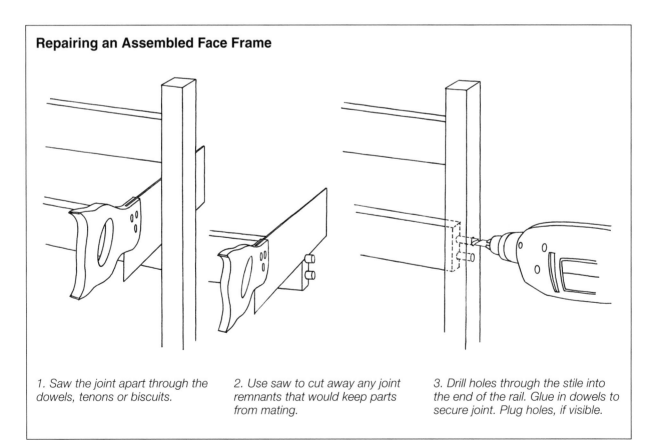

1. Saw the joint apart through the dowels, tenons or biscuits.

2. Use saw to cut away any joint remnants that would keep parts from mating.

3. Drill holes through the stile into the end of the rail. Glue in dowels to secure joint. Plug holes, if visible.

Cutting a bad joint apart

When a defective joint can't be disassembled by steam, heat or force, cutting the joint apart is your only recourse. You might need to cut a bad joint apart anyway, if it is between interlocked parts and forcing the joint apart would ruin a more complex assembly. When joints like mortise and tenons, biscuits or dowels don't drive home completely and can't easily be disassembled, it usually makes for a cleaner repair to leave things alone until after the glue sets, rather than frantically trying to take them apart. After the glue is dry, use a thin-bladed saw, such as a razor saw or a Japanese *dozuki,* to cut the joint apart at the dowel, tenon or biscuit. Then you can redrill holes for new dowels, cut slots for new biscuits, or, in the case of mortise and tenon joints, mortise both components and fit loose tenons.

If a part can't be removed from its assembly for new joinery to be fitted, use the saw to cut the joint apart and to trim the ends of the dowels or tenons so the mating surfaces of parts can meet flush (see the drawing on the facing page). Then drill or mortise through one part into the other and drive dowels or a loose tenon into the other part. The end of the dowels or tenon can be trimmed flush to look like a through joint, or the holes can be plugged to hide their presence.

When edge-glued boards made into a panels become badly misaligned (and there isn't enough extra thickness to plane the panel flat) the best solution is to saw the panel apart along the bad seam and reglue it. Unless the dimensions of the panel are critical, cutting it apart with a bandsaw, saber saw or with a thin-kerf blade on the table saw will result in very little loss in overall width (see the photo at right). If plate-joinery biscuits or dowels were used, the joinery should be redone after the panel is cut apart.

Truing up a twisted assembly

Few things are as maddening as twisted doors that won't shut properly or an out-of-square wall-hung cabinet that won't mount flat on a wall. Twisted assemblies often result when the parts aren't clamped flat during glue-up, and sometimes they can be straightened after the glue has set.

San Raphael furniture maker Griffin Okie advises that you can often rescue a twisted drawer or cabinet carcase by reclamping it, if the problem is discovered within a few hours of glue-up. With the drawer's bottom or cabinet's back removed, set a bar or pipe clamp diagonally between the corners that measure farthest apart. Apply force gradually, until the assembly twists a little in the opposite direction. Assemblies will often "pop" audibly as pressure is applied. After removing the clamps, make sure that your persuasive clamping has not

If edge-glued boards are out of alignment after glue-up, cut the panel apart along the bad glue line with a thin-kerf blade, then reposition and reglue the parts.

A twisted frame can be straightened soon after glue-up. The frame is set atop blocks on the workbench and clamped and weighed down in the direction opposite the twist.

cracked or separated any of the joints. If it has, you might need to inject glue into the joint, as described on p. 113. If you suspect that squaring has weakened a carcase, you can add reinforcing glue blocks wherever they won't show.

I learned the following method for removing the twist from a distorted cabinet door or frame from woodworker and Illinois Institute of Technology instructor John Kriegshauser. Put the afflicted frame on a benchtop with blocks set under the opposing "low" corners that contact the bench. At the two "high" corners of the frame that don't touch the bench, add clamps or put weights (sandbags, bricks or concrete blocks) that are heavy enough to distort the frame in the opposite direction of the twist (see the photo above). Everything is then left to set overnight or longer; the cure may take a day or so. Unless the frame is really bad, this process will give the frame a "tension set," straightening it enough to make it serviceable again.

Cutting in and wedging a twisted frame

Frames sometimes twist because the stock was warped when the joints were cut. Frame members that don't lie flat on a radial-arm-saw table or chopsaw base will end up with unsquare shoulder cuts. Likewise, sawing a tenon on a bowed rail using a table-saw tenon jig results in tenons with out-of-square cheeks. When these flawed parts are assembled, you can bet that the resulting frame won't be flat and true.

Serious twist in heavy frames, such as for household doors, must be remedied with major surgery: The frame should be cut apart and rejoined, as described on p. 107. But small degrees of twist in lighter frames, such as for cabinet doors, can often be flattened by cutting in and wedging: Each skewed joint is sawn partially through and a thin wedge driven to true up the joint.

Start by checking the surface across each joint for flatness, as shown in the photo at right. Mark the concave side of each non-flat corner. Now using a razor saw, fine-toothed dovetail saw or Japanese *dozuki*, make a cross-grain cut on each marked corner as close to the joint line as possible (see the photo below). Cut as far down as the tenon, dowel, biscuit or spline, but don't cut through it. Make thin wedges from scrap frame stock (the grain in the wedges running lengthwise), apply a little glue into each kerf and tap a wedge in. Check for flatness across the corner and drive the wedge deeper if need be. If the corner still

Sighting for light under a square placed across a frame joint quickly shows that the adjacent surfaces aren't flat, but concave on the top surface.

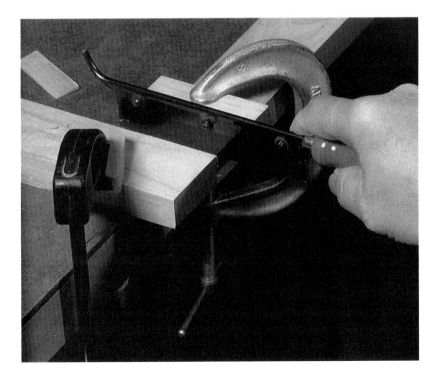

A square-edged block clamped to the frame guides a razor saw used to crosscut partway through the rail at the joint. A small long-grain wedge, seen in the background, will be coated with glue and driven into the kerf to flatten the frame joint.

isn't flat after the wedge is in, you might need to cut in at the joint on the opposite side, apply glue and reclamp the frame to press the kerf closed. The area around each joint can be cleaned up and sanded again after the glue is dry.

Leveling wobbly furniture

Another sort of twisted assembly that might need truing is a chair, stool, case-on-stand or other piece of furniture or cabinetry with legs or feet that don't all touch a flat floor at once. While there are sneakier ways of curing this sort of tippiness (see pp. 85-86), the easiest way is to scribe and trim the feet so the piece will sit flat.

First set the tippy troublemaker on a truly flat, level surface, such as the top of a table saw or other machine tool. Carefully set wedges under the two shorter legs (possibly more, if the piece has more than four legs) so that they are level relative to each other and the piece is sitting solidly. Now make a shim that's the same thickness as the distance between the end of the two wedged feet and the saw-table surface. Atop this shim, tape down a short pencil that's been sanded halfway through, flat-side down (this puts the point on level with the top of the shim). Keeping the shim bearing on the table, scribe a line around the legs that are unwedged (see the photo below). Trim these legs to the line using a handsaw, rasp, low-angle block plane, chisel or abrasives, checking occasionally to see if the piece sits flat. To prevent tearing the grain running up the leg, chamfer each end before trimming.

The legs on a tippy furniture piece can be evened up by first leveling the piece atop a flat surface using wedges under the legs that don't touch. Then, the touching legs are scribed, using a half pencil (sanded flat on one side) atop a shim that's as thick as the amount that the non-touching legs have been wedged up.

An electric detail sander is handy for cleaning up tool marks or rough surfaces on parts after assembly. It can get into spaces too confined for conventional power sanders.

Tackling difficult tasks after assembly

Little jobs, such as finish sanding or driving screws for hardware, are easy to do on carcase parts when they are separate but can be a pain if you leave them until after assembly. Sanding in tight corners to clean up a holiday (a spot you forgot to finish), a previously unnoticed tear-out or a rough area from which glue has been removed can be an ordeal. To ease the pain of those unexpected little sanding jobs, nothing fills the bill better than one of the detail sanders that have come on the market in the last few years. Models by Bosch, Fein and Ryobi all share a similar design, with a vibrating triangular head at the end of a handle that houses a small universal motor. The projecting head and low profile of the tool allow it to fit easily into nooks and crannies that are hard to clean up by hand (see the photo above). The Bosch sander I use (as well as the Fein) can be fitted with a thin extension pad, allowing it to sand between louvers or in other very tight spaces.

Another hassle is drilling holes and driving screws for metal drawer slides or for mounting cabinets inside cramped carcases. These tasks are often difficult by hand, and impossible with a standard electric drill. There are a number of compact angled-head drives that can be chucked into any hand or electric drill (corded or battery powered) and can work in spaces with only as couple of inches of clearance. If you do a lot of installation work, you might want to buy an angled drill/driver, like the one made by Sioux (see Sources of Supply on pp. 196-197). Robertson-type square-head screws are ideal for cramped work because they stay on the end of the driver by themselves, and their heads that aren't likely to strip out like straight-slot or Phillips screws.

Fixing Glue Failures

Accurate woodworking often calls for cutting, planing and chiseling to a line and not beyond. Gluing up is really no different: You must apply enough glue to avoid starved joints, yet not so much that you will make a mess. Even if your glue-bottle dispensing technique is flawless, there are many factors that can hinder successful glue-ups. Bad joints can result from glue contamination, improper curing or resins in the wood itself. Such difficulties can also cause blisters and delamination in wood veneers. Glued-up carcase sides and tops can fall apart if the edges being joined have been glazed by dull tools during machining. Worse, a whole assembly can fall apart if the glue is bad (see p. 189) or if your shop temperature plummets before the glue has cured (see p. 184). Like other woodworking dilemmas, gluing disasters can be remedied if you take the appropriate steps.

Glue-starved joints

Joints of obvious poor fit are usually repaired soon after they are cut, as described on pp. 31-39. But, sometimes, bad joints aren't discovered until after the parts have been assembled. In the haste of gluing up, or in an effort to avoid excessive glue squeeze-out, you might apply too little glue and end up with starved (dry) joints. When the surfaces of two mating parts haven't had enough adhesive spread on them, they won't bond properly. Starved joints can also result from not allowing enough time prior to clamping for the adhesive to soak into the wood, or from too much clamping pressure. In either case, the glue squeezes out before the bond is achieved. And often, starved joints occur during the hurried assembly of a complex piece—a big face frame or chair legs and stretchers. When many parts need to be coated with glue, assembled and clamped before the glue sets, glue is applied hastily, and a joint or two might not get a proper application.

Starved joints are considerably weaker than properly bonded ones. You can often spot a starved joint by the lack of glue squeeze-out. Ideally, every joint should have a tiny row of glue beads at the juncture of the mating parts. A starved joint is likely to make itself known the first time you test a newly assembled chair: You'll feel the legs and stretchers rack. And a starved edge-to-edge glue joint in a panel often can be separated just by applying twisting force on either side of the joint line with your hands.

The strongest way to repair starved joints glued with hide or PVA glue is to disassemble the piece (see pp. 104-106), reapply glue (this time more liberally) and clamp it up again. This approach works with PVA-glued joints that have not had a chance to cure, which takes about 24 hours. Fresh glue re-emulsifies the dried glue, and the molecules intermingle to form a strong bond. The same is true of hide glue, except that more hot glue can be introduced to strengthen the joint at any time during the life of the piece. That's what makes hide glue the easiest among all adhesives to repair.

If you suspect a glue-starved mortise and tenon, loose tenon, dowel or biscuit joint that is otherwise tight fitting, the least disruptive way to restore its full strength is to inject more glue into the joint (within 24 hours, for PVA-glued-joints). The procedure calls for a special high-pressure syringe (available from several woodworking supply catalogs) like the one shown in the photo below. One or more small holes must be drilled into the joint for glue injection. These can usually be located on surfaces that won't be seen, or can be puttied and touched up later. The 1/32-in. dia. holes (to match the size of the syringe nozzle) should be placed where they will deliver glue to the center of the joint, so the adhesive has the greatest opportunity to spread throughout. Insert the syringe nozzle firmly into the hole and keep the pressure up until squeeze-out emerges from around the hole or from other parts of the joint. The syringe (which is designed for water-based glues only) must be cleaned out between uses.

If you discover a dry joint in an otherwise sound frame, you can strengthen it by injecting glue into the joint. Here, two holes are drilled on the back (cabinet) side of the face frame, and yellow glue is injected with a special high-pressure syringe.

Failed joints in exotic woods

Certain exotic woods are difficult to glue with water-based glues. This problem arises because the resins and oily extractives naturally present in the wood concentrate on the surface as the lumber dries. These inhibit bonding by making the wood surfaces water repellent (for more information, see p. 183). I once built a small wall-mounted coat rack with a shelf above it for my first one-man furniture show. I wasn't able to resist using a beautiful exotic species called yellow putumuju. (This was in the dark days before it was considered politically incorrect to use rare woods.) I noticed that the wood was rather oily as I cut and planed the parts to shape. It was only after glue-up that I realized what a big problem those extractives were: The shelf, coat pegs and mounting board literally fell apart as they were unclamped.

The process I used to repair that putumuju coat rack is the one I recommend for fixing any glue joints that fail when bonding resinous wood parts. The good news is, changing glues can solve the problem. Several adhesives, including epoxy, resorcinol, Behlen's "Rivet" and polyurethane glues (e.g. Gorilla Glue, Excel), have a low sensitivity to oil contamination, which is a problem with exotic species. Polyurethane glues and 3M's 5200 should be applied very carefully: They contain isocyanates, unstable acids that can cause serious skin and respiratory irritation. The bad news is that the mating edges and joint surfaces must have any and all remaining glue machined off them. Joints must have glue scraped off. Boards edge-joined into panels and carcase parts should be run over a jointer set for at least a $\frac{1}{32}$-in. deep cut.

Glue failure due to dull cutters

Even the machining process itself can cause gluing problems when dull jointer or planer knives burnish the edge or surface of a board rather than shearing the wood fibers cleanly. A burnished, or glazed, edge won't readily absorb a water-based glue, and hence the joint will be prone to failure (surface glazing can also impair wood's ability to absorb stain and finish, creating a blotchy, unnatural appearance). The telltale sign of a glazing problem is that glue beads up rather than flowing out smoothly. Also, edge-glued parts that can be broken apart easily with hand pressure will show few wood fibers embedded in the film that has torn away from one side of the joint.

The solution for burnished edges is the same as for glue failures caused by wood extractives: Remachine the joints, of course this time with sharp knives installed in the jointer or planer. A very fine cut—a mere $\frac{1}{32}$ in.—should be enough to remove the burnished wood surface and expose cleanly sheared fibers that will absorb glue properly.

Rebonding loose or blistered veneer

Although we do our damnedest to glue veneers down firmly on a stable substrate material, they occasionally don't obey us and blister or otherwise come unglued. Unless the material is a burl veneer that wasn't properly flattened before application (see p. 87), veneering defects are usually due to one of four causes: not enough glue; not enough clamping pressure; air trapped between veneer and substrate; and contamination of the veneer or substrate, either in the form of dirt on the surface or extractives in the veneer that inhibit bonding (see p. 183).

Blisters—little raised bumps in a veneered surface—are probably the most common problem and are usually the easiest to fix. While some blisters rise up enough to be obvious, you should also check for more subtle blistering before you apply a finish: Lightly and quickly run your fingertips over the veneered surface (or lightly tap)—if blisters are present you'll hear a loose, hollow sound.

The way to flatten the blister, or other small area of lifted veneer, depends on the adhesive used to lay the veneer in the first place. If the glue is thermoplastic—contact cement (either water or solvent based), PVA (white and yellow glues), hide glue, or Glu-film hot-melt adhesive veneer bond sheet—you can usually rebond the veneer to the substrate (or crossbanding) by simply going over the area with a regular household iron set to medium-high heat. Apply pressure to the repair area, using a clean cotton cloth or a few sheets of white paper between the iron and the veneer to prevent scorching. After each pass, lift the iron and see how things are going; stop as soon as the blister doesn't rise again when the iron is withdrawn. Incidentally iron-on wood edgebanding often lifts at the ends or falls off because it wasn't heated long enough during application. Repair it by ironing on a new piece, this time letting the iron heat the banding until tiny beads of the thermoplastic glue form at the edges.

If veneer blisters don't stay down after ironing, you'll need to inject fresh glue and clamp the area back down. If the veneer was glued down with PVA, hide glue or urea formaldehyde, inject that same kind of glue with any type of disposable syringe (see Sources of Supply on pp. 196-197). To effect the least noticeable repair, make a small slit in the blister (don't try to skewer it) and insert the tip of the needle, as shown in the photo at right. Inject just a drop of two of glue; more will just end up squeezing out and you'll have a mess to clean up later. This method works well for rebonding lifted areas of veneers applied with the "iron-on" technique (see pp. 184-185). If contact cement was used originally to lay the veneer, apply a small amount of cyanoacrylate,

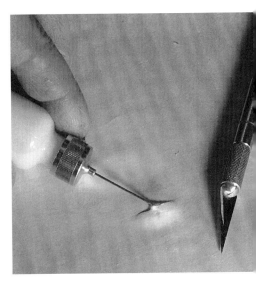

If ironing fails to persuade a veneer blister (laid with a thermoplastic glue) to flatten out, make a small slit in the blister and inject a drop or two of the same kind of glue used to glue the veneer down in the first place.

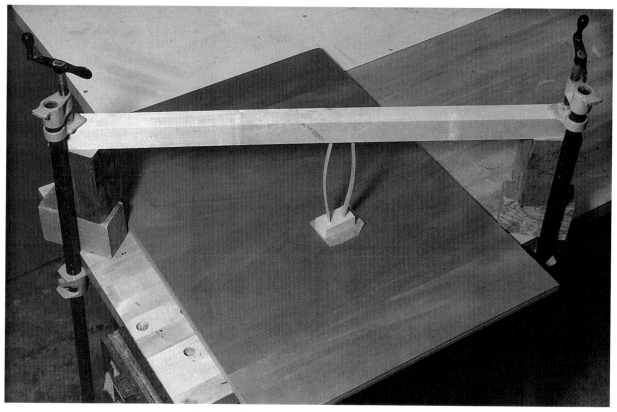

To apply clamping pressure to glue down a blister or a patch in the middle of a panel, use go-bars—springy sticks wedged between the work and a fixed surface, here a crossbar temporarily clamped above the panel.

which will bond with the neoprene in the cement (this might also work to rebond lifted areas of veneers applied with a hot-melt sheet adhesive; you'll have to experiment).

After gluing, clamp the repair area flat immediately, though this can be tough, since blisters are often in the middle of a panel. If your clamps don't reach, try weighting down the area with lead weights or sacks of sand. You can also apply pressure by using "go-bars," a clamping method commonly used by guitar makers for gluing down delicate braces to the inside surfaces of an acoustic guitar's top and back. Go-bars are thin, springy sticks that are wedged between the work and a fixed surface—a rafter or the ceiling in your shop might serve well. An alternative method is to clamp a crossbar temporarily above the work, as shown in the photo above.

Dealing with Excess Glue

A certain amount of glue squeeze-out is a good thing. It shows that the glued-up parts have had enough adhesive spread on them to wet their surfaces—essential for a strong bond. But like most other things in life when present in excess (with the possible exception of love and money), too much glue is a problem. Glue drips, rivulets, puddles and smears can turn your neat, well-prepared wood surface into a wasteland of blotches and pock marks. The best remedy, of course, is to use only enough glue to get a line of fine glue beads at the joint line. And there are a couple of other good methods to prevent excess glue from becoming a problem (these are described on pp. 185-187). But excess glue can be successfully removed, and here's how.

Knowing when to take it off

When you remove a glue drip is as important as how you do it. As much as one's first inclination is to wipe up and clean off excess glue as soon as it is discovered, resist this temptation with all your might. In most cases, you'll end up making things worse by contaminating a larger area with glue, especially if you are gluing and then staining open-pore woods such as oak and mahogany. Wiping off a water-based glue with a damp rag almost guarantees that the glue will soak deep into the pores of the wood and wreak havoc at finishing time (unless you're using hide glue, which stains and finishes like wood).

Instead of taking action immediately, inspect each assembly a short time after clamping it up, and note the location of all exuded glue. Wait for 20 minutes to one hour (less on a hot day) before removing the glue, which by then should be dried only rubbery hard. You can remove glue that has dried harder, especially small flecks. But with larger drips and corner fillets, you stand a greater chance of tearing the wood surface beneath the dried glue as it is removed. How you should go about removing errant glue depends on the size of the spill.

Flecks, drips and rivulets

Tiny flecks of glue—around pinhead size—can be excised with a well-tuned cabinet scraper. Small droplets and drips no bigger than a lentil can usually be popped off with a sharp chisel. For this purpose I reserve a special chisel on which I've rounded the edges with a file, as shown in the photo at right. The sharp corners of a regular chisel tend to dig into the work surface and cause scratches and gouges that warrant further repair. Working with the bevel side up, I push the chisel up to the edge of the drip and remove it with one clean motion. I work with the grain of the wood and keep the chisel's edge slightly skewed to the direction of travel, to prevent it from digging in. Small rivulets of glue can also be removed in one clean motion, if care is taken. Chisel-

Small glue droplets are easy to pop off once they have dried rubbery hard. Use a chisel that has had its corners rounded, because sharp corners may accidentally gouge the work surface.

To remove a glue rivulet cleanly, keep the edge of the chisel skewed to the direction of push and work with the grain to avoid pulling up wood fibers as the rivulet is lifted. Use one hand to push the chisel and the other to keep it flat.

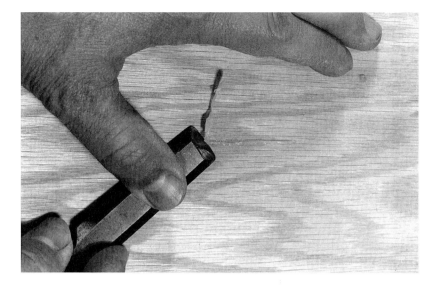

ing with the grain is essential because the glue film is likely to pull up wood fibers as it is lifted. Use one hand to push the chisel and the other to keep it flat, as shown in the photo above.

Inside corners, puddles and smears

Removing glue squeeze-out from an inside corner is easy if it is in the form of little beads (as is ideal). Carefully press the edge of a sharp, wide chisel into the corner, keeping it bevel side up and at a very low angle. Then press the chisel in from the other direction to pop the beads out. If a lot more glue has squeezed out and formed a corner fillet, you'll need to work the chisel all the way along the corner, pressing it into the glue fillet from both directions before attempting to pull it out in one strip. A really terrific tool for performing this excision without marking up the wood surface is a chisel plane, such as the one made by Lie-Nielsen (see the photo at left).

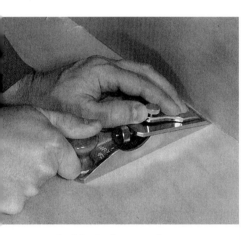

A chisel plane makes an easy job of cleanly removing excess glue from an inside corner. The edge of the plane's blade is pressed into the corner (working alternately from both sides), and the glue fillet pops out.

Really big drips and puddles will still usually be liquid in the center even when the outer skin is quite dry and leathery. With these, it's best to remove the inner goo before removing the rest of the puddle, to avoid smearing it on the wood and causing more problems. Do this by cutting into the top of the puddle and using a coffee stirring stick to spoon out the glue. Now carefully use the chisel to get under the puddle, gradually working it up at the edge all the way around.

Glue smears, which often result from getting glue on your hands and handling wood parts, are usually thin enough to scrape or sand off. Prominent smears that have been scraped away won't pose problems at finish time unless you've introduced other contaminants to the surface, the result of smearing the glue on with dirty fingers. Such dirt and grease might mark blond, open-pored woods like oak even after the glue is gone, so take care to scrape them off completely. If the smear is minor, nothing more than a slight smudge, you might do well just to sand it away. Yellow glues sand poorly, clogging the paper readily, so choose a not-too-fine grit paper, such as 100 or 120. In all areas where glue has been removed, it's important to make sure you've scraped or sanded away absolutely all of it before commencing with finishing, as described on pp. 188-194.

Besting biscuit pucker

Strictly speaking, biscuit pucker is not caused by too much glue, but by too much wood swelling due to the glue. Biscuit pucker (no, it's not the sound that overaffectionate biscuits make) occurs when plate joinery is used to couple thin parts ($\frac{1}{2}$ in. thick or less), or when slots have been cut too close to the surface. When the joint is glued up, the compressed-wood biscuits expand from the water-based adhesive, in turn swelling the wood and causing a small lump at the surface.

The first reaction of most woodworkers is to plane or sand these little lumps away, but this is not a good solution. If you're working with plywood that has thin face veneers, there will be bald spots where you've sanded through. If you flatten biscuit-pucker lumps in solid wood, you'll end up with "biscuit dimples" when the swelling subsides and the wood shrinks down close to its original thickness—a process that could take several days or more. Therefore, if you experience biscuit pucker, wait at least a few days before flattening the surface.

To avoid biscuit pucker on subsequent joints in thin wood or plywood, switch to thinner biscuits, such as Lamello H9s or Woodhaven's "Itty-Bitty" biscuits. Slots for the H9s are cut with a special $\frac{1}{8}$-in. thick plate-joinery machine blade. Slots for the Itty Bitty biscuits are cut with an $\frac{1}{8}$-in. thick router kerf cutter. Another way to avoid pucker problems is to choose regular biscuits that fit snugly in their slots and bond them with epoxy, which will fill any resulting gaps and won't cause the biscuits to swell.

CHAPTER 7
Conquering Finishing Failures

I still remember my first major woodfinishing blunder with painful clarity: Barely a teenager, I decided to make my own crossbow by screwing a child's fiberglass bow to a stock I made from 4/4 redwood. I designed a trigger mechanism that would release the bowstring and fabricated it by pouring lead into a crude mold: aluminum foil pressed into the dirt. Amazingly, the contraption worked fairly well. All it needed was a finish. So I checked the shelf in the garage, where our home's previous owner had left several cans of old paint, and turned up a nearly antique can of shellac.

I brushed on a thick coat of that stinky orange shellac, and proudly I set my weapon aside to dry. A day was a long time to wait for anything at that age. But when a week had passed and the shellac finish was nearly as wet as the day I applied it, I knew I'd have to intervene. After trying in vain to "wipe the finish dry" with an old rag, I was desperate. I took my crossbow out to the backyard and rubbed dirt into the finish until the shellac was no longer sticky. Believe it or not, the dirt actually improved the look of the finish, making that crossbow look like a relic of the War of the Roses. Little did I know at the time that if I hadn't applied that drastic dirt treatment, the shellac finish might still be wet to this day!

Unfortunately, few woodworkers would be satisfied with the look of their precious furniture project after it had been rubbed with dirt. But while it's chemically impossible to make old shellac dry, most finishing problems are repairable, using techniques that don't require you to strip off the finish and start over again. Some of these solutions work as if by magic, such as clearing up a blushed lacquer finish or re-amalgamating a crackled varnish film. Other finishing quandaries can be put right in more than one way, such as staining or toning to adjust color, and touching up puttied patches or scratches with a brush or a special marker pen.

Altering the Color of Wood

It's been said that it's not nice to fool with Mother Nature. While the beauty of a gorgeous piece of wood is hard to improve upon, there are circumstances in which changing wood's color results in an improvement. There are times that you need to darken or lighten the color of a cabinet or furniture piece to make it fit in better with other furniture pieces or with the color of the room. Processes such as selective staining, toning and bleaching can also be used to hide sapwood or adjust the color of one part in a piece, say a drawer face, so the wood will better match the surrounding cabinet parts. And various methods of touching up allow you to alter the color of wood in small areas to repair problems or hide defects.

Selective staining

Cabinets and furniture pieces are not usually built from a single board or even out of wood from the same tree. While color variations between different parts of the same furniture piece are usually acceptable, there are times when drastic differences in the color of adjacent parts detract from the overall look of the piece. I've seen this problem often in furniture and cabinets made from mahogany, walnut and cherry. The most expedient way to remedy this visual shortcoming is to stain the entire piece to even out the overall color.

Pigmented stains can perform this trick most effectively, since they are essentially thin paints that will easily cover up the wood's own color (as well as defects in poor-looking wood or to make plain, inexpensive woods look darker and richer, a trick that has been used for decades by the production furniture industry). To control the shade, wipe off more or less of the stain, or repeat the application for a darker effect. However, pigmented stains also tend to cover up the natural grain pattern and obscure the beauty of the wood.

A two-step dye staining process can serve to even up the color of wood as well as enhance its beauty. The sample here shows (from top to bottom): unstained cherry, a yellow ground stain over the cherry, and a reddish-mahogany final stain over the yellow.

Dye stains offer a more transparent coloration, and they're also among the most repairable of stains, in case you accidentally sand through the top coat during finishing. One popular staining technique that's good for for evening up color uses dye stains in a two-step process. First, a ground stain is applied, then a final stain is applied over that (see the photo on p. 121). The ground-stain color should be compatible with the natural color of the wood, but contrasting. For example, you can use a yellow ground stain on mahogany, or light purple or orange on walnut. If you mix your own dye stains, say with anilines, you can control the darkness of the color by making the mixture more or less concentrated. The final stain that goes over the ground stain may be chosen for whatever effect is desired. With a yellow ground stain, use a rosewood stain for a reddish mahogany look, or a walnut stain for a brown mahogany look. On walnut, the lavender ground stain with a walnut final stain creates that rich brownish-purple look that aged walnut gets. In addition to evening up the wood, the two-part staining process also brings out highlights in figured woods. You'll see flashes of the ground stain when the wood is viewed at certain angles relative to light, a subtle but most pleasing effect.

As with any stain combination or mixture, you'll want to make a finish sample before staining the actual piece (you might want to make two or three samples, choosing wood pieces that reflect the color variation in your piece). That way you can evaluate final color under the same kind of lighting that the piece will be seen in to avoid any unpleasant surprises. (Different light sources do funny things to color; see the discussion on metamerism on pp. 192-193.)

Concealing sapwood

Selective staining can also be employed for evening up the tone of woods with sapwood that differs drastically in color from heartwood. Such woods include walnut, rosewood, cherry and koa. Start by carefully staining only the sapwood areas with a stain that approximates the natural color of the wood. Test the color of your "sap stain" on a sample first (see the photo on the facing page). Check the color of the wet sap stain by wetting the adjacent heartwood with water (if using a water-based stain) or mineral spirits (if using a solvent-based stain). Once you're happy with the sap-stain color you've chosen or mixed, apply it to the sap areas of the work using a brush, cotton swab or the tip of a wound-up rag for an applicator. After the sap stain has dried, coat the entire piece with a lighter version of the same stain. You can thin solvent-based stains with naphtha or dilute a water-based gel stain, such as Clearwater, with clear extender—not water. If the light sapwood still stands out too much for your taste, you can repeat the process, switch to a pigmented stain or use toning (as described in the next section) to darken the sapwood and obscure color differences.

Selectively staining the sapwood will even out the color of woods with distinctly different sapwood and heartwood, such as the Hawaiian koa shown here. For a better color comparison, wet the heartwood on your test sample with clear water before brushing stain on the sapwood.

Adjusting wood color by toning

If you plan to complete your project with a film-type top coat, such as a lacquer, varnish or polyurethane, another option for adjusting the color of the wood (from lighter to darker) is to tint the color of the finish by toning it. Toning is the process of applying a layer of finish that has colored dyes and/or pigments in it. The process is also called tinting or glazing when the finish is applied by wiping or brushing. Toning gives you a much greater range of color changes than staining does: A tone can get the wood much darker than dyes or even many pigmented stains. While a tinted finish can be applied to raw wood parts or parts that have been previously stained or bleached, the great thing about toning over a surface that has already been sealed or clear finished is that the color you apply won't change much during subsequent topcoating, so what you see is what you get.

Toning is ideal for blending in areas where you've accidentally rubbed through a finish and created a light spot in the stained wood below. It's a terrific way to hide spots where you've sanded through the face veneer on a hardwood-plywood part (a mistake that's hard to fix any other way). Toning is also good for balancing the color of mismatched parts that aren't discovered until after topcoating with clear finish. For example, I once built a large dining table with extension leaves from mahogany that was stained a dark reddish-brown. Using a water-based gel stain, I was very careful to make sure the color on the top surface of the leaves matched the main tabletop in terms of degree of dark-

Spraying on an aerosol toning lacquer is a quick way to darken the tone of wood to match the color of parts after finishing. Walnut toning lacquer, sprayed here over clear finished maple, is translucent when sprayed thin, but obscures the grain when sprayed heavily, characteristics you can use to advantage when trying to hide defects.

ness. However, I didn't discover that the color of the 4-in. thick edges on the table and the leaves didn't match until after the table had been sprayed with lacquer. Instead of removing the finish and restaining, I masked the edge of the leaf from the adjacent top and sprayed on a tinted lacquer until the shades of color matched beautifully.

The easiest way to tone woods finished with lacquer or shellac is with aerosol tinting lacquers. These come in handy spray cans (see the photo above) in a wide range of popular natural and stained hardwood colors, such as mahogany, walnut, oak, cherry and maple (earth pigments, such as raw and burnt umber, as well as black and white tints are available for handling a wider variety of color-adjustment situations). It's best to spray the desired part with a series of thin coats to build up a darker color, rather than applying one thick coat. Also remember that tinting lacquers have pigments in them; therefore, the more coats you spray, the more opaque the finish gets. Therefore, it's usually better to start with a darker tint color and spray fewer coats for more transparency that will let the wood's grain show through. However, if you are working with a dark-stained wood that has lots of knots, putty, patches, etc., the opacity of many layers of tinting lacquer can be put to advantage to hide the defects.

To tone the color of wood finished with an alkyd varnish or polyurethane, start with the same finish you used for clear coating and thin it with naphtha about 10% to 25%. To add color to the finish, mix in a small amount of the desired universal tint, as described on p. 126.

You can also create toning oils by adding universal colors to Danish, tung or other oil finishes. Because these finishes dry slowly, it's easy to adjust the color you apply if it isn't just right: Just wipe off the toning oil and apply a mixture of another color.

Whenever you apply a tone, it's important to topcoat the parts afterwards, to protect the layer of color. With lacquers and shellacs, this can be done a short time after toning is complete. Varnishes and polyurethanes should dry for the same length of time as normally required between subsequent coats. Oil finishes should be allowed to dry for several days before the application of a final protective top coat of clear oil.

Bleaching parts that are too dark

As we have seen so far in this chapter, most color correction requires that a lighter wood surface be darkened to match a darker one. But there are circumstances where that approach just isn't practical, such as when a single part is much darker than the rest of the piece. In this case, you'll be better off bleaching the dark part lighter with a two-part wood bleach (also called an A/B bleach), then staining it to match the surrounding wood.

In order to be most effective, a bleach has to be able to soak into the raw wood. Before applying an A/B wood bleach, therefore, clean the wood surfaces to rid them of waxes or residues of any kind. You begin by flooding the surface with the A part of the bleach (typically a moderately strong alkaline solution, such as sodium hydroxide), using a synthetic sponge or brush as an applicator. After a few minutes, while the wood is still wet with part A, apply a coating of part B (typically hydrogen peroxide) using a separate brush or sponge. A slight amount of foaming is a good indication that the bleach is working. Bleaches are strong chemicals that can easily burn your skin or eyes, so wear protective gloves and goggles and work in a well-ventilated area. The reaction slows down after a short while. Give the wood surface a good rinse with clear water or vinegar and water to ensure a neutral surface pH and to remove any remaining residue. After the wood has dried, you can stain it (if necessary) to match the prevailing color of the piece, as described on pp. 121-122.

The right touch-up color can be obtained by mixing dry fresco powders with a padding lacquer. Storing the powders in a plastic seven-compartment pill box (available at drug stores) keeps them clean and separated, and pouring the padding lacquer into a squeeze bottle makes it easier to add a little at a time. Colors are mixed in an artist's plastic paint palette before trying them out on the finish sample.

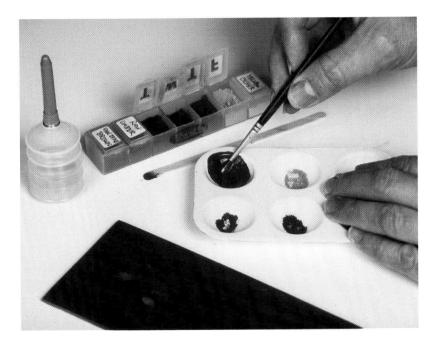

Touching up

Just as a little makeup can transform pockmarked skin into a blemish-free complexion, a touch-up brush and color can turn an obvious puttied patch into one that's really hard to see. Holes that were puttied in raw wood with a commercial putty are especially good candidates for touch-up, since the putty color chosen for raw wood rarely matches after staining and/or finishing. It's best to perform touch-ups on the wood after it's been filled, stained and sealed but before topcoating. The traditional method of touch-up requires that liquid tints or dry powders be mixed into a medium (usually lacquer or shellac) and brushed over the defect. The idea is to make the patched area match the color of the surrounding wood and blend in. Universal tints are more readily available (at paint stores) than dry powdered pigments, and, since they are liquid, are much easier to mix into finishes. Powders tend to form clumps unless you premix them with a small bit of finish.

For touch-ups on lacquer, shellac or varnish finishes, mix tints or powders into a padding lacquer, such as Behlen's Qualasole. I like to put small amounts of different color powders in the dimples of a plastic paint palette (an inexpensive purchase at any art-supply store), then test various color mixtures on my finish sample (see the photo above). Color mixing calls for an artist's eye, and more than a little patience.

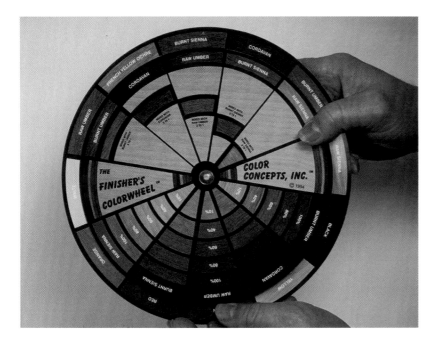

Mixing the right color for touch-ups is easier if you use a Finisher's Colorwheel. The device has two rotating discs: You align the colors you want to mix on the outer and inner discs and view the combination in the window below.

A Finisher's Colorwheel (see the photo above) is helpful for figuring out what color pigments need to be mixed together to get just the right color to match the repair area. The wheel is made by Mohawk (see Sources of Supply on pp. 196-197).

A more forgiving way to touch up with fresco powders, which Chris Minick taught me, is first to seal the repair area with shellac, then rub powder onto the dried shellac with a cotton swab. You can mix, blend and streak colors as needed with the tip of the swab. If you don't get good results on the first try, just wipe off the dry powder and start again (or wipe down the area with a little denatured alcohol). When the repair looks right, seal it in by spraying or brushing a little shellac over it, then topcoat the surface with your regular finish.

If you're working on wood with prominent grain and are trying to hide a more egregious defect, say a really humongous puttied patch, you stand a better chance of hiding the repair by first brushing on fine grain lines to match the grain of the wood. This technique is especially effective on open-pore wood grain that has been filled with a dark filler. After the grain lines are brushed on, you can overcoat with touch-up colors that match the overall wood tone. Applying the graining first and then adjusting the background color makes it easier to get a good match. Once you're happy with the look of the touch-up, topcoat the part to protect the touched-up area.

Touch-up pens can make quick work of covering up small scratches or blending in puttied repairs with the surrounding wood, such as on one of the author's geometrical tulipwood end tables. After color is applied, the excess is immediately wiped off.

Touch-up pens A modern alternative to mixing and brushing on repairs, touch-up pens are an extremely easy way of concealing putty patches or small surface imperfections and small rubbed-through areas in a finish. Since touch-up pens are so handy to use, I carry them in my tool kit for on-site repairs of little accidents that can happen during delivery or installation, such as scratches, scraped edges or spots rubbed into the finish from hold-down straps used during transport.

Touch-up pens work just like colored felt-tip marker pens and can be applied directly over the defect to darken the spot and match that area with the surrounding wood (see the photo above). The pens come in dozens of wood tones (see Sources of Supply on pp. 196-197), and because the colors are translucent, you can lay one color over the other to get just the shade you need. Special graining pens are also available: These fine-tip touch-up markers come in dark colors designed to simulate the grain lines present on open-pore woods. The fine tip makes it easy to draw on grain lines to help the repair area blend in. Both touch-up and graining pens are compatible with all finishes and, unlike stationery-store marker pens, bite into a finished surface so they won't wipe off once dry. You don't have to apply a top coat over them, but it's a good idea to do so, when practical.

Removing Spots

Just like Lady Macbeth, many a woodworker has had occasion to cry: "Out, damnèd spot." Any stain or spot that mars a pristine wood surface is no less traumatic than discovering a mustard stain on your favorite shirt. Fortunately, it's probably easier to clean up that wood spot than to wrestle the stain from your shirt.

Water spots on raw wood

Water spotting occurs when droplets of clean water (or spit from a sudden sneeze) accidentally sprinkle onto an otherwise dry wood surface. The result is small patches where the grain of the wood has been raised, hence the pores are more open and absorb stain or finish more readily than the surrounding wood (see the photo at right). It's an insidious problem because it often goes undetected until it's too late, and you find mysterious dark spots in the middle of your tabletop.

You can easily cure water spotting by treatment before finishing: Simply wipe down the entire surface of the part with clear, tepid water, let the wood dry completely and finish sand with fine-grit paper (220 to 400). Wiping with water raises the grain of the entire surface equally, and then the fine sanding knocks it back down. In fact, the action of wetting and sanding the entire surface of a project just before finishing both prevents water spotting and keeps grain raising from any finish (especially water-based finishes) to a minimum.

If you discover dark spots due to water spotting while applying an oil finish, flood the area with oil and sand the surface with 400-grit paper. This may not completely eliminate them, but at least it will make them much less prominent. If you discover spots after wiping on an aniline dye stain, let the surface dry, then lighten the dark spots by carefully brushing chlorine bleach over the area, which will decolorize many dyes—especially anilines. Standard supermarket-variety chlorine bleach is quite weak (typically a 5% concentration of sodium hypochlorite in water) so you might have to apply it more than once to lighten the surface to the point where restaining will conceal the area where the spots were. Chlorine is an effective oxidizer and will dissolve natural fibers (so use a synthetic brush), but it doesn't need to be neutralized after application.

The subtle spottiness of this maple surface is due to raindrops that dried on the raw wood. This caused the light stain to soak in on those spots more than the surrounding wood. If the surface had been washed down with clear water while the raindrops were still wet, spots wouldn't have formed.

Stain spots

While stains are capable of enhancing and enriching the appearance of wood, a stray stain spot can seem like spray-painted grafitti on a clean wall. As described in the previous section, chlorine bleach is the solution of choice for removing dye stains and anilines that accidentally splatter onto raw wood surfaces. But getting good results requires an unexpected step prior to bleaching: staining the entire surface first with the same dye that splattered on it. Bleaching afterwards then removes the color from the entire surface at once, resulting in a more uniform appearance than if you had selectively treated only the stained spots. If a dark dye leaves the wood tainted with color after bleaching, try using a more concentrated chlorine bleach, such as liquid pool chlorine.

If spots are the result of spilled pigmented stain (or a stain that's a mixture of dyes and pigments), you'll have to color the entire surface, then bleach with an A/B type wood bleach (see p. 125). Since even A/B bleach won't lighten all types of pigments, alternative treatments include planing or sanding the surface back to raw wood or covering up the spotted surface by toning it, as described on pp. 123-125. Of course, if you happen to like the color of the spilled stain, you can always stain the entire piece to match.

Spottiness in an oil finish

Oil finishes, such as Danish oil or tung oil, are very popular with woodworkers because they are easy to apply and repair. But when these oils are wiped on liberally over open-pore woods, an undesirable result often occurs: spots or small rings of gummy oil that keep reappearing after the surface has been wiped dry (see the photo below).

An unpleasant side effect of applying oil finishes to open-pore woods, such as this red oak, is that undried oil continues to exude from the pores, leaving gummy oil spots, as seen here.

Although the wood surface appears dry, oil continues to ooze eerily from its pores, often even after the wood has been wiped down many times. The problem is that any finish with a high oil content expands as it dries. As the oil increases in volume it has nowhere to go except out of the pore, where it forms a spot or a ring. This, in turn, changes the surface tension of the thin layer of oil around the pore, creating a capillary-action-like force that continues to pump oil out of the small reservoir inside the pore.

The most immediate way to deal with this problem is to keep wiping the surface down until the oil in the wood's pores has been depleted. But this solution isn't always practical: I once finished a large koa stereo cabinet at the end of my workday and had to set my alarm several times during the night, so I could keep wiping the wet oil spots down. If you don't catch the spots in time and they dry enough to become gummy, you can smooth them by reapplying the oil finish and scrubbing the surface lightly with a fine plastic abrasive pad (such as 3M gray). If the oil spots have dried hard, you can flood the surface with oil finish and scuff-sand with 320-grit or 400-grit paper until smooth. In either case, to keep spots from reappearing, you'll have to wipe the surface down repeatedly. To keep this chore from interfering with your sleep, plan to start finishing early in the day, or switch to another kind of finish for your open-pore wood projects.

There is another solution that involves doctoring the oil finish you're using. First, pour off enough of the finish to coat your project into a can and thin it down with VM&P naphtha (available at paint stores). Add the naphtha a little at a time, checking the viscosity of the mixture with a paint cup (see the photo below). A full Zahn #3 cup should

The viscosity of a thinned oil finish can be checked with a paint cup and a stopwatch; the thinner the finish, the less time it takes the cup to empty. Once the finish is correctly thinned, adding a few drops of cobalt dryer will help prevent the oil finish from bleeding from the pores of an open-pore wood, such as oak.

empty in about 13 seconds; a #2 or #4 Ford cup (the most common types of cups sold at paint stores) should empty in about 25 seconds. Once the finish is thinned, add a cobalt dryer (available in the oil-painting rack of an art-supply store) to the mixture—about 10 to 15 drops per pint of finish. When a thin coat of this doctored oil finish is applied over the wood, the film dries faster, leaving no time for fresh oil to ooze out.

Rescuing a Contaminated Finish

Bubbles, brush hairs and bugs are three common contaminants that can mar a finish. Bubbles often form in slow-drying film-type finishes, such as varnish and polyurethane. The best way to control bubbles is to discourage their formation in the first place. First, never shake these finishes to mix them. Instead, stir them with a clean stick. Second, if you're brushing the finish, gently tap the bristles of the brush from side to side against the side of the container to remove the excess finish. Also, avoid using flagged bristle brushes with water-based finishes, as these tend to encourage bubble formation. Tapered bristles, often found on nylon brushes, work well. Third, don't apply finish to a wood surface that's been left in the sun, especially if it is an open-pore wood. The heat seems to encourage bubbles to form, especially if the finish is brushed on. Bubbles that do form in a finish can usually be burst by lightly blowing on the surface with filtered compressed air. You can also use your breath, but I suggest blowing through a thin handkerchief, so you don't accidentally get spittle in the wet finish.

Brush bristles should be picked out as soon as they are discovered. You can use your fingernails or a pair of tweezers. Then tip off the area immediately to smooth out the ridges left by the bristle. Tipping off (discussed on p. 136) will level any unevenness left after objects have been picked out of the finish, and it will also remove small bubbles in the film. If you find more than one or two bristles in the finish, save yourself further grief and change to a new brush immediately.

Bugs are kamikazes in the war you fight for a good finish. Unlike inert objects that end up in the film, live bugs don't die right after taking a header—if not noticed and removed quickly, they can track across a surprisingly wide surface, often leaving a trail of torn-off legs and wings along the way. A stuck moth in its death throes is the worst, with flailing wings that can deposit a coating of shiny dust as they thrash. A surprisingly effective way of removing live or dead bugs and their parts from a still-wet finish is to dab at them with a piece of sticky tape. You can then go back in and tip off the area. If the finish is gummy, you'll have to wait until it is completely dry and scrape the area clean, as described below, then recoat it.

If bug swarms in your area reach Biblical proportion, the only way to ensure a pristine finish is to build or suspend a temporary tent frame around your piece and cover it with fine mesh or sheet plastic (vapor barrier from a construction supply works well). Leaving a flap open for ventilation, work inside the tent, then seal it up until the finish is dry (also see the section on dust contamination on p. 195).

Scraping off a contaminated coat of finish

Years ago, I was pulling an all-nighter trying to complete a hall table (shown on p. 145). While spraying a final coat of lacquer onto the table's laminated maple top, I watched in horror as the gun suddenly spewed little bits of frothy blue paint all over the clear blond wood! After overcoming the urge to commit hara-kiri, desperation led me to discover what professional wood finishers already know: that a sharp cabinet-scraper blade is a sensitive, powerful tool for removing some or all of a lacquer finish. I was able to scrape the paint flecks off and re-finish the top before the first glint of morning light.

Scraping works best for removing harder film finishes, such as lacquer and shellac. More elastic finishes, such as varnish or polyurethane, must be completely cured, and even then don't scrape off as cleanly. Scraping will also remove embedded dust, a poor touch-up or drips and sags. The scraping technique I use is the same as to take a fine shaving on a panel: I hold the blade held with both hands, using my thumbs to deflect the blade into a slight curve, then draw the scraper toward me to take a fine cut. Veritas makes a scraper-blade handle that has a built-in screw for adjusting the curve of the blade, as shown in the photo at right.

A scraper is handy for removing a finish from a flat surface. Here, shop assistant Ann Gibb uses a Veritas scraper-blade handle, which makes the blade easier to hold and scraping less fatiguing.

Scraping away swirl marks

Swirl marks are corkscrew-shaped scratches that are an unfortunate by-product of powered orbital sanding. Most commonly besetting smooth-grain hardwoods, such as cherry and maple, swirl marks are often hard to detect until stain or finish has been applied, when it's too late to sand them out. Once again, a sharp caabinet scraper is the tool du jour for scraping below the finish and removing the offending swirl marks. In the future, you can detect swirl marks before finishing by wiping down sanded surfaces with naphtha. You can avoid creating them by not pressing down too hard on your electric orbital machine when sanding.

Repairing Clear Finishes

If you're reading this section to try to fix a shellac or varnish finish on your piece that just won't dry (see p. 120), I'm afraid you're out of luck. Most of the blunders that involve the use of over-age finishing materials or incompatibility between coats of different finishes are fatal: You must chemically strip or scrape off the old finish and start over again. (You can sidestep problems with old varnish if you catch them beforehand; see p. 189.) But more minor problems, such as scratches, drips, cracks and witness lines, can be cured, which will save you the agony of starting the finishing process from scratch.

Drips, runs, sags and curtains

Brushing or spraying on a too-thick coat of finish often results in all kinds of unpleasant problems, such as drips, runs, sags and curtains. Drips are individual stray drops of finish that hang off of edges or pool on a surface; runs are small rivulets of excess finish that run down a vertical surface; sags are excess finish that droops on a vertical surface, creating a thick bulge of film at the bottom (see the drawing below); curtains occur when the excess finish runs on an entire section of a vertical surface, creating a theater-curtain-like series of runs.

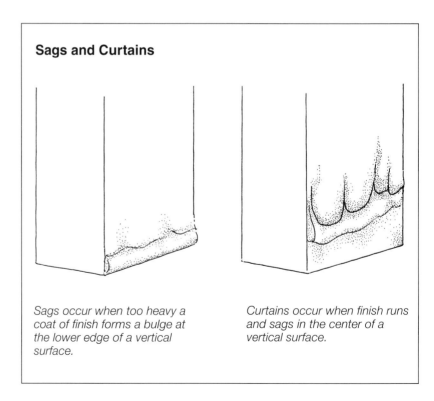

Sags and Curtains

Sags occur when too heavy a coat of finish forms a bulge at the lower edge of a vertical surface.

Curtains occur when finish runs and sags in the center of a vertical surface.

To reduce the likelihood of these defects forming on vertical surfaces, turn them upside-down after finishing—reversing the effects of gravity tends to keep them at bay. Interestingly, even if small runs, sags or curtains form on a surface, they will be less noticeable if the fatter rounded part of the defect is oriented up rather than down.

If you can catch the problem while the finish is still wet and pliable, all these defects can be remedied with a clean brush by tipping off, as described on p. 136. For drips on the lower end of a part, lightly pat the side of the brush against the bottom edge. In both cases, excess finish will be drawn up into the brush's bristles via capillary action.

If you don't notice a defect (or decide to wait) until after the finish is dry, you can usually slice off an offending drip or run with a sharp chisel without disturbing the surrounding surface (don't wait with water-based finishes; wipe off offending drips and runs immediately). First, make sure the drip is dry inside by pushing the tip of a toothpick into it (the same way you'd check to see if a cake is cooked all the way through). Now bring the edge of the chisel to bear at an angle, using a slicing action to keep from tearing the finish film, as shown in the photo at right. Touch-sand the area with 400-grit paper, and apply another coat as necessary.

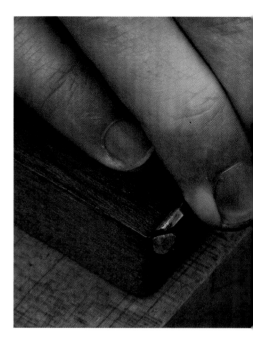

A drop of dried varnish at the bottom of a panel can be cut off using a sharp chisel. Using a slicing action prevents the chisel from tearing the finish film surrounding the drip.

Streaks and roughness

Smoothing out the final surface of a piece coated with a film-type finish by "rubbing out" is a tried-and-true method; for a good description of the technique, see Michael Dresdner's *The Woodfinishing Book* (The Taunton Press, 1992). But it's also time-consuming and problematic if you rub through a layer of finish—or the stain underneath. One way to avoid or at least minimize rubbing out is to get your final top coat as smooth as possible.

If you are spraying on a clear lacquer finish that isn't laying out well, you might end up with a surface that has a regular pattern of small bumps, something like a relief map of the moon. To smooth out a surface beset by so-called "orange peel" or by brush marks, spray a final coat of lacquer that has a small amount of a retarder additive mixed into it. This final coat will redissolve the previous surface (as lacquer normally does), while the retarder keeps it from drying too quickly, allowing the surface to flow out smooth and level. In lieu of mixing your own, you can use a "slower" lacquer thinner or an aerosol lacquer leveler, available in convenient spray cans (see Sources of Supply on pp. 196-197).

To smooth out ridges and streaks left after brushing on a coat of lacquer or varnish, lightly drag the tip of brush across the surface, a process known as "tipping off."

Streaks and ridges can result when a film-type finish is brushed on unevenly. How you repair them depends on the type of finish used. The best way to smooth a rough varnish or polyurethane film is while the material is still wet by "tipping off" the film. This process is performed by lightly dragging the tip of an unloaded brush across the wet finish (see the photo above). Tipping off can also remove streaks from a slow-drying brushing-lacquer finish, although you might do better to load a clean brush with lacquer thinner, then brush lightly over the area, using a deft touch.

If your varnish finish is too dry to tip off, you can try the method advocated by Chris Minick: Wait for the surface to dry to the touch, then rub it down thoroughly with a soft, lint-free cloth, applying lots of pressure. The idea is to burnish the irregularities out of the partially dried film. Minick says the method takes some experience to master (so experiment with a scrap first) but he adds that it does a nice job of smoothing out ridges left by heavy brush strokes.

If your finish has dried completely before the surface irregularities are discovered, a possible remedy is to overcoat a gloss or semi-gloss finish with an eggshell or flat finish. Like a flat paint, the minimized surface reflection of a flat clear coat tends to hide irregularities or even dust that might have embedded itself in the surface.

Small scratches

Small scratches in a finish can be an annoying distraction on an otherwise flawless piece of work. (Scratches from fingernails, belt buckles or even buttons on a shirtsleeve can easily occur as the piece is carried or transported from shop to house.) Repair is based on the kind of finish used. Oil finishes are the easiest to fix. Simply dip the tip of a cotton swab or rolled-up rag into the oil finish and rub it over the scratch. Shellac and lacquer are also easy to fix. Fresh shellac, or a padding lacquer such as Qualasole, can be "padded" over a scratched area (you can also add tints or pigments to padding materials to tone the color of the repair). Padding is done with a balled-up rag, like a tampon you would use for French polishing, as shown in the multiple-exposure photo below. Of the film-type finishes, varnish and polyurethanes are the most difficult to repair. You can carefully flow fresh finish into the scratch with a fine brush, then topcoat the surface to even up the repair. Small, less prominent scratches can usually be hidden by coloring them with a touch-up pen, as described on pp. 128-129.

A scratch in a lacquer finish can be covered by applying padding lacquer with a balled-up soft cotton rag. Lightly stroke the scratch area with the rag in an arc motion, just as if you were French polishing.

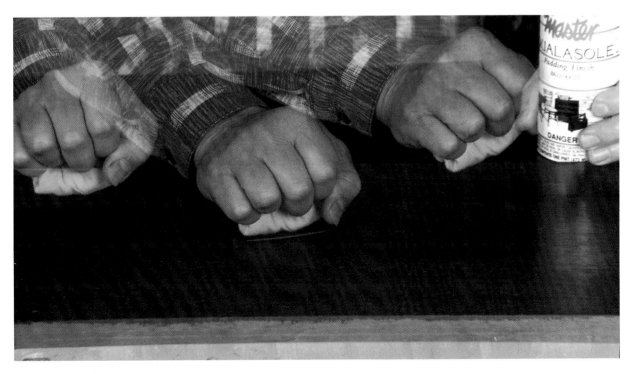

Witness lines

In contrast to evaporative finishes, such as nitrocellulose lacquer or shellac, where subsequent coats meld into one thick coat, applying a coat of a reactive finish, such as varnish and water-based or catalyzed lacquer, over a previous coat, will not redissolve the old coat. Subsequently, if you sand through one or more coats of a reactive finish, say to clean up a sag or to remove brush marks, it's likely that you will see a faint line or lines around the border of the sanded area (see the drawing below). The only way to get rid of these "witness lines" is to top-coat the entire surface. As with any top coat, make sure the surface is clean and free of sanding debris and scuff-sand the whole surface with 280-grit or 320-grit paper, to give the new coat a better bite.

Crackled finishes

Exposing a warm, freshly finished surface to a cold draft may cause "cold checking," which looks like a latticework of tiny cracks running all over the surface. Lacquer finishes are the easiest to heal, by over-spraying with regular lacquer thinner to reamalgamate the surface. You can use an aerosol product referred to as amalgamator to fix a cold-checked shellac, varnish or lacquer finish. The amalgamator, which can be brushed or sprayed over the damaged finish, temporarily dissolves the finish while corrective plasticizing agents help the finish to flow back together into a continuous film. It's a good idea to topcoat the amalgamated finish with a padding lacquer in order to seal in the amalgamator, so the problem won't happen again.

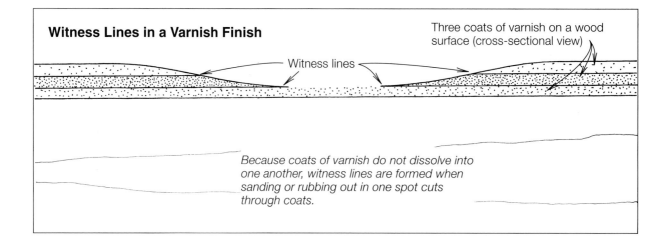

Witness Lines in a Varnish Finish

Three coats of varnish on a wood surface (cross-sectional view)

Witness lines

Because coats of varnish do not dissolve into one another, witness lines are formed when sanding or rubbing out in one spot cuts through coats.

Another cause of a cracked or "alligatored" surface is finish incompatibility. This can occur when one kind of finish is applied over another, such as lacquer over varnish (goodness knows why you'd want to do this, but we all experience moments of bad judgment). The cause of the cracking is similar to what happens when a layer of ice forms over mud: as the wood moves, the flexible varnish can flex, but the more brittle lacquer does not and cracks. In this case, the only remedy is to remover the lacquer, using lacquer thinner, which will leave most of the varnish coat underneath in place. Then scuff-sand and apply another coat of varnish.

Repairing Special Lacquer Problems

Some finishing problems occur only with lacquer finishes. These maladies, including blush, fisheye, pin holes, cobwebs and pebbliness due to overspray, can affect nitrocellulose, acrylic or water-based lacquers.

Blush

If you work in a humid climate and like to lacquer your woodwork, you've probably already had to deal with blush. When blush occurs, all of a sudden your crystal-clear finish turns cloudy white in patchy areas. Blushing is most likely to occur if there is moisture in the air and/or if you're spraying on thick coats. But just as mysteriously as those cloudy patches appear, they can be made to vanish: Simply dilute the lacquer with a slower-drying lacquer thinner, or add a small amount (about 10%) of a commercial lacquer retarder (which is usually butyl cellusolve) to the lacquer mix already in the gun's cup and respray the surface. Alternatively, you could spray the surface with "No Blush," an aerosol product made by Mohawk (see Sources of Supply on pp. 196-197). In any case, the blushed film should quickly turn clear again (a common explanation is that the solvent temporarily dissolves the film, allowing trapped moisture to escape; but I have it on good authority that what occurs is a considerably more complicated chemical process). If you don't have a retarder or slow thinner on hand, you can reshoot the surface on a less humid day with regular lacquer. However, as you probably want to undo the blushing on the same humid day as it took place, the slower-drying lacquer mixture will prevent blushing from occurring again.

Fisheye

An all-too-common lacquer problem, fisheye looks like little craters that are about ⅛ in. in diameter. It occurs after a surface has been contaminated by silicone, a common ingredient in some machine-tool lubricants and rust preventives, as well as in spray waxes, such as Pledge. The silicone reduces surface tension in the contaminated area, causing the lacquer to flow out better in that spot than on the surface surrounding it (see the drawing below). Just as taking the "hair of the dog that bit you" is said to cure a hangover, the solution to fisheye is to add silicone to the lacquer, in the form of fisheye eliminator, and respray the surface. The addition of silicone reduces surface tension evenly over the entire film of lacquer, and also improves the flow-out properties of the lacquer. A few important caveats though: Once you've added fisheye eliminator, all future coats must contain it, lest fisheye problems be renewed. Most important, once you've used silicone-doctored finish in a spray gun, that gun will always be contaminated—you just can't remove all traces of silicone. Therefore, you'll might want to buy a cheap spray gun (or dedicate an old one) just for fisheye repairs.

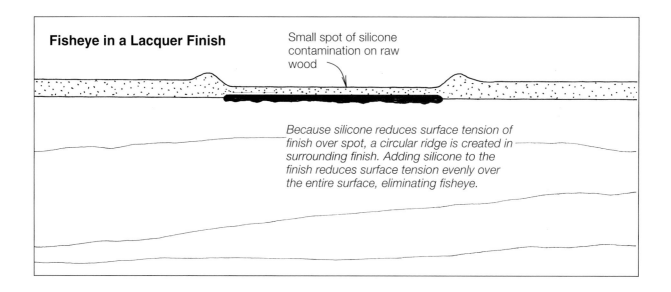

Fisheye in a Lacquer Finish

Small spot of silicone contamination on raw wood

Because silicone reduces surface tension of finish over spot, a circular ridge is created in surrounding finish. Adding silicone to the finish reduces surface tension evenly over the entire surface, eliminating fisheye.

Pin holes

Surface tension can also play tricks on you if you get a little heavy handed when spraying lacquer on unsealed, large-pored woods. The result is little holes above the large pores that look like pin pricks. The simplest fix is to overspray the surface with plain lacquer thinner, which allows the lacquered surface to flow out and reamalgamate.

Cobwebs

Sometimes lacquer sprayed on a hot day dries so quickly that it is a sticky powder by the time it hits the surface of the work. The result is a stringy mess that looks remarkably like spiderwebs. These cobwebs, as they are called, are most likely to form in dry, hot weather. There's no need to get caught in a tangled web though; the remedy is a cinch. Wait a few moments and wipe the surface with a clean cloth or scrub it down with a gray Scotchbrite pad. Now reduce the air pressure at the gun and spray on a new coat. Any minor remaining cobwebs will be redissolved. If that doesn't help, add a small amount of retarder to the lacquer (or use a slower thinner) to extend the time it takes the finish to dry.

Overspray roughness

A dry, rough texture on a sprayed lacquer surface is often due to atomized particles of overspray landing on the surface after the finish has tacked (the surface of the finish has dried); the particles don't flow out. Because each new coat of lacquer dissolves the previous coats, you can easily smooth out the problem by shooting a nice wet coat over the affected surface. If roughness problems continue, try using a lower air pressure or reduce the width of the spray pattern at the gun's nozzle. If you're plagued with overspray from trying to shoot inside assembled casework, shoot the top areas first and bottom last (also see p. 181). You can also significantly reduce overspray by using an HVLP (high-volume/low-pressure) spray system. As the name indicates, HVLP guns deliver finish at low pressure, producing relatively little overspray. A simpler, but less effective solution is to place the intake side of a portable fan near the cabinet you're shooting, to draw overspray away before it has a chance to settle. Just work in a well ventilated area, so fumes don't accumulate. Do not try this with solvent-based finishes, which can pose an explosion hazard.

PART 2

Avoiding Woodworking Mistakes

Thus far this book has dealt with fixing mistakes—what to do when things go wrong, how to make the best of a bad situation. But rather than just curing problems as they occur, it's to your advantage to avoid them by developing foresight and work habits that discourage them from happening in the first place. Because each step of a project—designing, drawing, constructing, assembling and finishing—presents an opportunity for disaster to strike, the number of things that can possibly go wrong is far too great to cover in just a few short chapters of a book (in fact, I doubt that a multi-volume set could contain them all). However, you can get a head start in the race against regret by exploring the more common—and avoidable—pitfalls that can waylay you. Errors due to design and measurement can be kept at bay by sketching and modeling, by planning around potential problems and by learning to measure accurately. These topics are dealt with in Chapter 8. Errors of cutting and machining, discussed in Chapter 9, can be headed off by sensible shop practices, as can problems in assembly and finishing, discussed in Chapter 10. The strategies presented in these three chapters (supplemented by your own experiences) will help you develop a kind of "mistake radar"—a little buzzer in your head that automatically goes off before trouble takes a toe hold and the expletives start flying.

CHAPTER 8
Good Designs and True Measurements

Anything can exist in the mind's eye. Unfortunately, the landing strip that provides ideas with a place to enter the physical world is strewn with all manner of unattractive, untenable and poorly functioning work. The first steps required for transforming an imagined thing into a satisfying object made of wood are design and measurement: The first gives form to the idea, and the second gives it scale and proportion. This is the time to develop drawings, cobble up models and make patterns for parts. It's also the time to consider how well the intended piece will fulfill its duties. Will the cabinet have enough room for the stereo components it's going to accommodate? Will the window seat fit into that opening beneath the bay windows? Is the chair wide enough for Aunt Louise?

At perhaps no other time is a woodworker more in control of the destiny of a project. For while a badly made joint can be recut or too-short part replaced, few of us have the time—or initiative—to rebuild a project completely because its proportions are poor or the design doesn't quite work. Poor planning can mean major reworking of a piece if its structure is unsound or it falls apart because the joinery was ill conceived, if it's the wrong size or doesn't do what it's supposed to—or if it doesn't fit through the door of the house in the first place. And poor measurement practices can lead to an entire stack of parts that are 1 in. too long or a cabinet that's 1 ft. higher than the ceiling.

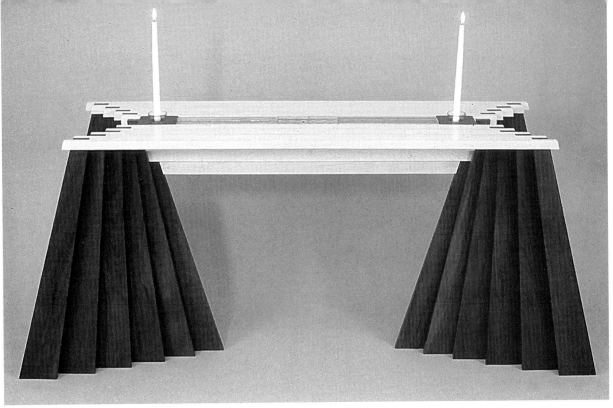

Envisioning Reality

If you were a child growing up in the early 1960s, you probably re-member those ads in the back of comic books for sets of "realistically molded" plastic soldiers. An illustration I saw when I was eight years old made a set of Civil War soldiers look dramatic and exciting. But the excitement abated considerably four to six weeks later when the let-ter carrier finally delivered the prize. The small, cheesy plastic figures were as flat as pancakes, with features molded in less-than-breathtaking $\frac{1}{32}$-in. deep relief.

Most of us learned early on of the enormous difference between how something is represented on paper and how it looks in reality. I don't know a single woodworker who hasn't experienced serious disap-pointment on a project that didn't come out as envisioned. Our prima-ry tools for sidestepping such displeasure are accurate renderings and models. But not every woodworker is an artist (or even a good draftsperson), so here are a few simple methods for representing and evaluating crucial features of a piece quickly and easily—before you commit wood to its construction.

Despite the complex appearance of the piece, thorough planning, including the preparation of numerous drawings, construction models, joinery mockups and a step-by-step assembly diagram, helped the author build this Peruvian walnut and maple hall table from start to finish in only three-and-a-half days. It was delivered just in time for the opening of a furniture exhibit in Mendocino, California (the fused-glass tiles that run down the center of the top were added later). Photo: Nicholas Wilson.

Sketch from a viewer's perspective

Tables, desks and cabinets with tops that overhang their aprons or carcases often share a common problem: Features such as patterned drawer pulls, shaped aprons or decorative carvings are planned on a front-view elevation drawing. But when the piece is put into use, the overhang prevents a standing viewer from seeing or accessing salient features. After making this mistake once on a table with difficult-to-see contrasting inlays on the apron, I came up with a quick way for making sure that features will be visible at typical viewing angles and distances. Using graph paper with a standard ¼-in. grid, draw a side view (elevation drawing) of your piece at a convenient scale, say ¼ in. equals 2 in. (see the drawing below). Now, using the same scale of

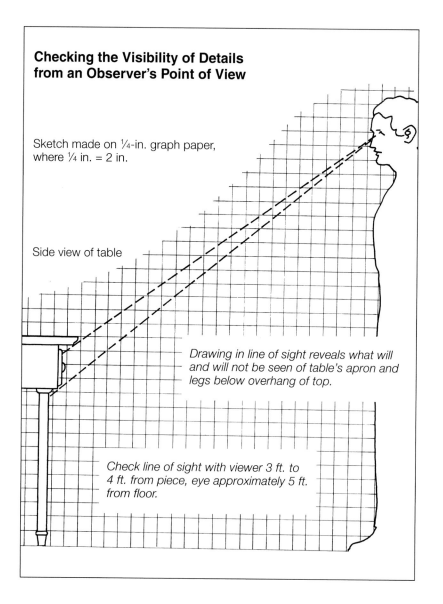

Checking the Visibility of Details from an Observer's Point of View

Sketch made on ¼-in. graph paper, where ¼ in. = 2 in.

Side view of table

Drawing in line of sight reveals what will and will not be seen of table's apron and legs below overhang of top.

Check line of sight with viewer 3 ft. to 4 ft. from piece, eye approximately 5 ft. from floor.

measure, add the point of perspective of a viewer standing 3 ft. or 4 ft. away (I make the eye about 5 ft. from the floor; typical for a person who is 5 ft. 6 in. tall). Now draw a straight line between the viewer's eye and the feature in question. If you can't do it, try reducing the overhang of the top, making the apron wider or locating features farther down. The sketch also reveals things that may be hard to get to, such as top drawers that may be difficult to manipulate because of an overhanging desktop—in which case you can either change the overhang or switch to full-extension drawer glides (see p. 27). You can also use the sketching technique to determine if the user will be able to see and/or reach the contents of a high shelf.

Construct simple models to evaluate form and proportion

Scale models are great for seeing a piece in three dimensions before you actually build it. A good model, even if simply done, will give you a sense of the overall proportions of a piece and their often complex interrelationship. For example, function might dictate the width, height and depth of a chest of drawers; but a quick cardboard box cut out with the same proportions will tell you if the piece will look fat, squat or clunky. Likewise, a quick cutout model of a side chair will tell you if its legs look too thin or fat, if their taper appears elegant or awkward, and if the back looks good at a three-quarter profile.

Another important use of a model is to evaluate how the piece will look and function at human scale. It's much easier to judge a relatively complex piece, such as the lectern shown in the photo at right, if you place a human figure, cut to the same scale as the model, behind it (scale the figure to average height, about 5 ft. 6 in. tall). By placing your eye at the same height it would be at that scale, you can get a good idea of how a person standing behind this podium would look from different vantage points. Similarly, models and cutout figures can be used to evaluate the visual and functional merits and shortcomings of chairs, benches, desks and cabinets.

Unless you're using a model to sell a client on a commission, don't bother with much in the way of details; you aren't building dollhouse furniture here. The carcases of most cabinets can be made by cutting and bending cardboard into box forms, then taping or hot-gluing on tops and legs. With these temporary fasteners, it's simple to remove and rework components that don't seem right. To make forms easier to judge, I often darken the outline of each form or component with a

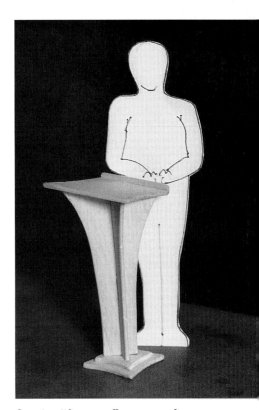

A cutout human figure, made to match the scale of the model, such as the lectern shown here, can help you evaluate the proportions of the piece before you make final plans and cut lists.

You can get away with building just half of a complex model, such as the nesting set of tea tables shown here, by placing the half-model against a mirror. The mirror is set atop a dark base, for contrast, and supported with a pair of wooden cam clamps.

marker pen. If the form of the piece you're modeling is complicated but symmetrical, a mirror will allow you to see the overall visual impact, but build only half the model (see the photo at left).

Make crude full-size mockups

A scale model, even built as accurately as full-sized work, is only so effective for predicting the qualities of a fully built piece of furniture. It's like looking at a tiny paint chip and trying to imagine what a whole room would be like painted in that color. It's hard to appreciate how a big piece of furniture will change the entire feeling of a room, and whether it will clash or harmonize with the room's colors and other furnishings. One quick way to avoid surprises is to make a very crude full-size representation of the piece and look at it in situ, at its final location. This mockup doesn't have to be exact; it can be nothing more than a big piece of paper or cardboard cut out to the approximate shape of the finished piece (painted, if necessary). Tacking this up in the room where the piece is intended to go will give you a pretty good idea how that piece will interact with the rest of the room.

Furniture that must accommodate the human body will require more extensive modeling. Crudely built full-size chairs, benches and desks can give the future user a chance to try the piece—and give the builder an opportunity to refine dimensions—ahead of final construction. Build such models from cheap plywood fastened together with drywall screws, so the components can be reworked, repositioned or replaced as the design is refined to suit the user.

Model selectively

Another way to use simple, full-scale modeling is during the construction phase itself. Let's say you are building a sideboard. Once the basic carcase is assembled, you can cut out full-size cardboard parts to represent components such as legs or drawer fronts to check their look before making them. This is also a good way to evaluate decorative details, such as carved plaques or contour-cut borders, both for suitable appearance and mounting position on the carcase.

Selective modeling is also useful for mocking up tricky joints and connections to make sure they're going to work. Mocking up the parts of a joint allows you to develop a sense of how the assembly is going to go and will let you experiment with the order of gluing up parts (subassemblies). And you'll also get a great picture of how the finished joint will look, an important consideration if the joint is in a prominent location, such as the corners of a Parsons table or the connection between shelves and their supports on an étagère. After mocking up a joint, you may decide to reduce the dimensions of the final joinery to make it look less heavy. Or, you might anticipate the need to make

Mocking up a joint or small section of a mechanism can help you avoid problems ahead of building the actual components. This model of a tambour assembly is being used to check for clearance between the track and the inside of the carcase.

joints stockier for better strength. Mocking up part of an articulating assembly, such as a tambour door, can prevent problems such as making the track too sharply curved for smooth motion or allowing too little clearance between the track and the carcase (see the photo above).

Planning around Problems

There's more to designing a cabinet or furniture piece than its form and proportion. There are practical matters that require advance planning, if your project is to come off without a hitch. The joinery, in addition to being strong (and possibly attractive), should also allow for the seasonal movement of the wood. Cabinets should be designed to accommmodate the stuff that's supposed to go inside them, and they should be easy to install cleanly. Even the path from shop to installation needs consideration, if the delivery of that much-awaited project is to go smoothly.

Design joinery for expansion and contraction

Problems that arise from poorly designed construction, such as cross-grain construction that doesn't allow wood to expand and contract, often result in disastrous consequences: a tabletop that buckles like an enormous potato chip, aprons that crack apart where the legs are joined, an entire carcase that explodes. Don't let the rapture of design inspiration lead you away from good building practices that accommodate wood's changeable nature. I've seen very few designs that couldn't have been adapted to incorporate floating (rather than fixed) cross-grain joints. If you must "breadboard" (cap the end of a panel or top with a cross-grain member), use a spline along its length to keep it registered and fasten it only at the center portion. This allows the end caps to float on the ends of the panel as it swells or shrinks with the changes of season.

To reduce the effects of cross-grain problems, frame rails wider than 4 in. to 6 in. should have twin rather than single tenons on their ends. Also, never try to surround even a plywood panel with a mitered frame that is more than 4 in. wide. If the wood in the frame shrinks, the miter joints eventually open up and look very poorly made, even if they were as tight as clams when first glued up. Instead, make the entire top from plywood and create the look of a frame and central panel with veneer. Indeed, plywood and veneer will let you create all sorts of visual effects that would be foolish to try with solid wood.

Sidestep the trap of "standard" sizes

Cabinets and furniture are very often designed to accommodate things like electronic components, appliances and cushions. But while you'd never build a TV cabinet without first measuring the size of the TV, many woodworkers have gotten into trouble by assuming that the components they built for were standard sized. Common items, such as wine bottles, can vary considerably in length and diameter, and most wine racks won't handle champagne bottles. Most musical compact discs are the same size—except the double albums and the new issues with environmentally friendly packaging. The worst offenders are "standard size" bed mattresses and box springs. Fulls, queens and kings of different brands and models typically vary 1 in. in width and can vary up to 3 in. in length! Kitchen appliances are notorious for special electrical, plumbing and ventilation requirements. Follow the specifications in the manual for the actual unit that the cabinet will house whenever possible. When in doubt, make spaces bigger—trim can always be added to conceal open spaces (see pp. 26-27). This same strategy can be employed when making stereo and television cabinets. By adding a trim frame, the cabinet will neatly accommodate a 23-in. set; with the trim removed, it will house that super-duper 27-in. TV when you upgrade in a few years.

Include a fudge factor

I have a poster hanging in my shop that says "Murphy was an Optimist." The poster lists a number of Murphy's Laws (e.g., Anything that can go wrong, will), and it serves as a reminder that I don't live in a perfect world, and therefore should build my furniture accordingly. That doesn't mean I accept poorly made joinery or sloppy finishes. But I also don't try to create built-in cabinets that will "piston fit" into their intended wall spaces, or wardrobe cabinets that are "exactly" short enough to clear the ceiling in the bedroom they are destined for. By easing measurements and building in a little margin for error, I add what I call a "fudge factor" to many pieces I build.

One such fudge factor that most professional cabinetmakers use is to add scribes to their built-in cabinets. In most cases, a scribe is a wide face-frame member that overhangs its carcase (see the drawing below). A cabinet that must fit flush with an interior wall or mate to other cabinets can be fitted simply by trimming the edge of its face frame—not the

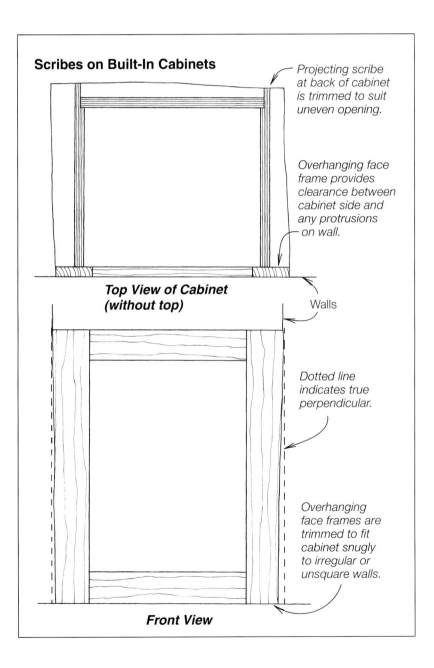

Scribes on Built-In Cabinets

Projecting scribe at back of cabinet is trimmed to suit uneven opening.

Overhanging face frame provides clearance between cabinet side and any protrusions on wall.

Top View of Cabinet (without top)

Walls

Dotted line indicates true perpendicular.

Overhanging face frames are trimmed to fit cabinet snugly to irregular or unsquare walls.

Front View

A face frame that overhangs the side of a cabinet can be scribed and trimmed so the cabinet butts up flush to irregular or unsquare walls. A simple pencil compass is used to transfer the profile of the wall to the face frame.

entire cabinet side. Besides allowing you to compensate for inexact measurements or carcases that are slightly out of square, a scribe also lets you deal with the irregularities of sheetrocked walls, which are rarely straight or plumb. The process of scribing—transferring the contour of the wall to the cabinet's face frame—can be done with a simple pencil compass, as shown in the photo above. In lieu of an overhanging face frame, you can add a scribe strip, like a plain molding, to the edge of or on top of the face frame to hide the juncture of cabinet and wall or gaps between adjacent cabinets.

In order to compensate for out-of-plumb walls when trying to hang upper kitchen cabinets true, cabinetmaker Cliff Friedlander also adds a scribe to the back of his cabinets (see the drawing on p. 151). This is done by making the rabbet for the cabinet backs about $\frac{3}{4}$ in. in from the back edge of the cabinet sides, top and bottom. Once the $\frac{1}{4}$-in. cabinet back is installed, about $\frac{1}{2}$ in. is left that can be trimmed to suit the wall contour, just like the face-frame scribe discussed above.

To add a fudge factor to large carcase pieces, such as wardrobes, chests and entertainment centers, consider building them as modular components that will be assembled on site. Large traditional pieces, such as highboys and chest-on-chests, were usually built this way, with separate carcases, drawer chests, cornices and bases. Modular construction makes it easier to install tall cabinets where there is limited ceiling clearance. If the dimensions of the piece are incorrect (or you just don't like the style of the curvaceous plinth base you copied from *Sunset* magazine), modularity makes it a lot easier to make changes. Take just the base back to the shop for alterations or make a new one that suits your taste. And if the crown molding on a big armoire is too tall and gouges your cottage-cheese sprayed-on acoustical ceiling, it's a whole lot easier to change the feet on the base or cut down the cornice than to rework the entire carcase.

Design for delivery

We've all read those stories in *Reader's Digest* about plucky retirees who have single-handedly built rather large sailboats in their basements or garages—only to discover that they had to dismantle part of a wall to get them out! The path you must take to deliver a completed piece of furniture or cabinetry—into cars and vans, through doorways, up stairs, into elevators—should be made a part of your design and measuring process from the very beginning of your project. A narrow passage might require that you redesign an entire section of a large cabinet, perhaps build it in modular sections and assemble them on site. Corner units for base kitchen cabinets (typically 3 ft. square) are often too big to fit through standard residential doorways. Kitchen-cabinet expert Cliff Friedlander recommends that you build these with a separate base at the kickspace. With no top or base, a corner cabinet can be maneuvered through a typical 32-in. wide doorway with the door removed from its hinges.

Avoiding Bad Measurements

All woodworkers must deal with numbers that represent the sizes of things in both the represented world of drawings, models and cut lists and the real world of wood parts and assembled carcases. But while numbers can serve as steadfast messengers to help transfer sizes between represented forms and real materials, they can quickly become heedless saboteurs that jumble dimensions, leading to individual parts—and whole pieces of furniture—that don't fit.

There are many ways to avoid mismeasurements when working with rulers and tape measures, and even ways to dispense with numerical measurements entirely. But regardless of how you work, the best advice regarding measurements is to perform the most critical steps when your mind is fresh. For many of us, that means first thing in the morning, before the day's events can fill our heads with distractions.

Transfer measurements from drawing to cut list

Mistakes are terribly easy to make when sizing parts directly from a scale drawing, especially if you're using a regular ruler and converting for each dimension (let's see, $\frac{1}{4}$ in. on the drawing equals 1 in., so $3\frac{7}{16}$ in. equals...?). It's much safer to use an architect's or engineer's ruler of the proper scale and read the full-size dimension right off the scale. To avoid accidentally taking a measurement with the wrong edge of a multi-scale ruler (triangular ones with six different scales are particularly confusing), put tape over every scale but the one you're using. If you're transferring a curved part from a scale drawing to create a full-size pattern, first lay out any critical edges and the position of the joints, then transfer the curve using a pantograph, or use the enlarging feature found on many up-scale photocopy machines.

Be extra careful when sizing components like window and door sizes from an architect's or builder's drawings. The standards nomenclature for such architectural components lists them in feet and inches: A 60-in. tall window is labeled as "5-0." The problem is clear: If you interpret the 5-0 measurement as 50 in., you'll end up with a window that's 10 in. short. And since such labels don't always correspond to their scale measurements on a drawing, it's prudent to check dimensions with a scale and question all inconsistencies.

A couple of other pitfalls are worth mentioning. When taking measurements or developing patterns from a drawing, be wary of parts that are foreshortened because they have been rendered as a projection in the particular view in the drawing you are looking at. For example, take a look at the splayed legs of the picnic table in the drawing on the facing page. Also, when building from plans published in a

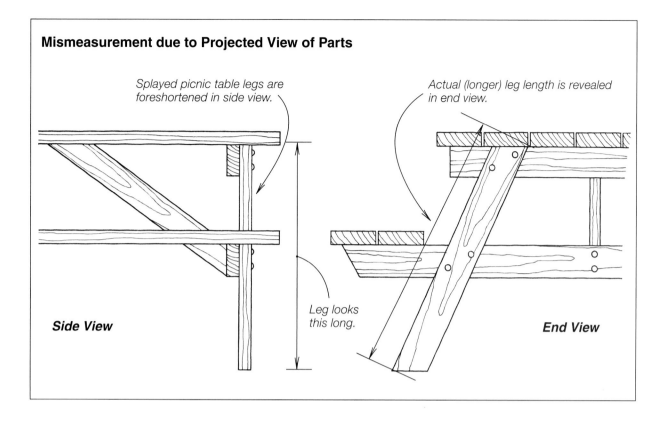

Mismeasurement due to Projected View of Parts

Splayed picnic table legs are foreshortened in side view.

Actual (longer) leg length is revealed in end view.

Leg looks this long.

Side View

End View

book or magazine, double-check all measurements and cut lists before commencing. Despite the best attempts of the author and editor to get it right, errors do have an insidious way of sneaking into print.

Calibrate your tapes and rulers

I kept getting an annoying discrepancy whenever I would cut frame members to length on my chopsaw. To save time, I had mounted a long fence to the saw, complete with a stick-on steel ruler and FasT-Track flip-stop system. I had zeroed the stop and checked to make sure that the 12-in. mark was exactly 1 ft. from the blade. But cutoffs that were 2 ft. or longer always seemed to come up just a tad short. When I finally compared the entire length of the scale with my trusty Starrett tape measure, my suspicions were confirmed: The increments on the two scales didn't match!

The lesson here is that we should make sure that the measuring devices in our shops match, including all rulers, yardsticks, graduated squares, stick-down scales and tape measures. If you discover that a cheap yardstick or your "bargain" imported steel rulers don't correspond to your standard scales, throw them out (or mark them as defective and use them only as straightedges). Otherwise, they will bring you no end of misery. Stop systems on radial-arm saws or other cutoff saws should have the accuracy of the stick-down tape checked before the tape is attached and zeroed to the blade.

Tape measures need to be checked occasionally, especially if they are subject to abuse, because the rivets that attach the end hook can loosen, destroying the accuracy of the tape. The best way I've found to ensure the accuracy of outside measurements taken with a tape is to set the position of the end hook carefully, then fix the rivet in place, as shown in the photo below. Setting the end hook dedicates the tape for outside measurements; you'll have to use another tape for inside measures. Incidentally, you can ruin any tape's accuracy by consistently allow its strong spring to retract the tape at full speed, which slams the end hook into the case. Instead, slow it down with a little finger pressure.

You can improve the accuracy of a tape measure by fixing its sliding end hook to make it dedicated for outside measurements. After the position of the hook is confirmed with an accurate ruler, set the rivets that secure the hook to the tape using an arbor press or a small hammer.

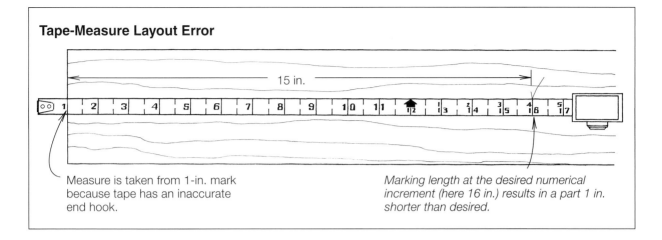

Tape-Measure Layout Error

15 in.

Measure is taken from 1-in. mark because tape has an inaccurate end hook.

Marking length at the desired numerical increment (here 16 in.) results in a part 1 in. shorter than desired.

Avoid errors when measuring from the 1-in. mark

One of the most common errors I've encountered is when tape measures are used to take readings from the 1-in. mark. The reason for this is that many tapes have inaccurate end hooks, so many woodworkers use the 1-in. mark as the zero point of measurement. Measuring a 16-in. long part this way will yield a reading of 17 in. If you forget to subtract the inch when you cut a matching part, you'll end up with a piece 1 in. longer than needed.

The more serious problem is when you want to lay out a new part that's 16 in. long. If again you use the tape's 1-in. mark as zero and forget to *add* 1 in. and mark the part at the tape's 16-in. increment, you'll end up with a part that's an inch short (see the drawing above). To avoid the risk of error, take your outside measurements using the end hook on a tape that's been properly calibrated, or switch to either a metal ruler, a folding rule, a yardstick or a dedicated outside measuring tape, made as described in the previous section.

Overcome errors due to throat-plate deflection

One machine component that's often responsible for causing depth-of-cut inaccuracies is the insert plate or "throat plate" found on most table saws and router tables. The problem is that many of these plates flex (see the photo on p. 158). When the workpiece is pressed down over them during cutting or routing, you end up with an inconsistent depth of cut for grooves, dadoes and joint cuts. This is how it happens: The height of the blade or bit is first checked by measuring with a small ruler, which applies little downward pressure on the plate. Then, when the workpiece is run through, the plate flexes and the depth of cut mysteriously increases, usually sporadically, since hand-feed pressure varies over the course of the operation.

Any deflection or sag in the insert plate on a router table can lead to cuts of inconsistent depth. Even relatively stiff phenolic plates, like this one, can sag over time when they must support a hefty router mounted underneath.

To cope with the deflection, I fit my saw and router table with more rigid throat plates (some of aluminum, some of thick phenolic plastic). On cuts with a critical depth, I fit a featherboard or a wheeled hold-down over the dado blade or cutter, set to roughly the correct depth of cut, then fine-tune it by testing on an extra workpiece or sample that's the same width and/or thickness as the workpiece.

Eliminate numbers by using a story stick

Just as some satirists have speculated that "the problem with society is people," many experienced builders will say that the problem with measuring is numbers. Each distance we can measure has a different set of numbers associated with it, and numbers are entirely too easy to mix up. We read numbers wrong from a ruler, forget them between the time they're measured and a saw stop is set, jot them down erroneously, accidentally transpose them ($8^3/_{16}$ in. becomes $16^3/_8$ in.) and more. Measurements can be awkward to interpret in terms of the numerical scales we use—for example, a table leg that is $25^{11}/_{32}$, plus a tad. Adding up fractions is always dangerous: Quick—what's $25^7/_8$ plus $11^{13}/_{32}$? And what about when you're trying to figure in the thickness of a sheet of metric plywood with the size of a box, built using inches. Common sense often warns us when numbers have been fumbled and a particular measurement "is just too big to be correct." But subtle mismeasurements have occasionally been the downfall of woodworkers one and all.

The best way to make certain that you will never stumble on account of numbers is to eliminate them. Instead, substitute marks recorded on a on a story stick (also called a story pole). The marks represent the exact sizes of parts: the width of a door, the depth of a carcase side, the length of stiles and rails in a face frame. This serves as a physical means, or "analog," for setting up tools and machines when cutting parts to size, as shown in the photo below. After all, if parts are cut to exact size and fit, who cares how long they are numerically? One story stick can hold all the essential data for building a single piece of furniture or an entire kitchen's worth of cabinets.

To make the marks on the stick in the first place, you can use regular measurements made with a tape or a yardstick. Some measurements, such as the distance between walls where a cabinet fits, can be transferred directly from the room. Each distance is then labeled. Just make sure you double- and triple-check your measurements and labels. If you put the wrong marks on your story stick, you might not discover the error until the entire piece is complete...and doesn't fit!

Setting a table-saw fence with a story stick decreases the chances of measurement errors because no numbers are involved. All vital dimensions for a cabinet or piece of furniture are marked as labeled increments on the stick.

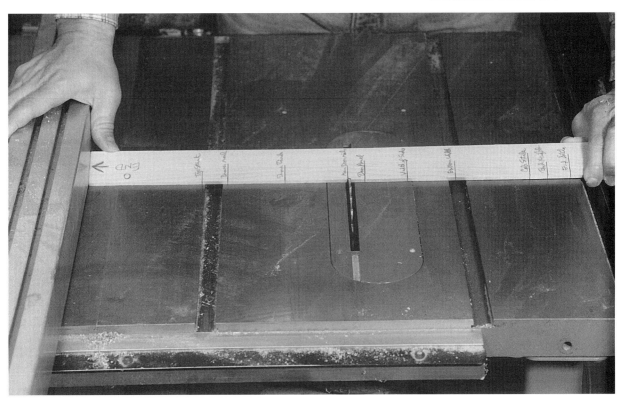

CHAPTER 9

Good Practices for Cutting and Machining

There's no substitute for abundant experience and skilled hands when making parts for a project. As the movie character Forrest Gump might say: "skilled is as skilled does." If you simply do everything right the first time, then you won't have to worry much about making mistakes. But as any woodworker who has put tool to plank knows, there's really nothing simple at all about doing everything right. Even if you've honed your woodworking abilities to razor sharpness, the way you implement them probably has just as great an effect on the outcome of your project.

The best way I know to avoid the twin perils of error and bodily injury is to apply your workmanship methodically at each step of construction. This includes the selection and handling of lumber, the marking out of individual joints and parts for assembly, and the order and manner in which machine operations are performed. Even the way that tools and jigs are set up and labeled can make a difference in how much time you'll be spending scratching your head rather than reveling in the routine of making clean shavings.

Taking a "nose cut"—trimming the end of a board to reveal hidden checks—is one way to prevent splits from occurring later. Here Toshio Odate uses a Japanese log saw to take a nose cut on the end of a walnut plank.

Steering Clear of Lumber Problems

While there are plenty of ways to deal with lumber defects and fix cracks, splits and more if they find their way into your projects (see Chapter 5), there are lots of little things you can do to keep many of these problems from occurring in the first place. The very way you select, dress and machine a plank of raw lumber can prevent many defects from emerging at later stages of machining and assembly of parts, when problems are much less convenient to deal with.

Take "nose cuts" to curtail checks

End checks in air-dried or kiln-dried boards commonly form during the drying process. But a hairline check that's barely visible at the end of a board can suddenly erupt into a full-blown split later on, after you've gone to the time and trouble of making a part. To keep end checks at bay, traditionally trained Japanese *shoji* maker Toshio Odate recommends a process he calls "taking a nose cut." Trim a short length from the rough end of a board; if the short cutoff falls apart or shows any sort of split or fissure, take another short trim cut. Repeat this process until the cutoff piece is solid and free from cracks. Nose cuts will also often reveal problems with honeycombing in thicker stock (see pp. 97-98).

Set parts aside to season

If you're like most woodworkers—in a hurry to finish projects—then the rush is usually on to cut out parts and immediately machine them and glue up joints and assemblies. The trouble is that parts often warp minutes or days after you cut them. If you can be patient and temporarily set parts aside, it will keep you from having to take time later to correct parts that have warped. Cutting narrow parts on a table saw or resawing thin parts on a bandsaw brings new surfaces into direct contact with the air, and moisture is exchanged. Thin parts, such as slats for tambours or back splats, spindles for balusters, or narrow moldings, can distort tremendously. If the board you're cutting comes from a tree that developed tension during growth, it might be unleashed at the time parts are cut. Parts cut from reaction wood may buckle abruptly and often bind against the blade; discard these parts, as they will cause you grief down the line. Distortion due to moisture exchange might take several days to develop to a point where the part is twisted, bowed, cupped or crooked enough to make it unusable.

To get a better idea of whether warpage will be a problem, give all parts a chance to acclimatize after cutout by stacking them in the shop and leaving them alone for at least a few days. Don't stack them directly on the ground or on a cold concrete slab, and sticker between layers to allow free air circulation. Obviously, you'll have to cut extra parts so that you can cull any that are warped beyond usability. Discards are often good enough to be recut into smaller or shorter parts.

Shun sticker stain

Blond woods like maple and birch purchased from a lumber dealer will often show signs of sticker stain. These bands of discoloration form at the spots where thin, narrow stickers separate layers of freshly sawn boards and allow air circulation during the drying process. The stain is caused by tannin or other chemicals in the stickers leaching into the wet stock, or by fungal growth. Lumber salespersons will usually tell you not to worry about those marks, claiming that you can simply belt-sand or thickness-plane them away. That's true—if you want to end up with $\frac{1}{2}$-in. thick parts from 4/4 stock!

Sticker stains usually run deep, and they aren't easily eliminated. Many stains don't even bleach away easily. Therefore, it's best to avoid buying any lumber that shows signs of sticker stain. If you find a couple of boards in a stack that are clearly affected, examine any other boards carefully before selecting from that stack. Sticker stains are sometimes fairly subtle until you've reached the final sanding stages and just can't get rid of their little dark ghost images. Stain or finish might even make the stain more apparent, an especially tragic outcome if it happens to be right in the middle of a tabletop or prominently located door panel.

Prevent splits with holes and chamfers

Because a board is composed of bundles of fibers that run lengthwise, any stress or pressure that follows the grain tends to cleave those fibers apart, resulting in splits. A stopped saw kerf cut with the grain, say for a wedged tenon, is an intentional split that has a tendency to enlarge and spread (due to stress or seasonal movement) beyond the desired point. To squelch a split, bore a hole at the kerf's termination. The hole disperses stress forces, preventing them from traveling along the split.

When force is applied across the end grain of a board, as when hand planing or jointing, bundles of fibers tend to split away. Chamfering the edges of solid-wood end grain (or plywood) will keep these splits from starting.

Leave horns on mortised parts

Most woods have very little strength across the short grain and are inherently predisposed to splitting—just see how easy it is to break a short cutoff scrap in half across the grain. To protect the ends of frame stiles and other members from splitting when mortised close to their ends, leave a little extra length on them. This nub, often called a horn, adds strength across the width of the stock, making it more substantial and less likely to split from the considerable forces generated during mortising. Horns are equally effective if mortising is done by hand, with an auger and chisel, or by machine, with a hollow-chisel mortiser. After mortising, the horns are "polled" (a cattleman's term for cutting a cow's horns off) when the member is trimmed to final length.

Marking Parts

Lines marked on lumber can do more than just indicate where a tool cut should be made. Simple marks can show you which side of the line the sawblade should cut on, or which part of a joint to cut away. A simple markilng system will also help you keep track of the orientation of multiple parts in a complex assembly, and prevent you from confusing left-hand and right-hand parts during cutout and template routing.

Cut on the right side of the line

When you mark a part for trimming to length, the distinction between the good side of the line and the waste side is usually obvious: The shorter piece is the waste. But often the waste piece and the good piece are nearly the same length, and sometimes two parts are cut at different ends of the same board (with a knot in the middle left for waste). Confusion about which side of the line to cut on can result in a part that's exactly one sawblade thickness too short. While the waste

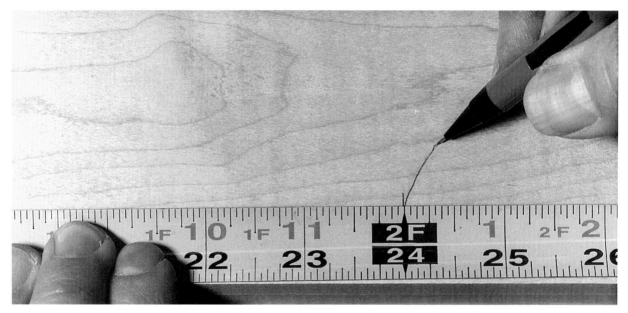

To keep you from accidentally cutting on the "good" side of a marked line, flick a quick pencil mark to indicate the waste side.

side of cuts can be marked with an X or any other mark you choose, it can be done just as effectively with a flick of the pencil: After marking the cutoff line, just pull a pencil line quickly toward the waste side of the cut, as shown in the photo above. This can be done just as easily if you're marking with a try square; just set it on the good side, and strike the waste-side mark away from the square.

A variation of the "good side/waste side" dilemma can beset you when a stack of parts not marked individually is being cut to length on a radial-arm saw (or chopsaw) using a fence and stop system. Typically, the parts have been squared up on one end first, the stop is set and the other end of each part is to be trimmed to final length. The trouble is that if parts get flipped, you can lose track of which ends remain untrimmed. I avoid this pitfall by carefully pulling each part from the saw after the first cut and leaving it with the squared end to my far right. After all parts are squared on one end, I strike a quick line to designate the end to be trimmed on the entire stack. This way, there's no doubt about which end to trim, even if the stack is fumbled—or if I get interrupted by a phone call—before I can complete the job.

Mark waste on joints to be cut out

In the same way that you can cut a part too short by sawing on the wrong side of the line, you can absolutely ruin a joint if you cut the waste from the wrong side of the layout lines. Consider, for instance, the botched dovetails shown on the cover of this book and in the photo

In the same way that you can cut a part too short by sawing on the wrong side of the line, you can absolutely ruin a joint if you cut out the wrong parts, as in the botched pins of the dovetail joint at left.

above. It's easy to get distracted and confused and cut away the pins and/or tails themselves, instead of the waste between them. If you miscut both halves of a finger joint in this way, you'll end up with a pair of negative profiles that will interlock only if one member shifts up a finger. Miscutting is even more likely if you cut finger joints using a table-saw jig, where joints are not laid out before they're cut. It also pays to mark the waste portions of twin mortises that are close together. There's a good chance you won't see all the layout lines and chop out the wood *between* the mortises, as shown in the photo at right.

The bottom line is that it's worth taking a few moments to strike a pencil line through the waste portions of any joint, just to prevent confusion during the cutout process. This is an especially good idea if you mark out joints on Tuesday and don't cut them until Thursday. (By the way, it's best to cut out and assemble joints on the same day that you dress the stock and mark them out. This will prevent changes in stock dimension due to expansion or contraction from ruining the fit.)

Mark assemblies with a triangle

Because cabinets are usually symmetrical, most assemblies require parts that have the same length, width and joinery, only cut in mirror symmetry, with a set of right-hand parts and a set of left-hand parts. This deceptively simple arrangement can nevertheless become as confusing as distinguishing right and left when giving driving directions. When parts get flopped in the course of machining, you can end up with all right-hand stiles, or two sets of backwards parts that don't fit correctly on either side.

If you don't mark the waste on closely spaced mortises, you might accidentally chop the area between them. Setting stops on a hollow-chisel mortising rig can also prevent miscuts.

One device to help you keep track of alignment is to mark assemblies with a cabinetmaker's triangle. This simple method entails drawing a triangle across adjacent parts, say, several boards that will be glued edge to edge for a tabletop or slats for a tambour door. The surface marked becomes the face-side up of all parts. The top point and sloping sides of the triangle indicate which ends are up, and the two lower corners show left and right. The marks are usually made with a pencil, but Florida woodworker Mark Hensley says chalk works just as well and is easier to remove when the parts are finish sanded.

One or more triangles can be used to indicate the alignment of more complex frame assemblies (see the photo below). This way, parts can be chosen and arranged for best grain pattern or color, then trimmed to length and have their joints machined, then be reassembled without mixup. The marks allow you to keep all parts face up (or, if you prefer, face down) while joinery is cut. This method ensures that any variation in stock thickness ends up all on one face, where it can be easily planed or sanded away.

For parts to be shaped by template routing, make sure to mark which side of the template should face up. Unless the part itself is symmetrical, mounting the template upside-down will result in parts that are cut out backwards. If the same template is used to shape both right-hand and left-hand parts, mark the correct side up for lefts or rights. In this case, it helps to mark the top side of the part blanks as well, as a safeguard against cutting all left-hand or all right-hand parts.

Marking two cabinetmaker's triangles (one on the three stiles, one across the six rails) confirms the positions of all the members in this face frame. They can be instantly returned to the right relative position, even if they are mixed up while the joinery is cut.

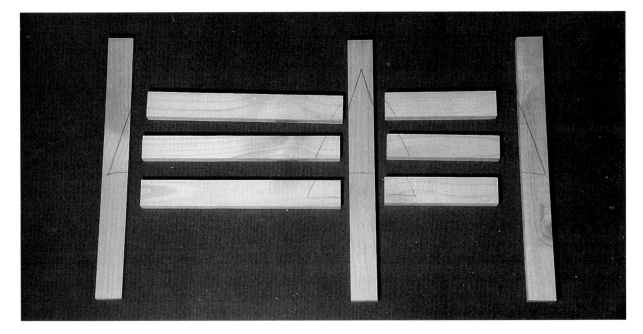

Working in a Logical Order

Carefully arranging the order in which you perform machining operations needed to build a project can prevent errors and make it less stressful to recover from any blunders that do occur. Often, parts are easier to make and turn out more accurately if the machining order is correct, as the following three examples show. First, if you want to make a countersunk hole, countersink first, then drill the hole through. The countersink won't chatter (the way it does when boring into a hole), and the conical depression it leaves will make it easier to center the drill bit. Second, if you want to cut a groove that runs all the way around the inside of a frame, cut the groove in a long piece of stock first, then miter the four pieces to length and assemble the frame. This way, the grooves will line up more consistently at corners where members meet, even if the groove cut wantered a little. Third, consider the curved parts for a solid-wood border on a circular table, as shown in the drawing below. It makes more sense to trim the ends

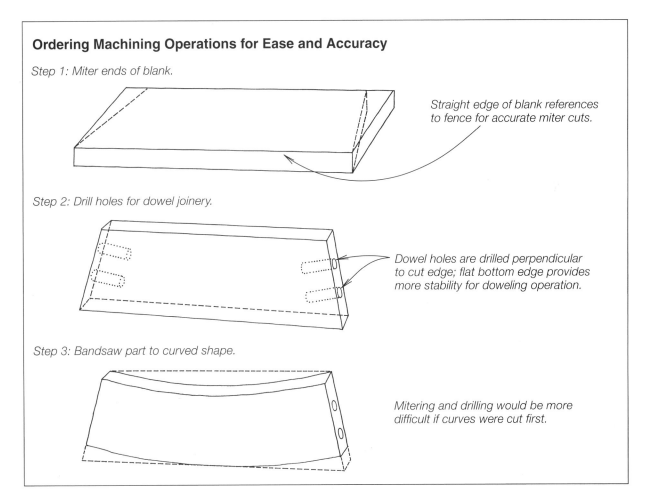

Ordering Machining Operations for Ease and Accuracy

Step 1: Miter ends of blank.

Straight edge of blank references to fence for accurate miter cuts.

Step 2: Drill holes for dowel joinery.

Dowel holes are drilled perpendicular to cut edge; flat bottom edge provides more stability for doweling operation.

Step 3: Bandsaw part to curved shape.

Mitering and drilling would be more difficult if curves were cut first.

of a rectangular part blank to the proper angle, as well as to cut the joinery on each segment before cutting it to its final curved profile. The straight-sided part blank is easier to reference to the fence on the crosscut saw and the table on the drill press (for the dowel holes). You could probably make the part either way, but accuracy is likely to be more difficult to achieve if the joinery is done after the part is cut to its curved shape.

Cut longer parts first

During the course of a large project, such as making face frames for an entire kitchen, back splats for a set of dining chairs or *kumiko* (mullions) for a large *shoji* screen, you need to cut dozens of parts to different lengths. In these cases, it's most sensible to cut the longer parts before the shorter ones. That way, if things go awry—wrong measurements, tearout during cutting—a longer part can still be used as a blank for a shorter part. Alternatively, if defects are discovered in a longer part, several short parts can be cut out around the defect. Also, when cutting parts to length from long lengths of stock, you'll end up with offcuts suitable for the shorter parts.

Rout in multiple passes

When taking a heavy cut with a big shaper cutter or router bit, if you take the cut in several light passes, the experience will be less harrowing . Save a fine pass for last to clean up any tearout that may have occurred during previous passes. To reduce tearout when freehand-routing curved shapes following a template, try routing with end- and shank-mounted bearings and making your cuts run with the grain for both situations, as shown in the top drawing on the facing page.

When routing a groove in multiple passes to increase its width, set the fence to take the first pass at the position farthest from the edge of the stock, then reduce the distance between the bit and the fence for the final pass (see the bottom drawing on the facing page). That way, if the fence pulls away from the edge during the first pass, resulting in a wavy line, you can take a second pass to clean up the glitch, then reset the fence to widen the groove (just make sure to keep the fence bearing steady on subsequent passes). For the same reason, it's a good idea to cut with the fence closest to the blade when taking two or more passes with a dado blade in the table saw. Move the fence farther from the blade on subsequent passes.

Machine all parts with the same setup

When two or more parts need to be cut to the same width or length, try to cut all of them at the same time. This will not only overcome slight variations in size that can creep in when a fence or stop has to be reset to the same measurement, but also decrease the likelihood

Avoiding Tearout when Freehand-Routing Curved Forms

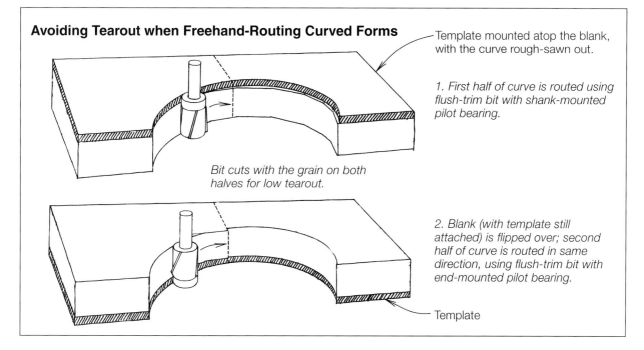

Template mounted atop the blank, with the curve rough-sawn out.

1. First half of curve is routed using flush-trim bit with shank-mounted pilot bearing.

Bit cuts with the grain on both halves for low tearout.

2. Blank (with template still attached) is flipped over; second half of curve is routed in same direction, using flush-trim bit with end-mounted pilot bearing.

Template

Routing a Groove Wider than the Diameter of the Bit

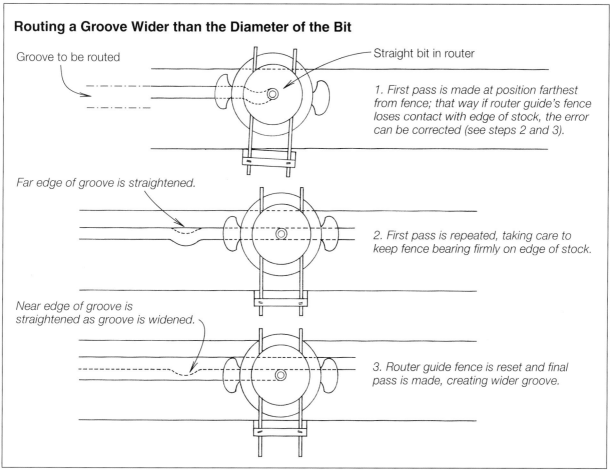

Groove to be routed

Straight bit in router

1. First pass is made at position farthest from fence; that way if router guide's fence loses contact with edge of stock, the error can be corrected (see steps 2 and 3).

Far edge of groove is straightened.

2. First pass is repeated, taking care to keep fence bearing firmly on edge of stock.

Near edge of groove is straightened as groove is widened.

3. Router guide fence is reset and final pass is made, creating wider groove.

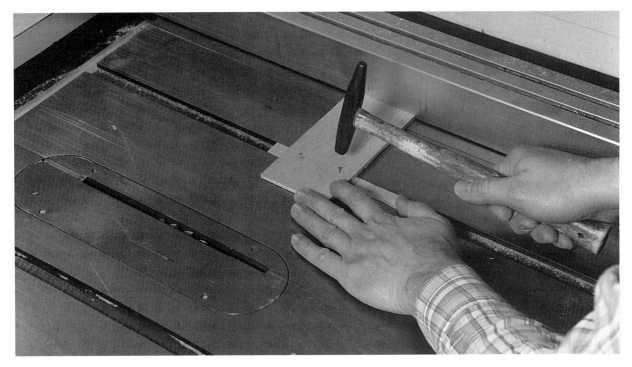

A quickly made setting gauge ensures that your table-saw rip fence can be reset to repeat an important cut later. The gauge is made by nailing a crosspiece to a bar press-fit into the miter slot. The fence butts up to the end of the crosspiece.

that you'll reset the fence incorrectly and miscut parts entirely. However, this approach can be impractical on machines such as table saws, which are needed for a wide variety of cuts during the construction of a project. To make the rip fence faster to set for accurate repeat cuts, you can quickly hammer together a setting gauge, as shown in the photo above. This presses into the saw's miter-gauge slot and provides a positive stop for positioning the fence. Flip stops allow the stops on a cutoff saw to remain set but leave the saw available for other work. These can be shop made (see pp. 104-108 in my book, *Woodshop Jigs and Fixtures,* published by The Taunton Press) or purchased commercially, such as the FasTTrack flip-stop system shown in the photo on the facing page.

Assemble the carcase before making doors and drawers

Often, discrepancies of cut carcase parts may be insignificant, if you measure a part at a time. But when you add up these little deviations, the cumulative error can be startling. For example, let's say that you're building an armoire that has three banks of drawers across its width. If each rail has been cut $1/16$ in. too short and each stile is $1/32$ in. too narrow, the assembled carcase will be more than $1/4$ in. too narrow. This can be a most egregious error if you've already made a stack of drawers that now prove to be too wide to fit!

For that reason, it's prudent to wait until a carcase is assembled before making the doors, drawers or shelves that fit into it. Take your measurements for these secondary parts directly from the carcase and cut the components accordingly. Ordering the work in this fashion allows you a maximum amount of slack to compensate for any unexpected errors. This is especially important if you're making flush-fitting drawer fronts and doors, which call for tight tolerances. Even if carcase size deviates by only a tiny amount, it's nice to be able to fit doors and drawers without spending extra time trimming them into place.

If you cope and stick your door frames, it's wise to not cut and raise panels until you can dry-assemble the frames to check the final dimensions. If you cut, shape and sand the frame and panels at the same time and the frame is undersized, you'll have to trim the panel to fit, then raise and sand it again—all of which is very time-consuming. Also, be extra careful when making frames for glass panels. If there's a slight fit problem, you'll have to adjust the fit by remachining the frame. It isn't easy to trim small amounts from the edge of a glass pane.

Flip stops, such as the FasTTrack system used here with a cutoff saw, can reduce cut-list errors: You can set different stops to necessary measurements and flip them down whenever needed.

Making Extra Parts

In post-World War II issues of *Popular Mechanics,* there were often articles about projects that involved cutting out parts for an entire piece of furniture from one sheet of plywood. I must admit, there's great satisfaction in cutting it close when estimating materials, provided that your estimate is correct and you end up with a perfect finished piece and just enough scraps and sawdust to kindle a small fire. But buying more wood than you strictly need can actually save you more than the extra materials cost, in the long run. How? By accepting the possibility that you might botch an operation or two and by having extra stock and parts on hand, you're likely to save yourself the time and trouble it would take to run back out to the lumberyard to buy more wood. And if the yard is out of stock that matches the grain and color of the wood you're using, you'll end up fooling around with the board-stretching techniques presented on pp. 7-9. Instead, you can save yourself needless grief by following the precautions presented below.

Spares to replace miscut parts

Anyone whose car has broken down in the middle of nowhere knows the value of having spare parts on hand. Imagine the joy of simply bolting on a new water pump rather than waiting around in Podunk for one to arrive. The same holds true for many furniture parts, especially if they are complex and require several steps to manufacture. As old Murphy (author of the infamous Murphy's Laws) would predict, if a table leg takes five different operations to machine, it's most likely that the part will be ruined on the last step. Then, even if you have extra lumber on hand, you'd have to go back and perform each and every step of machining, and very likely have to go through setup procedure for one or more steps, which takes loads of time, all for one part.

Save yourself the bother and spend a few moments to create an extra part at the same time you make all the others. You'll likely want to make more than one extra part under these circumstances:

- The part is really complex, requiring many different setups on the same tool, such as a curvaceous drawer front shaped on the router table using four or five different bits.

- The part is created by processes that are inherently risky, such as steam bending, shaping with big bits or freehand carving with a body grinder, and some failures are inevitable.

- The wood is highly figured or is prone to tearout, warping or splitting; you're going to end up with more defective parts when working with problematic woods.

- Your project requires lots of identical parts, and, odds are, you'll need more extras because the same percentage of error will result in a greater number of rejected parts.

- Several extra parts may need to be sacrificed for setting up subsequent machining operations, as discussed below.

Parts used for setting up operations

If you're having trouble justifying the time and materials required to make extra parts, consider that all your parts are more likely to end up accurately made if you use expendable extra parts to set up and test operations at each stage of machining. Scales and rulers used to set up machines and jigs give us a pretty good idea of what to expect—a rip fence set 4 in. away from the blade should yield a part 4 in. wide. However, inconsistencies often arise when an actual part is cut. For example, a ruler might tell you that the dado blade projects exactly 1 in. above the saw table, but the actual dado in the part might end up $1\frac{3}{32}$ in. deep because the workpiece pressed down on the saw's throat plate and caused it to deflect (see pp. 157-158). Had you tested the cut first, you'd have been able to fine-tune the blade depth before ruining a whole run of parts. You can use any old scrap for checking some cuts, but more often, the test piece should have the same size, shape and dimensions of the real parts. Sacrificing a spare part this way helps to ensure that more of your regular parts will survive each machining step.

Spares for repairs

I'm not the kind of guy who needs encouraging when it comes to saving things. If Hungary (my country of origin) has a native packrat, I'm surely a descendant of that species. Like me, you might not have all the room in the world to keep scraps and cutoffs around during or after the course of a project. But you'll reap the rewards of keeping scraps around if you need to make patches or other repairs to save your piece. Even if you have loads of walnut in your lumber stash, it's not certain that any of that stock will quite match the color and grain figure of the material you've been using for a particular project. Larger scraps can be used to create finish samples, so you can accurately envision the effect of fillers, putties, stains and clear coatings on your piece. Smaller scraps will be essential for all kinds of small repairs during construction, such as splits and patches, as described in chapters 3 and 4. I like to keep cutoff scraps in a bag, labeled so I know what piece they were the by-products of. When the project is completed, I dump most of the scraps into the kindling bucket. However, if your finished project will be subjected to teething puppies, toddlers or teenagers, you might want to keep that bag of scraps for future repairs.

Making Machining More Certain

Control and precision are the names of the game when you're working wood: You want parts exactly so long, grooves precisely so deep, holes just so far from an edge, and so on. But overseeing all that exactitude takes a lot of brain power, and if your attention wanders, you're likely to botch a part. The solution could be to take "smart pills," but it's far more practical to use common shop devices, such as stops and dedicated (operation-specific) jigs to take some of the burden off your constant attention. These devices "lock in" dimensions, such as the length of parts, location of holes and depth of slots, so that you don't have to position each part yourself. A good friend and woodworker colleague of mine, Roger Heitzman, calls this making an operation "fool resistant" (since nothing is completely foolproof).

Use stops

Stops are among the simplest—yet most versatile—devices in a woodshop. A simple square block clamped to a fence can control the length of an entire stack of crosscut parts, limit the length of a groove in a panel edge, or position an irregular part on a drill-press table for an accurately located hole for mounting hardware. Stops create consistency when handling lots of parts. You are more assured of accurate length if you slap the end of a board against a stop than if you mark it for length, then line up the mark with the sawblade. In addition to their use with power tools such as cutoff saws (see the photo on p. 171), stops can also come in handy for many hand-tool operations, such as sawing to a predetermined depth when cutting joinery, as shown in the photo below. For more about stops, see Chapter 4 in my book, *Woodshop Jigs and Fixtures,* published by The Taunton Press.

Adding a clamped-on wood stop will prevent you from accidentally cutting too deep when making delicate joints with a handsaw.

Limit free motion whenever possible

Flaws that occur during freehand routing and other power-tool and hand-tool operations are often the result of something most of us usually can't get too much of: freedom. Whenever you entrust your hands (and concentration) to control the motion of a tool or workpiece, you open yourself up to unexpected glitches that result in undesirable motion...and defects. For example, when shaping an edge using a router table, you must not only move the workpiece through the cut while keeping it flat on the table, but you must also keep the edge of the part firmly against the fence, lest the edge be shaped irregularly.

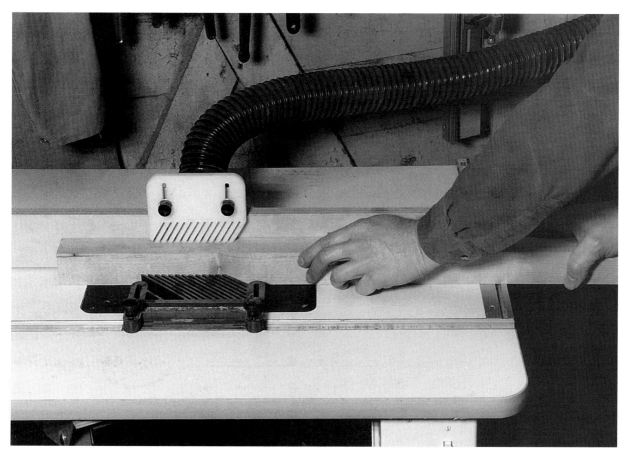

Featherboards can help keep the stock flat and bearing against the fence on a router table, making it easier for you to feed the stock steadily, for a smoother cut.

A second fence clamped to the left of the workpiece keeps it from accidentally drifting away from the main fence when cove cutting on the table saw.

Although it's not always practical or possible, take some of the pressure off yourself by making your jigs do more of the work. Use featherboards or wheeled hold-downs when sawing or routing, as shown in the photo on p. 175. Another way to keep parts from being ruined is to use a second fence, such as shown cove cutting on the table saw in the photo above. This auxiliary fence keeps the work from drifting away from the main fence and ruining the cove.

Control your power cords

We've all had the experience of belt-sanding a panel and running out of power cord; the sander, pulled up short, tips and gouges the surface of the work. One way to keep electrical cords from getting in the way (or worse, causing injury) is to suspend them above the work. I sometimes use regular elastic bungee cords for this, using one hook to hold the cord, and the other on a nail in a rafter above the work table. Just don't try to hang the power tools from these (belt sanders don't take to bungee jumping any better than most sensible humans do). Another way to keep power cords clear is to add a stiff wire tether to

the edge of your benchtop or to the base of a jig (see the photo above). Made from a bent coat-hanger wire, the tether works like the one on some household ironing boards, keeping the cord out of harm's way.

Keep portable-tool power cords from getting in the way and causing problems by supporting them with a tether bent from an ordinary wire clothes hanger.

Label your jigs
One more way of keeping good lumber out of the fireplace scrap box is to label your jigs with all the pertinent information about the operation: what blades or bits were used, how the tool was set up (depth of cut, fence settings and the like), what cuts were taken and in what order, the positioning of the workpiece in the jig (or how the jig is fastened to the tool). Include any pertinent information that will allow you to repeat the operation successfully at a future time—next week to make a replacement part (oops!) or next year, when you want to make parts for a duplicate project, but don't remember exactly how you did it the first time.

CHAPTER 10

Smooth Assembly and Finishing

It seems ironic that the same woodworkers who spend many hours practice-cutting fine dovetails or hand-planing complex moldings will slam together a cabinet without checking the fit of the joints, using whatever glue happens to be on hand. Then, they will slap a finish they've never tried over that expensive wood, applying it right out of the can with no more forethought and preparation than it takes to make ice.

If you've performed each step of your project with great care, from re-fining the design to accurately machining the parts, why stop short of a perfect conclusion? An ounce of prevention in seeing a project through its final assembly, glue-up and finishing is worth considerably more when you consider the amount of time you've already spent getting to this stage. Things like trial assembly, careful selection and use of glue, and applying a previously sample-tested finish under optimum conditions will thwart most avoidable disasters. Such good practices will help you elude vexations caused by glue-smeared carcases with joints that didn't clamp up right, or a blotchy, dust-laden finish that must be stripped off and finished all over again.

Dry assembling a carcase or frame helps you make sure that things will go smoothly when the glue is applied. A trial run provides a chance to check joint fit and the squareness of the assembly (as done by the author here), and also to make certain that there are enough clamps to do the job.

Before You Assemble

You're undoubtedly eager to see all those parts scattered across your benchtop meld into one great glorious form. But try to restrain yourself for a few more minutes and carefully consider your game plan for the final stages of assembly. The first order of business should be a dry run, where you confirm that the parts will assemble smoothly and that you have enough time and clamps. And making a trial run is essential if you plan to glue up using a vacuum-bag setup. Depending upon the design of your project, you might also want to finish parts before gluing up, to save time and end up with a better overall finish.

Do a dry run

It usually takes only a few minutes to perform a dry run of the assembly process. But a quick trial run can save you a tremendous amount of trouble, if a glue-up goes badly. What can go wrong? Plenty. Here are just a few of the horrors I've personally experienced (and I'll bet you could add your own to the list): joints that are too tight or don't fit together at all, clamps that are too short to reach, not enough clamps to close up the gaps between members, clamps that slip on rounded or angled edges of parts, not enough time to apply glue to all the joints in the assembly before the glue starts to set. Trial fitting gives you a chance to prevent these problems. You can adjust the fit of poor joints (as described on pp. 31-39), and you can make sure you have enough clamps of the right length and that clamping blocks are set to prevent marring and provide good purchase. You can save time and frustration by taping clamp blocks or pads directly to clamp faces, or to the edges of the parts themselves. You can also reduce the amount of frantic clamp handling by using clamp racks and stands, commercial or shop-made, that position clamps in readiness to receive the work. To avoid dents and splintered edges, use soft-face rubber or dead-blow mallets when driving joints home.

If you're assembling a project that has too many parts to glue up at one time, you have two ways of preventing an aborted glue-up. You can switch to a glue with a longer open time (as discussed on pp. 181-182). Or you can divide your glue-up into multiple stages. It's almost always possible to split up even the most complex frame, carcase or furniture piece into two, three or more subassemblies. The idea is to end up with fewer joints to glue up at any one time.

Circumvent vacuum-bag disasters

Trial runs are an absolutely essential part of vacuum veneering. In addition to the problems discussed above, the use of a vacuum pump, vinyl bag, and various platens and cauls inside the bag introduces another level of complication—and more things that can go haywire. For starters, make sure you can get your glued-up assembly into the bag in the first place. As crazy as this sounds, I've heard more than one sad tale of expensive wood being ruined when the piece couldn't be bagged after the veneer was glued and cauls were applied.

Dry parts should be set into the bag, positioned, then run through the vacuum procedure. That way you will discover if the bag leaks (the telltale sign is a vacuum pump that cycles frequently or doesn't switch off at all) and if there are problems with sharp corners on the cauls or on the piece itself that might pierce the bag. You might also discover areas of the bag that aren't getting evacuated properly, a situation you can remedy by adding channels to your cauls or by repositioning the assembly on the platen.

Another thing to watch out for, if you're veneering a hollow structure: Make sure the piece is adequately reinforced inside to resist the pressure of the vacuum (that is, the pressure of the atmosphere due to the evacuation of air, which is 13.7 psi). If the interior of the box flexes, you might end up with a veneered surface that's seriously cupped or sunken. Or the entire cavity might suddenly implode like a sunken Nazi U-boat, ruining your entire assembly! If implosion seems even remotely possible, choose another way to veneer your hollow form.

Finish first

A carcase or furniture piece often has cramped interiors, nooks and cubbies that are difficult or impossible to get at after assembly. You can save a tremendous amount of time and trouble if you do your final sanding and finishing of these surfaces before gluing them up. This allows you to finish both sides of the carcase sides and panels equally, something you should always do (especially with panels you've veneered) to prevent uneven moisture exchange on the two sides of a surface, a common cause of warpage. If you finish with a spray gun, finishing ahead of assembly is a must, since spraying into confined spaces will put more finish back into your face than is deposited on the wood (at least leave the back off cabinets until after finishing). Finishing ahead of assembly can also thwart contamination of wood surfaces from excess glue squeeze-out (see pp. 185-186).

The only precaution you must take when finishing before assembly is to keep the finish from contaminating joints and edges that are to be glued. If you brush on a finish, all you have to do is be aware of the glue surfaces and avoid them. If you plan to spray finish, you'll need to cover up the glue surfaces. For best results, don't use regular masking tape, which has a rubber-based adhesive that can leave a residue that might prevent water-based glue from being absorbed properly into the wood. There are several tapes, such as 3M's blue #2090, that use a special adhesive that doesn't leave a residue. Another important caveat: Never let a taped surface sit in the sun or close to a stove or other heat source. Heat can cause the viscous adhesive on the tape to flow into wood pores and lock in; to get it off again, heat the tape with a heat gun or blow dryer (hair dryer), scrape it off with a cabinet scraper and remove the residue with lacquer thinner or naphtha.

Guaranteed Glue-Ups

Modern adhesives are so strong and effective most of the time that we often take them for granted, that is, until that fateful day when a piece falls apart after the clamps come off. There's more to getting a strong glue joint than uncorking any old bottle of stickum and letting the goo flow. Here are a few things to consider when selecting adhesives.

Choose a glue with enough open time

Even though there are dozens of different adhesives on the market, woodworkers tend to stay with a product they know. Hence, they will rush through a big glue-up on a complicated face frame using regular PVA (yellow aliphatic-resin glue), which has a relatively short open time (the time between glue application and clamp-up)—typically 10 minutes at 70°F, and less at higher temperatures (see p. 184).

You'll work at a more comfortable pace and reduce the risk of dry joints, or dreaded "can't clamp it together, can't get it apart" joints, by switching to a slower-setting glue. Traditional choices that are readily available include resorcinol, urea-formaldehyde and hot hide glue. If you like the working properties of PVA and want to stick with it (no pun intended), Garrett Wade sells a special "Slo-Set" PVA with an open time of about 30 minutes (see Sources of Supply on pp. 196-197). You can also extend the drying time of a regular PVA yellow glue by adding propylene glycol to it: about an ounce to a pint of glue (experiment before you try this on your project). The additive slows the evaporation rate of water in the glue and retards the coalescence of its resins.

Wet joint surfaces adequately

Believe it or not, many poor or failed glue joints are due to inadequate application of glue. Whether it's to limit the amount of glue squeeze-out or to save on glue, woodworkers who apply glue sparingly are risking failed glue joints. Other factors besides inadequate application, such as high resin content or surface glazing, can limit absorption; see the discussion on the facing page. If *both* surfaces of a joint don't absorb glue, the bond will not develop properly. Even if you apply copious amounts of glue to one surface of the joint, it may not transfer evenly to the other surface. Therefore, judiciously apply glue to each bonding surface, and spread it evenly. A printer's brayer (available from art-supply stores) works great as a glue roller on flat edges and surfaces (see the photo below), while a coffee-stirring stick, dowel or small brush allows you to work glue into joints and grooves.

A rubber printer's brayer is used to spread a layer of adhesive evenly on the edge of a board before it is glued up. Even spreading ensures good surface wetting and a strong joint with minimum squeeze-out.

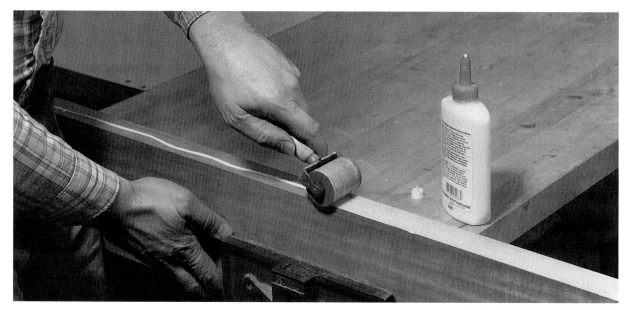

Give special attention to resinous woods

Resinous woods, such as rosewood and teak, can be reluctant to absorb adhesives, especially water-based glues. Hence, getting a good bond can pose a problem. You can check to see how resistant the surface of the wood is to glue absorption by performing a simple test: Place a droplet of water on the surface of the edge or joint you intend to glue (see the photo at right). If the water stays beaded up for more than 30 seconds, you know that the wood will repel the water in the glue and prevent a good bond.

One common practice is to wipe down the surface of a resinous wood with lacquer thinner or acetone prior to gluing. But, in fact, the action of the evaporating solvent actually tends to wick fresh resins to the surface. The best thing to do is machine the mating edges of parts and joints just before gluing up, to reveal clean wood where resins haven't had a chance to collect on the surface. If machining is not practical, switch to a glue that's less oil sensitive, such as an epoxy or a polyurethane glue (Excel or Gorilla Glue).

Eliminate surface glazing

Dull knives in a jointer, thickness planer, shaper or other machine don't shear wood fibers cleanly. They burnish the wood as they cut, leaving a glazed surface that is likely to be resistant to absorbing water-based glue. Surface glazing can also hinder absorption of stains and finishes, resulting in a blotchy-looking surface. You can check for this problem by performing the water-droplet test, described above. Keeping knives sharp with regular honing and occasional regrinding will prevent glazing and poor glue joints.

Don't use too much clamping pressure

While having too many tools (or too much money to buy them) is rarely a problem woodworkers must face, it is possible to have too much clamping pressure during glue-up. Heavy clamps torqued to the max can easily squeeze all the glue right out of a joint, especially if you're gluing parts made from a dense hardwood, such as maple. Don't be afraid to tighten the clamps until you see some glue squeeze-out, but save your brute force for the weight machine at the gym. Remember, any two well-machined surfaces that are adequately wetted with glue can be rubbed together and set aside and will still adhere more than adequately. (Glue blocks rubbed on to reinforce the underside of a carcase assembly are a good illustration of this principle.)

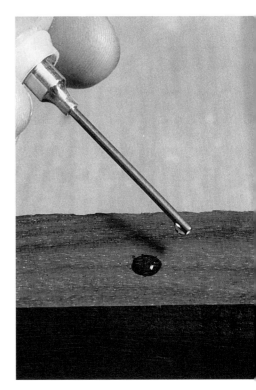

If you're using a water-based adhesive to bond resinous woods, check the moisture resistance by applying a single drop of clean water to the edge or surface to be glued. If the drop stays beaded and doesn't flow out, remachine the surface before glue-up.

To prevent slippery glue-coated edges from sliding out of position when clamped up, here's a neat little trick I've used for years: Put a minuscule pinch of salt in a spot or two along the glued edge or surface. I use coarse Kosher salt, available at most supermarkets. Just a few jagged-edged grains provide just enough bite to keep parts in place as clamping pressure is applied.

Factor in temperature and humidity

Like finishes, all glues have temperature and humidity ranges recommended for optimum results. High temperature is mostly a nuisance because it reduces the open, "working" time of the glue. For example, PVA's open time shrinks from ten to only about five minutes at 90°F. Low temperature is a more serious problem. You are likely to face gluing failures when the mercury plummets and both adhesives and wood parts get too cold. An easy way to make sure it's warm enough is to smear some PVA glue on a wood scrap and wait five minutes; if the film turns whitish and powdery-looking, it's too cold to glue up. Even if you keep your shop toasty during working hours, low-temperature failure can still sting you if clamped parts are left to dry overnight in an uninsulated shop that takes on the character of an icebox. Storing glue in a cool basement will extend the useful life of most adhesive, but freezing any water-based glue will ruin it. You can tell if the glue has frozen (or is too old) because it has a snotty, stringy consistency. Subzero temperatures won't hurt solvent-based glues (epoxy, polyurethane, etc.), but they must come back up to room temperature before they can be used.

While low humidity can also reduce an adhesive's open time, excess humidity can be a mixed blessing. If the humidity goes up, open time increases too: Between 70% and 90% humidity, open time might increase by 50%. However, high humidity also makes a glue dry more slowly, so you must increase clamping time by 50% or more, lest your project fall apart if the clamps are pulled off prematurely.

Ensure a good bond when ironing on veneer

Many woodworkers have had success laying down veneers with the "iron-on" method, a technique where veneer and substrate are coated with PVA (a thermoplastic adhesive), allowed to dry, then bonded with a hot iron (for details, see *Fine Woodworking* #108). However, some unfortunate individuals have experienced disastrous failures: Heat from the iron can shrink and crack the veneer, and blisters and lifting can result from poor bonding. To prevent shrinkage, pre-iron the veneer before applying the glue, and always cut veneer pieces oversize and trim them after application.

To forestall bonding failures, first, apply enough glue: apply a 1-mil thick layer of a white PVA glue, which bonds more easily and at a lower temperature than yellow PVAs, to both veneer and substrate (a 1-mil layer is thick enough for the spread wet glue to obscure the wood grain). If you plan to use a water-based finish, apply a coat of shellac to the underside of the veneer as a water barrier. Second, use enough heat: After the glue has dried clear (45 min. to one hour; but not more than a few hours later) use an iron adjusted to the wool setting to bond the veneer to the substrate. Press *hard,* and move the iron slowly on a flat surface, very slowly if the surface is curved (less contact on a tangent means less heat to the veneer). When in doubt, iron longer; too little heat is the most typical cause of bond failures.

Prevent excess glue squeeze-out

Excess glue that exudes from a joint and contaminates a clean wood surface is a pain to clean off. Worse, beads of glue that dry on your workbench can dent and ding the smooth surfaces of your projects. Clean off drips after glue-up, or better yet, cover your bench or assembly table with a disposable layer of kraft or butcher paper.

The best way to prevent a river of excess glue from messing up pristine raw wood surfaces is not to apply too much in the first place (see p. 182) Prefinishing parts using a film-type finish will prevent excess glue from being absorbed into the wood, as described on p. 181. Another good method for preventing glue contamination is to apply a layer of really thin, clear tape to the surfaces nearest the joint before glue up (see the photo below). Use a tape that has a weak adhesive, such as Scotch 2770 (which uses the same adhesive used in Post-it

To prevent glue from squeezing out of a joint and fouling the surface of an open-pore wood (oak is shown here), apply a layer of removable transparent tape to surfaces adjacent to the joint. After glue-up, excess adhesive should be wiped off before it hardens.

An easy way to prevent adhesive from squeezing out and contaminating a wood surface is to rout a shallow groove near the edge of one of the parts. Here, the groove is being cut with a small veining bit in a laminate trimmer fitted with an adjustable guide fence.

notes). Available at paint stores, Scotch 2770 tape is designed for masking sensitive surfaces, so it won't pull up wood fibers when you remove it after gluing. Once glue has squeezed out, you can carefully use a damp sponge to clean it off the tape surface, taking care not to contaminate adjacent raw-wood surfaces. If you wait for the glue to dry, you will need to chisel it out of the corners, as described on p. 118. Open-pore woods, such as ash and oak, are especially good candidates for tape protection around glue joints.

Another good trick for keeping glue from gushing out between parts is to rout a groove in the mating edge of one part, as shown in the photo above. The groove acts like the blood groove around the perimeter of a meat carving platter; the excess adhesive floods into this groove instead of out of the joint or seam and onto a visible surface, where it must be scraped off.

Make sure glue squeeze-out is gone

Even after careful scraping and sanding, glue can remain in the pores of the wood, only to confront you at the most inconvenient time: during finishing. Glue drips and splatters will show up as little light spots after staining or clear coating. It takes only a moment to check for renegade glue spots. Just wipe down all surfaces suspected of contamination with mineral spirits or VM&P naphtha (available at hardware

To reveal hidden glue drips and smears before they interfere with finishing, wipe down raw wood surface with VM&P naphtha, then watch for telltale light spots.
Wear gloves to keep the solvent off your bare skin, and immerse rags in water after use to prevent combustion.

and paint stores), as shown in the photo above. You can also use water, if you plan to raise and knock down the grain before finishing. Then watch for light dots or streaks. These occur because the adhesive prevents the solvent or water from being readily absorbed. Remove the offending glue remnants with a scraper or chisel, as described on pp. 117-119.

If you run a production shop and don't want to be bothered trying to spot every stray glue drip before it ruins the finish, you might consider investing in a "Glue Spotlight". Available by mail order (see Sources of Supply on pp. 196-197), this glue detection system includes a special powder that's added to white or yellow PVA adhesive. After normal glue-up, a special UV fluorescent light bulb is used to illuminate the wood in a darkened room. Any errant squeeze-out—drip, smudge or bead—is instantly revealed and can be targeted for removal.

Good Finishing Practices

One of the first steps to becoming a good wood finisher is to learn the basic things you can do to dodge the most avoidable kinds of finishing blunders. Practices such as testing a finish on a sample, keeping your finishing area warm and dry and making sure the finish you're using is fresh are elementary, but easily overlooked. Other practices, such as using a simple shop-built light booth to evaluate the color of stained or puttied wood under different light sources, employ methods long known to professionals, but little used by small-shop finishers.

Watch the thermometer

Most finishes have a temperature range that's recommended for good results. As with adhesives, the lower end of this scale is usually more problematic, especially if you live in a cold climate and work in an un-heated or poorly insulated shop. Most finishes perform best at around 70°F. You can usually get away with finishing down to about 50°F, but this is pushing it for most film-type finishes as moisture tends to condense onto wood surfaces at lower temperatures, causing finishes not to bond well. Higher temperatures can help the application and flow-out characteristics of many finishes. However, it also makes them dry faster, a particular problem with sprayed nitrocellulose lacquer, which can dry before it hits the work, forming cobwebs (see p. 141).

There's another way you can get in trouble with temperature when finishing—that's if the temperature of the air in your shop (or finishing room, if you're lucky enough to have one), the liquid finish in the can and the surface of the work aren't fairly close to each other. Even if you're working in a shop that's at ideal finishing temperature (70°F), brushing on lacquer from a can that has been sitting on a cold concrete floor onto a wood cabinet can result in a crackled finish. To prevent problems of this sort, let cans of finishing materials acclimatize in your finishing area for several hours before use. Crackling, commonly called "cold checking," can also occur if a cold draft wafts into your warm shop and hits a freshly finished piece. (To repair cold checking, see pp. 138-139.) Low temperatures can also pose a threat to stored water-based finishes and stains, as discussed on p. 190.

Humidity can be a lacquer finisher's nemesis, commonly causing blush problems (discussed on p. 139). Ironically, even certain water-based varnishes and lacquers are susceptible to humidity problems. These materials contain both water, which functions as a carrier, and "tail solvents," which help the finish flow out in a continuous film. In high humidity, the tail solvents may evaporate before the water, before they have done their job of coalescing the film. As a result, you end up with a powdery residue on the wood, which you can quite literally blow off. The best practice is not to apply these finishes on humid days.

Keep your finish fresh

Freshness is obviously a big concern with perishable foods, such as milk, cheese and meat. But woodworkers who have experienced the exasperation of coating their painstakingly constructed project with a gooey finish that won't dry know that freshness is also of paramount concern with wood finishes. Most wood finishes are complex chemical soups with compounds that break down over time. The same processes that cause a finish to dry into a film when applied in a thin layer are also at work when the finish sits idly in a can on the shelf. Finishes such as varnish, catalyzed lacquer and shellac break down quickly (shellac in as little as six months), and eventually lose most of their ability to dry.

How can you tell when a finish has gone bad? Unfortunately, not all finishes show their age as obviously as water-based finishes, which turn snotty and stringy looking, like old glue. The way to avoid ruining your project with bad finish is to test any marginal cans on a sample; if the finish doesn't dry properly, dispose of it promptly, following your local sanitation department's or landfill's approved methods of disposal. Even an old finish that dries may have lost some of its best qualities, so when in doubt, throw it out.

Varnish, however, is the one exception to the rule. Old varnish can be rejuvenated by replenishing its dryers, which naturally de-activate over time. Simply add a little cobalt dryer, available at art-supply stores (check the section where they sell supplies for oil painting). A few drops of cobalt dryer per pint of varnish should be about right; the exact amount isn't critical. Incidentally, adding Japan dryer (commonly sold through woodfinishing supply catalogs) by itself to the varnish won't do the trick. Most Japan dryers contain primarily zirconium dryers, which function properly only when cobalt dryer is active in the varnish.

The best way to prevent an old can of over-the-hill shellac from ruining your finish is to mix it fresh every time you need it. Shellac flakes and buttons are available from many suppliers (see Sources of Supply on pp. 196-197). A good general mixture for a sealer coat is a 1½-lb. cut, which means add 1½ lb. of shellac flakes to a gallon of denatured alcohol (proportionately less for smaller quantities). Make a heartier mixture for top coats, using 2½ lb. to 3 lb. of flakes to a gallon of alcohol. Use dewaxed shellac, because it's less sensitive to moisture.

Store your finish with care Always store and inventory your finishes carefully. Before buying a can of finish, check for freshness-dating information, which many manufacturers now include. Write the date you bought the finish on top of the can using a permanent marker. Most finishes should be tested on a sample before use on a project after they are more than six months old.

To keep finishes from aging prematurely in the container, try to store them in a space where the temperature doesn't fluctuate much. The optimum for storing a finish so it doesn't have to be heated before use is 70°F. If your shop is unheated, bring your finishes into the garage or house and store them in a utility closet on a shelf, rather than directly on a cold concrete floor. Most finishes last longer when stored in a cooler place, but they must be warmed up before use.

Never let a water-based finish freeze, or it will be ruined. A frozen finish is easy to spot: The resin particles in the finish agglomerate, and it looks like cottage cheese. In hot weather, keep finishes in a cool place: The reaction rate of most finishes doubles with every 18°F rise of temperature, so they go bad much more quickly.

Solvent-based oil finishes, such as Danish oil and tung oil, spoil in great part because of their exposure to oxygen. To keep them good longer, displace the air in any partially used container by throwing in marbles (available at a toy store) until the liquid level approaches the top of the can. Alternatively, you can displace the air with nitrogen from a can of "Private Preserve" gas (for preserving open bottles of wine), available at well-stocked liquor stores or mail order (see Sources of Supply on pp. 196-197). It's more expensive, but clean and quick to use.

Avoid blotchy stains

Some wood species, such as pine, birch, cherry and fir, have enough variation in the porosity of their grain that surfaces tend to absorb liquid in very different amounts. When you attempt to color these woods, the stain is not absorbed evenly, resulting in a blotchy appearance (see the photo on the facing page). Variable absorption is also to blame for the vast color difference between stained end grain and stained side grain; the soda-straw-like wood fibers soak up the stain faster on the end grain, resulting in a darker color. Solvent-based stains (containing either pigments or dyes) are the worst offenders; water-based dye stains are somewhat more forgiving. But you can also get blotchiness with a water-based stain if the wood surface has been glazed during planing by dull knives (see p. 114). You can check for this, as described on p. 183.

Variations in porosity can lead to a blotchy look when stain is applied (as on the right end of this board). But when a prestain conditioner is wiped on first (as on the left end of the board), the various wood surfaces drink in the stain more regularly. The color is lighter than if the stain is applied to untreated wood, but the effect is more pleasing.

If you do wish to use a solvent-based stain, preventing staining unevenness is as easy as preventing sunburn on your skin. Before applying a solvent-based stains, treat the wood with a prestain conditioner. This simple oil mixture is flooded onto the wood surfaces and is absorbed at different rates, more by end grain or earlywood and less by side grain and latewood. Once the wood is saturated, its overall degree of absorption is more even, so that when the stain goes on, the various wood surfaces drink in the stain more regularly. The overall effect will be lighter than if the stain is applied to untreated wood, but the stain color is much more even, as shown in the photo above.

Prestain conditioners can be mixed in your shop or purchased commercially (McCloskey and Minwax both make them, and they are available at local hardware stores and paint stores). The recipe that finish chemist Chris Minick recommends is 1 or 2 cups of boiled linseed oil dissolved into 1 gallon of mineral spirits (usually sold as paint thinner). After a thorough stirring, a heavy coat of the mixture is brushed over the entire surface of the project (small parts and carvings can be dipped). Thirsty end grain may need to be recoated if it dries out after a few minutes. Excess prestain can be wiped off after 10 or 15 minutes, and solvent-based stain may then be applied immediately.

As with all finishing processes, it's best to apply prestain to a sample, then stain it, to test the degree of effectiveness and check the color. Because solvent-based stains usually contain both dyes and pigments (which settle to the bottom of the can), make certain that you stir a can of solvent-based stain well before application, both to the sample and to your project. I once made up a sample for a dark mahogany kitchen using a small, unmixed can of stain. When I was ready to stain the cabinets, I had the paint store agitate a gallon of the same type of stain. The result was a much darker color—fortunately not unpleasant, but an unsettling surprise nonetheless.

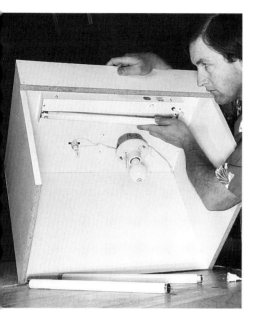

A light booth helps simulate different light sources, for more accurate color evaluation and touch-ups. Made from white melamine-coated particleboard, the booth has three fixtures: a regular incandescent light-bulb socket, a socket for a quartz halogen light, and a fluorescent fixture that accepts a cool-white, warm-white or daylight-type tube.

Conquer color problems due to metamerism

Speaking of color surprises, here's one that has baffled many wood finishers. We've all seen how vapid and sickly cool fluorescent light makes even a tan and healthy person look. Or how the warm light of a late afternoon sun gives even the palest skin a rosy glow. This is because different types of light bring out different colors in the things they illuminate. But while this basic physical fact makes the world around us more visually interesting, it can also create some insidious problems in the woodshop. Just as warm or cool light can change the quality of skin, so can it affect the perceived color of wood. The finish sample you raved over when viewed at sunset on the patio might disappoint you under incandescent light in the bedroom. The phenomenon is called optical isomerism, commonly known as metamerism.

The most direct way to eliminate differences in lighting as a variable in color choice is to view finish samples in the same light that the finished piece will be seen in. Better yet, check out the sample in the same space that the piece will occupy. The color of the walls or the outside light bouncing off a tree or a brick wall might alter the room's primary light, subtly changing the apparent color of the wood. If you're a professional woodworker who doesn't always visit clients (or if you work through an architect or interior designer) always send instructions along with your finish samples, that they be viewed *in situ*, before they're approved or rejected.

Once the color of a sample has been chosen, you'll get better results—and avoid many problems—if you do inspect your final finish under the same sort of light that the piece will be seen in. As it is highly impractical to install several different kinds of lighting throughout an entire shop, install them instead in a small "light booth" such as shown in the photo above left. Made out of white melamine-covered particleboard, this simple booth has three light fixtures in it: a socket for a regular incandescent bulb, a socket for a quartz halogen reflector-style bulb, and a 12-in. fluorescent fixture, which will accept either a warm white, cool white or full-spectrum (to approximate daylight) bulb. All three fixtures are wired to run off a single lamp cord, but separate on/off switches allow them to be used individually. I made my booth bottomless, so I can set it atop a piece of white melamine on the benchtop for viewing finish samples and small parts. Or I can place the booth directly over a work surface such as a tabletop (see the photo

Because the light booth lacks a bottom, you can set the booth over a large work surface, such as this walnut tabletop, when you are trying to match the color of puttied patches and touch-ups.

above). This allows me to keep an eye on the color match while puttying or touching up small defects. The light booth plays an important role in such repairs, because putty materials and touch-up paints are likely to reflect light differently than the surrounding wood. Therefore a patch or touch-up that's invisible under one type of light may actually stand out in another. That's just how insidious the phenomenon of metamerism can be.

Avoid finish contamination

There's more that you can do to prevent contamination than using a clean stick to stir your finish before use. If you brush on finish, clean the brush thoroughly after each use, using a comb to prevent partially dried clumps of finish from building up near the brush's ferrule and later ending up on your clean, finished workpiece.

If you're spraying finish with a compressed-air system and gun, be sure to use an air filter between the gun and the compressor. Coalescing filters work the best on removing water and oil mists that can leak from oil-lubricated compressor-pump cylinders. If you can, locate this filter fairly close to the spray gun end of your air line, especially if air must travel through a long hose or pipe to your finishing area.

Filters are essential to keep contaminants from spoiling a sprayed finish. An in-line filter, fitted on the air line just below the gun's handle, takes care of dirt particles in the compressed-air line; a screen filter slipped over the end of the gun's siphon tube stops contaminants that might enter the gun's cup.

An alternative is to use an in-line air filter (available from an industrial-supply store) attached directly at the gun (see the photo at left). To keep contaminants or lumps of unstirred finish from fouling the gun, filter the finish through a paint strainer as you pour it into the gun's cup. And to trap any bits of dried finish that might have stuck to the cup (these sometimes hide under the rim) or small debris that sneaks into the cup, a fine-mesh screen strainer slipped over the end of the gun's siphon tube is cheap insurance. (For both kinds of filters, see Sources of Supply on pp. 196-197.)

Smoothing the surface when sanding between coats can also lead to contamination of the finish. Stearates, which are incorporated into many modern sandpapers as lubricants, are waxy substances that can repel finish and should be blown or wiped away before the next coat goes on. Avoid using regular painter's tack cloths: these are saturated with gummy oils which, if rubbed too hard on a surface, can cause defects in subsequent coats. Common steel wool can create an insidious problem when smoothing coats of water-based finishes: Any steel fibers that remain trapped in wood pores or crevices will rust from subsequent coats of finish, and can cause deep stains in tannin-rich woods, such as oak and ash. Instead, use plastic abrasive pads or bronze wool. Bronze wool is like steel wool, only made from bronze filaments, which don't rust (see Sources of Supply on pp. 196-197).

Another kind of contagion that can seriously affect both a smooth finish and gluing performance is silicone contamination. Silicones are found in many spray waxes, machine-tool rust preventives and lubricants. They can taint a raw wood surface and repel water-based glues, cause fisheye in a lacquer film (see p. 140) and other problems as well. Avoid these problems by using silicone products sparingly; better yet, switch to a different form of lubrication, such as talc or paraffin wax.

If you suspect silicone has tainted a surface, apply a seal coat of shellac over the raw wood. Shellac will also prevent sap and resin from oozing out of knots or hidden pitch pockets and thus prevent the wood itself from contaminating the finish. In addition to sealing out contamination problems, versatile shellac can also be applied between just about any two coats of finish (or between a stain and a clear coat) whenever you suspect the finishes are incompatible (you can also use Mohawk's Barrier, a lacquer/shellac blend). Remember, when in doubt, test on a sample first (see the discussion on the facing page).

Keep the dust down

Dust isn't much of a problem when you spray on a lacquer finish. Unless it's loaded with retarders, the lacquer dries to the touch in just minutes. But dust accumulation over the hours it can take for a slow-drying finish, such as varnish or polyurethane, to dry can turn a smooth finish into a nubby mess. To avoid coating your work with sawdust, schedule your finishing for the end of the day so your project can dry in an undisturbed space. (Just maintain the heat of the shop during the night, as discussed on p. 184.) Keep dust to a minimum by vacuuming your shop or booth area thoroughly, and leave some time to let the lion's share of the airborne dust, stirred up during cleaning, to settle before proceeding. If you must finish parts during the day, do it first thing in the morning, before dust is stirred up in the shop. Immediately after coating, seal off the finishing area from the workroom with thin plastic sheeting. Alternatively, you could transfer it to a clean, dust-tight closet or a sheet-polyethylene tent constructed in a corner of your shop, in a shed or outdoors, if the weather allows.

Test the finish

As I've mentioned elsewhere in this book, a finish sample provides the most effective test of the viability of your finishing scheme. It will warn you if your finish is too old to dry properly, or if there are compatibility problems between coats. Samples provide a preview of final color with all stages of the finish applied and allows you to deal with unfortunate shifts in color due to metamerism (see pp. 192-193). They also allow you to test the color of custom-mixed putty patches and touch-ups, (see p. 62), as well as providing a safe place to practice doing these repairs before you tackle the project itself. I now make a couple of finish samples as a standard part of every project, thickness planing and sanding them right along with other parts. By testing a finish on these just ahead of finishing my project, I can also see how long it takes the finish to dry between coats and when it has cured and hard enough to be rubbed out. To determine this, I try sanding the sample with 180-grit sandpaper; if finish balls up into little pills that clog the paper, it's too soon to rub out.

If you're a spray finisher, here's a simple procedure to add to your pre-finishing checklist. After topping up the cup with finish, make a few passes with your spray gun onto a large piece of cardboard. This not only lets you hone your gun-handling techniques, but also allows you to check on the gun's pattern. If it's uneven, the tip is probably clogged and in need of cleaning. On more than one occasion, this little test firing has revealed a splattering of dried finish that I had failed to clean from the gun's passages. Better that this ends up on disposable (and even recyclable) cardboard than on a pristine wood surface.

SOURCES OF SUPPLY

These source listings, which contain numerous mail-order sources, should make it easier for you to obtain many of the tools and products discussed in this book. First look up the desired item in the list below. Once you have found the item, you can locate the address, phone and FAX number for its supplier or manufacturer in the list that begins on the facing page. This listing was compiled in spring 1995 and is subject to change.

Items Cited in the Text

Abrasive pads, plastic
Grizzly, Mohawk, Woodworker's Supply

A/B wood bleach
Garrett Wade (sold as "color dissolvent" and "decolorant"), Mohawk

Back plates (for pulls)
The Woodworker's Store

Barrier (spray finish)
Mohawk

Biscuits, extra small
Colonial Saw (Lamello H9), Woodhaven (Itty Bitty)

Bond-Aide
Mohawk

Box corners, brass
Woodworker's Supply

Brad pushers
The Woodworker's Store

Bronze wool
Jamestown Distributors, The Woodworker's Store

Casting epoxy
Gougeon Brothers

Chisel planes
Garrett Wade, Woodcraft

Clamps
Jorgensen #56 pipe clamps: Garrett Wade, Woodworker's Supply
Record clamp heads: Garrett Wade, Highland Hardware, Woodcraft

Cord grommets
McFeely's, The Woodworker's Store, Woodworker's Supply

Dead-Blow mallets
Trend-lines, Woodcraft, The Woodworker's Store

Detail sanders
Most catalog suppliers

***Dozuki* Japanese saws**
Garrett Wade, Hida Tool, Highland Hardware, The Japan Woodworker

Draw plates (dowel formers)
Constantine, McFeely's

Drawer slides
The Woodworker's Store (Accuride, Blum Epoxy), Woodworker's Supply (Amerock, Delta, Knape & Vogt)

Dremel tools
Hartville, Woodcraft

Drill bits, specialty
Lettered (set): Enco, Rutland Tool & Supply
Oversize: Woodworker's Supply
Wire-gauge (set): Leichtung, Trend-lines, Woodcraft
Tapered pilot-hole: Garrett Wade, Leichtung, Woodcraft, Woodworker's Supply

Drill/drivers, angled head
Hartville, McFeely's, Trend-lines, Woodworker's Supply

Escutcheons
Woodcraft, The Woodworker's Store

Finisher's Colorwheel
Mohawk

Fresco powders
Garrett Wade, Woodworker's Supply

Glue
Carpenter's Glue (Elmer's): Hartville Tool
Cyanoacrylate adhesives and accelerators: Garrett Wade, Hartville, Leichtung, Woodcraft, Woodworker's Supply
Epoxy: Garrett Wade, Gougeon Brothers, The Woodworker's Store
Gorilla Glue: Leichtung, Woodcraft, The Woodworker's Store
Polyurethane: Constantine, Grizzly, Trend-lines, Woodcraft, Woodworker's Supply
Rivit: The Woodworker's Store
Slo-Set: Garrett Wade

Glue-detection system
Glue Spotlight

Glue syringes
Regular: Leichtung, Renovators Supply, Woodcraft, The Woodworker's Store, Woodworker's Supply
High pressure: Leichtung, Woodcraft, Woodworker's Supply

Hardwood pulls
Recessed: The Woodworker's Store, Woodworker's Supply
Surface-mounted: Woodworker's Supply

Hot-melt adhesive sheet
The Woodworker's Store

Inlays, banding
Constantine, Woodcraft, The Woodworker's Store, Woodworker's Supply

Japan dryer
Mohawk

Lacquer leveling spray
Mohawk, Woodworker's Supply

Lacquer retarder
Mohawk, Woodworker's Supply, Van Dyke's Restorers (called self-leveling agent)

Locking pliers, long-nose
Rutland Tool & Supply

MiniSpot patching machine, patch trimmer and patches (Lamello)
Colonial Saw

Nail pullers, small
The Japan Woodworker (Tiger Claw), Woodworker's Supply

Nail set, double ended
Woodcraft

Nail spinners
The Woodworker's Store

No Blush aerosol
Mohawk

No-Mortise hinges
Woodcraft, The Woodworker's Store, Woodworker's Supply

Paint cup (viscosometer)
Campbell-Hausfeld

Paint palettes
Van Dyke Restorers

Plug cutters and plugs
Veritas: Hartville Tool, Lee Valley Tools
Snug-Plugs: Highland Hardware, Woodcraft

Pressed carvings
The Woodworker's Store, Woodworker's Supply

Padding lacquer (Qualasol)
Garrett Wade, Woodcraft

Private Preserve (aerosol nitrogen)
The Wine Enthusiast

Putty
Mohawk Finiishing Products (Bond-Aide, Fil-O-Wood), Van Dyke's Restorers (Araldite), 3M (Just Like Wood), The Woodworker's Store (Famowood, Wunderfil), Woodworker's Supply (color, Behlen's Master Wood filler, Quickwood, Wood-Tex Synthetic Wood)

Quick-Grip spreader
Woodworker's Supply

Router bits (specialty)
Flush and V-groove: CMT
Slot-cutter: CMT, Trend-lines, Woodhaven

Scraper blades, with handle (Veritas)
Lee Valley Tools, most catalog suppliers

Screw extractors
Rutland Tool & Supply, Trend-lines, Woodworker's Store, Woodworker's Supply

Screw-hole restorer
Hartville Tool (The Plugger),
Leichtung (Mr. Grip), Trend-lines,
Van Dyke's Restorers, The
Woodworker's Store (Mr. Grip)

Screw Medic
McFeely's

Screws, square-drive
McFeely's, Trend-lines, Woodcraft,
The Woodworker's Store,
Woodworker's Supply

Shellac, button or granule
Garrett Wade, Woodworker's
Supply

Shelf-pin sockets
The Woodworker's Store

Sliding-door track, hardwood
The Woodworker's Store

Slideez (lubricant)
Mohawk, Woodworker's Supply

Stick fillers
Garrett Wade (Retouch crayons),
Mohawk (Patchal Pencils), The
Woodworker's Store (Touch Up
Stik), Woodworker's Supply (Fill
Sticks)

**Strainers (for pouring finish
through)**
Jamestown, McFeely's,
Woodworker's Supply, Van Dyke's
Restorers

**Strainers (to fit over
gun's siphon tube)**
Woodworker's Supply

Tape
Jamestown Distributors (3M 2090
Scotch Long-Mask blue tape), 3M
(low stick Scotch 2770)

Threaded inserts, hex-drive
The Woodworker's Store

Touch-up pens
Mohawk (Instant touch-up markers,
graining pens), Woodworker's
Supply (Master Scratch Removers)

Transfil (for doping in)
Mohawk

Veneer punches
Woodcraft, The Woodworker's
Store

Veneers
Constantine, The Woodworker's
Store, Woodworker's Supply

Campbell-Hausfeld
100 Production Dr.
Harrison, OH 45030
(800) 543-6400

CMT Tools (manufacturer)
5425 Beaumont Center Blvd.
Suite 900
Tampa, FL 33634
(800) 531-5559 (orders/information)
FAX (813) 888-6614

Colonial Saw Machinery
100 Pembroke St.
Kingston, MA 02364
(617) 585-4364

Albert Constantine and Son
2050 Eastchester Rd.
Bronx, NY 10461
(800) 223-8087
(212) 792-1600
FAX (212) 792-2110

Enco (manufacturer)
5000 West Bloomingdale
Chicago, IL 60639
(800) 645-6094

Garrett Wade
161 Avenue of the Americas
New York, NY 10013
(800) 221-2942
(212) 807-1757

Glue Spotlight
PO Box 97
Carlisle, PA 17013
(800) 933-7963

**Gougeon Brothers
(manufacturer)**
706 Martin St.
Bay City, MI 48706
(517) 684-7286

Grizzly Imports
East: 2406 Reach Rd.
Willamsport, PA 17701
(800) 523-4777
West: PO Box 2069
Bellingham, WA 98227
(800) 541-5537

Hartville Tool
940 West Maple St.
Hartville, OH 44632
(800) 345-2396 (orders)
FAX (216) 877-4682

Highland Hardware
1045 N. Highland Ave., NE
Atlanta, GA 30306
(800) 241-6748 (orders)
(404) 872-4466 (information)
FAX (404) 876-1941

Jamestown Distributors
28 Narragansett Ave.
PO Box 348
Jamestown, RI 02835
(800) 423-0030 (orders)
(401) 423-2520
FAX (800) 423-0542

The Japan Woodworker
1731 Clement Ave.
Alameda, CA 94501
(800) 537-7820 (orders)
(510) 521-1810 (technical
information)
FAX (510) 521-1864

Lee Valley Tools
1080 Morrison Dr.
Ottawa, Ontario
Canada K2H 8K7
(613) 596-0350
FAX (613) 596-6030

Leichtung Workshops
4944 Commerce Pkwy.
Cleveland, OH 44128
(800) 321-6840 (orders)
(800) 542-4467 (information)
FAX (216) 464-6764

McFeely's
712 12th St.
PO Box 3
Lynchburg, VA 24505-0003
(800) 443-7937
FAX (804) 847-7136

Mohawk Finishing Products
4715 STHWY 30
Amsterdam, NY 12010
(800) 545-0047 (orders)
(518) 843-1380
FAX (518) 842-3551

Renovators Supply
Renovators Old Mill
Millers Falls, MA 01349
(413) 659-3773

Rutland Tool & Supply
16700 E. Gale Ave.
City of Industry, CA 91745
(800) 289-4787
(818) 961-7111
FAX (800) 333-3787

3M (manufacturer)
3M Center
St. Paul, Minn 55144
(800) 364-3577 (consumer product
information)

Tool Crib of the North
PO Box 13720
Grand Forks, ND 58208
(800) 358-3096 (orders)
FAX (800) 343-4205

Trend-lines
375 Beacham St.
Chelsea, MA 02150
(800) 767-9999 (orders)
(800) 877-3338 (automated
ordering)
(617) 884-8951 (information)
FAX (617) 889-2072

Van Dyke's Restorers
PO Box 278
Woonsocket, SD 57385
(800) 843-3320 (orders)
(605) 796-4425
FAX (605) 796-4085

The Wine Enthusiast
PO Box 39
Pleasantville, NY 10570
(800) 356-8466 (orders)

Woodcraft
7845 Emerson Ave.
Parkersburg, WV 26101
(800) 225-1153 (orders)
(800) 535-4482 (customer service)
FAX (304) 428-8271 (orders)

Woodhaven
5323 W. Kimberly Rd.
Davenport, IA 52806
(800) 344-6657
(319) 391-2386
FAX (319) 391-1279

Woodworker's Store
21801 Industrial Blvd.
Rogers, MN 55374-9514
(612) 428-2199
(612) 428-2899 (technical service)
FAX (612) 428-8668

Woodworker's Supply
1108 North Glenn Rd.
Casper, WY 82601
(800) 645-9292 (orders)
(FAX 505) 821-7331

INDEX

Editor: RUTH DOBSEVAGE

Designer: HENRY ROTH

Layout Artist: GRETA SIBLEY

Illustrator: FRANK HABBAS

Photographer: SANDOR NAGYSZALANCZY

Art Assistant: AMY L. BERNARD

Typeface: GARAMOND

Paper: WARREN PATINA MATTE, 70 LB., NEUTRAL pH

Printer: ARCATA GRAPHICS/HAWKINS, NEW CANTON, TENNESSEE